T0178329

Lecture Notes of the Institute for Computer Sciences, Social Informatics and Telecommunications Engineering 498

The LNICST series publishes ICST's conferences, symposia and workshops.
LNICST reports state-of-the-art results in areas related to the scope of the Institute.
The type of material published includes

- Proceedings (published in time for the respective event)
- Other edited monographs (such as project reports or invited volumes)

LNICST topics span the following areas:

- General Computer Science
- E-Economy
- E-Medicine
- Knowledge Management
- Multimedia
- Operations, Management and Policy
- Social Informatics
- Systems

Weizhi Meng · Wenjuan Li

Editors

Blockchain Technology and Emerging Technologies

Second EAI International Conference, BlockTEA 2022
Virtual Event, November 21–22, 2022
Proceedings

 Springer

Editors
Weizhi Meng (iD)
Technical University of Denmark
Kongens Lyngby, Denmark

Wenjuan Li (iD)
Hong Kong Polytechnic University
Hong Kong, China

ISSN 1867-8211 ISSN 1867-822X (electronic)
Lecture Notes of the Institute for Computer Sciences, Social Informatics
and Telecommunications Engineering
ISBN 978-3-031-31419-3 ISBN 978-3-031-31420-9 (eBook)
https://doi.org/10.1007/978-3-031-31420-9

This Springer imprint is published by the registered company Springer Nature Switzerland AG
The registered company address is: Gewerbestrasse 11, 6330 Cham, Switzerland

Preface

We are happy to introduce the proceedings of the second edition of the 2022 European Alliance for Innovation (EAI) International Conference on Blockchain Technology and Emerging Applications (BlockTEA), held online 21–22 November 2022.

Motivated by the success of cryptocurrency, blockchain technology has been emerging as a potential technology to be applied in various domains, including finance, computer science, electronic engineering, agriculture, healthcare and more. The blockchain-based emerging applications are able to aid current systems and networks by leveraging the benefits provided by blockchain technology, such as a decentralized, immutable, and cryptographically secured ledger. The aim of BlockTEA is to bring together researchers and practitioners from different disciplines and discuss recent advancements in blockchain and its emerging applications.

The technical program of BlockTEA 2022 consisted of 10 full papers in oral presentation sessions at the main conference, with an acceptance rate of around 30%. Aside from the high-quality technical paper presentations, the technical program also featured one keynote speaker, Siu-Ming Yiu, Professor and Associate Executive Director of HKU-SCF FinTech Academy, Department of Computer Science, University of Hong Kong, China. The talk title is Blockchain and Central Bank Digital Currency.

Coordination with the steering chairs, Imrich Chlamtac and Weizhi Meng, was important for the success of the conference. We sincerely appreciate their constant support and guidance. It was also a great pleasure to work with such an excellent organizing committee team for their hard work in organizing and supporting the conference. In particular, the Technical Program Committee, led by our General Co-Chairs, Jiannong Cao (Hong Kong Polytechnic University) and Abderrahim Benslimane (University of Avignon, France), and all the other chairs contributed to the conference organization and made a high-quality technical program. We are also grateful to all the authors who submitted their papers to the conference.

We strongly believe that the BlockTEA conference provides a unique platform for all researchers, developers, and practitioners to discuss all state-of-the-art and recent advancements that are relevant to Blockchain Technology and Emerging Applications. We also expect that future BlockTea conferences will be as successful and stimulating, as indicated by the contributions presented in this volume.

November 2022

Weizhi Meng
Wenjuan Li

Organization

Steering Committee

Imrich Chlamtac   University of Trento, Italy
Weizhi Meng   Technical University of Denmark, Denmark

Organizing Committee

General Chair

Weizhi Meng   Technical University of Denmark, Denmark

General Co-chairs

Jiannong Cao   Hong Kong Polytechnic University, China
Abderrahim Benslimane   University of Avignon, France

TPC Chair and Co-chair

Weizhi Meng   Technical University of Denmark, Denmark
Wenjuan Li   Hong Kong Polytechnic University, China

Sponsorship and Exhibit Chair

Javier Parra-Arnau   Universitat Politècnica de Catalunya, Spain

Workshops Chair

Jun Shao   Zhejiang Gongshang University, China

Publicity and Social Media Chair

Kambourakis Georgios   University of the Aegean, Greece
Jiangshan Yu   Monash University, Australia
Jianfeng Wang   Xidian University, China
Zhenliang Lu   University of Sydney, Australia

Publications Chair

Xuyun Zhang   Macquarie University, Australia

Web Chair

Wei-Yang Chiu   Technical University of Denmark, Denmark

Technical Program Committee

Owen Arden	University of California Santa Cruz, USA
Man Ho Au	University of Hong Kong, China
Xinxin Fan	IoTex, China
Xiapu Luo	Hong Kong Polytechnic University, China
Angelo De Caro	IBM Zurich, Switzerland
Jian Liu	Zhejiang University, China
Nikos Lenonardos	University of Athens, Greece
Yajin Zhou	Zhejiang University, China
Alberto Sonnino	Facebook Novi, USA
Ghassan Karame	NEC Laboratories, Germany
Ralph Holz	University of Twente, The Netherlands
Alessandro Sorniotti	IBM Research, USA
Bhaskar Krishnamachari	University of Southern California, USA
Ali Dorri	Queensland University of Technology, Australia
Christof Ferreira Torres	University of Luxembourg, Luxembourg
Wenjuan Li	Hong Kong Polytechnic University, China
Andrea Bracciali	University of Stirling, UK
Foteini Baldimsti	George Mason University, USA
Adam Eversspaugh	Coinbase, USA
Ittay Eyal	Technion – Israel Institute of Technology, Israel

Contents

Smart Contract

ID-Based Self-encryption via Hyperledger Fabric Based Smart Contract

Ilya Grishkov[1], Roland Kromes[1(✉)], Thanassis Giannetsos[2], and Kaitai Liang[1]

[1] Cyber Security Group, Delft University of Technology, Delft, The Netherlands
I.Grishkov-1@student.tudelft.nl, {R.G.Kromes,Kaitai.Liang}@tudelft.nl
[2] Ubitech Ltd., Digital Security and Trusted Computing Group, Athens, Greece
agiannetsos@ubitech.eu

Abstract. This paper offers a prototype of a Hyperledger Fabric-IPFS based network architecture including a smart contract based encryption scheme that meant to improve the security of user's data that is being uploaded to the distributed ledger. A new extension to the self-encryption scheme was deployed by integrating data owner's identity into the encryption process. Such integration allows to permanently preserve ownership of the original file and link it to the person/entity who originally uploaded it. Moreover, self-encryption provides strong security guarantees that decryption of a file is computationally not feasible under the condition that the encrypted file and the key are safely stored.

Keywords: Blockchain · IPFS · Self-Encryption · Security · Hyperledger Fabric

1 Introduction

The modern world is increasingly adopting blockchain technology. The first major market adoption of blockchain happened in 2009 when Bitcoin was introduced [12]. Interest in blockchain solutions grew over the years and lead to the invention of Ethereum - Bitcoin peer but with support for smart contracts which are digital codes enabling the description of complete business logic [1]. The introduction of smart contracts leads to further development in the field of blockchain and created demand for more industry-friendly solutions that allow to identify users of the system (Know-Your-Customer, Anti-Money-Laundering). Hyperledger Fabric was then introduced as a highly modular permissioned blockchain that allows great customization to suit particular industrial needs [3]. Given its customizability and modularity, Hyperledger Fabric (HLF) is a perfect platform for extending it with various trust and privacy preservation solutions.

According to Huang et al. [7] the main component of a blockchain that is being attack the most is a smart contract. High frequency of attack on a component designed to handle user private data suggests a need for an alternative approach to handling sensitive information other than just sending it raw to the

© ICST Institute for Computer Sciences, Social Informatics and Telecommunications Engineering 2023
Published by Springer Nature Switzerland AG 2023. All Rights Reserved
W. Meng and W. Li (Eds.): BlockTEA 2022, LNICST 498, pp. 3–18, 2023.
https://doi.org/10.1007/978-3-031-31420-9_1

ledger. An local data encryption prior to sending data to the smart contract could be a solution.

Self-encryption was introduced as a mean of encrypting files that "requires no user intervention or passwords" [9]. This algorithm can be used for local encryption of files, encrypted chunks of which will be later uploaded to a cloud-based storage or to a distributed file system (e.g., IPFS[1]) Pointers to the encrypted chunks are then sent to the ledger. It can be noted that storing only the hash values of the encrypted data chunks on blockchain ledger is vital when the data size is significant. The authors in [5] point out that sending data to a blockchain frequently, when the data size is large, can cause the entire blockchain network to crash. Sending only the hash values of the given data is more optimal as a hash value is usually 32 bytes long. While this solution allows to keep file content private, the file itself is not linked in any way to its owner. A variant of identity based encryption can tackle this problem. If a file is self-encrypted with owners identity used during the encryption process, this file remains linked to the person who initially uploaded it to the blockchain. This way original ownership can be preserved.

This paper aims at exploring trust and privacy preserving solutions in Hyperledger Fabric blockchain. More specifically the goal is to further investigate the utility of a combination of identity based encryption and self-encryption as means of improving security of the data in the HLF; extend the previously done research by [13] and implement ID-based self-encryption via Hyperledger Fabric smart contract. Hence, this work is aimed at finding a possible solution to combining ownership information with blockchain architecture. Another goal of the paper is creating a proof of concept solution for integration of ID-based self-encryption into a blockchain context in a generic way.

Within this paper an approach of integrating ID-based self-encryption is presented. Moreover a detailed description of prototype implementation is given. In addition to this implementation of ID-based self-encryption, a practical fully decentralized network architecture for storing encrypted data has also been deployed. In this proposed network, the data owner can use ID-based self-encryption to store encrypted data in a decentralized and secure manner. The encrypted data chunks are stored in an InterPlanetary File System (IPFS) which is a decentralized systems for file storage. To store the references (hash values) of the encrypted data chunks, the Hyperledger Fabric blockchain was used.

This work is structured as follows. Section 2 describes related works used to achieve the goal. Section 3 gives a background about the implementation of ID-based self-encryption. Section 4 discusses the inner workings and the proposed implantation of ID-based self-encryption. The performance analysis and the overview of benefits of the proposed implementation is presented in Sect. 5. Finally, the work is discussed in Sect. 6, and concluded in Sect. 7.

---

[1] https://ipfs.io/.

2. State of the Art

Blockchain is a distributed ledger technology that provides immutability and transparency of data to members of the blockchain network [19]. The blockchain is also a peer-to-peer network in which participants are known to each other. Authentication of participants is ensured using elliptic curve cryptography. Today's blockchains enable the deployment of complete business logic in a seamless manner. These digital business logic are also known as smart contracts.

Blockchain technology is used in several use cases such as smart city, smart agriculture, vehicle networks [10] and also healthcare [15]. In the latter two cases, the privacy and ownership of data transmitted from a driver and medical patient is particularly important, as this data may contain privacy sensitive information. It can be noted that in these latter use case using a private blockchain such as Hyperledger Fabric can be a more optimal choice as they can provide higher security and privacy level.

The topic of security and privacy of the Hyperledger Fabric has been thoroughly studied [4,16,18]. Moreover a research has been conducted this year by a student of Delft University of Technology [13] addressing similar issue of improving HLF security using self-encryption.

The concept of self-encryption was introduced by Yu Chen [2]. The approach of the original paper involves converting a file into a bit stream, extract the key by randomly selecting bits from the stream and then doing the encryption using that key. After the encryption the key and the encrypted file should be stored separetely, e.g. the key can be stored locally, while the encrypted file can be sent to a server.

The original encryption scheme was also extended by Moch Rezky Debby Rahardjo [14]. According to the paper, "The modification is located in dividing the plaintext and ciphertext into 1024-bit chunks at XOR process and using the date when encryption process starts as a seed. The modification also adds the database for the key management function". Storing the key and the encrypted chunks in separate places makes in computationally not feasible to get the original data.

The later industrial adaptation of the self-encryption scheme happened when a team lead by David Irvine made self-encryption the core of his company's (MaidSafe) product - SAFE Network [9]. Irvine's implementation of the self-encryption scheme will be the basis of this work, hence a more detailed explanation of the implementation of the algorithm will be given.

Figure 1 shows the encryption process. First, the original file is getting split into minimum of 3 file chunks. After the file is split into chunks the algorithm creates a data map, where the key needed for decryption will be stored. Each chunk is then hashed and those hashes are written to the data map. Parts of those hashes are used as a key and initialization vector for AES 128 algorithm that encrypts each file chunk. When encryption is done, each encrypted chunk is obfuscated with the previously computed hash values by applying a XoR function. At the end of the process the encryption scheme returns a data map that is going to be later used for decryption, and the encrypted file chunks.

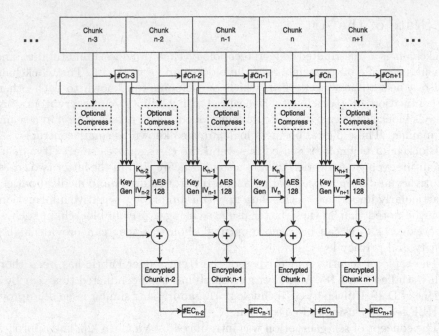

Fig. 1. Self-encryption process, adopted from [11]

3   Background

Original implementation of the self-encryption schema by David Irvine [11] was modified and used for this research. The use of rayon library (which adds parallelization to the code) was removed from the algorithm, due to the fact that the compilation target (WebAssembly) only supports single-threaded code. Additionally the code base was modified to include an interface for communication with the external code. Changes were also done to the Cargo.toml to make the code compatible with the target. Modified self-encryption algorithm was compiled to WebAssembly and run in a virtual machine (VM) and invoked from the code of the developed local application (which allows the interaction with the Hyperledger Fabric Smart Contract). A more detailed description of the process will be given in the Sect. 4. The benchmarks of this implementation will be provided in Sect. 5.

Hyperledger Fabric test network v2.4.3 was used. Test network was deployed to Docker based on the tutorials provided by Hyperledger Fabric[2].

Smart contract was then deployed (detailed in Sect. 4).

Encrypted file storage is handled by the IPFS, which is a distributed Torrent database, which uses hashes of files to address its content. IPFS node was also deployed to Docker. For IPFS deployment two directories (staging and data) were

---

[2] Usage of the command requires navigating to the root directory of the test-network, provided by the Hyperledger Fabric [8].

mounted on the host file system to persist the stored data, when the container is stopped. Hyperledger Fabric provides official software development kit (SDK) for 3 languages: Go, Java, Javascript. Go was chosen for implementation of the project, due to ease of integration with both Hyperledger Fabric and the IPFS. Encryption library is written in Rust and is compiled to WebAssembly, hence a way to call WebAssembly was needed. Go also provides support for Wasmer library that allows to call WebAssembly function directly from Go code.

4   ID-Based Self-encryption

4.1   Integrating Identity into the Encryption

This paper offers an extension to the algorithm proposed by Irvine [9]. Encryption step in the original algorithm is modified to include identity of a person who is running the algorithm into the encryption process. Instead of using part of the chunk hash as a key for AES 128, the result of XoR of the hashed identity and the chunk hash is used as a key. The identity can be any string of any length. If the length of this string is shorter than the length of the key, then the cycle function is applied to the string, which repeats the iterator of a string. The hashing function SipHash 1-3 is used to hash the identity of a user, before passing it to the XoR function. Figure 2 demonstrates the process of encrypting a file using the modified version of self-encryption with identity integrated into the encryption process.

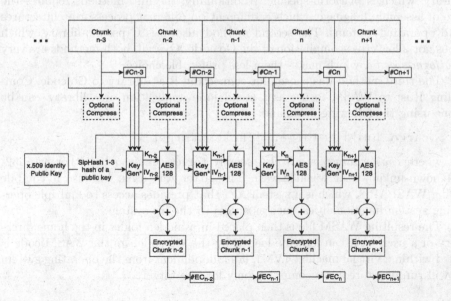

*The key is generated by performing XoR of a chunk hash and SipHash 1-3 of user's public key

Fig. 2. ID-based self-encryption process

Decryption of the file, that was encrypted using ID-based self-encryption, is similar to that of a regular self-encryption, with the key for AES 128 being the only different part. The decryption calculates the key the same way the encryption does it by applying XoR function to the hash of identity and the chunk hash from the data map.

The implementation of the encryption scheme can be found on GitHub[3].

4.2   Connecting the Encryption Algorithm and the Local Application

The implementation of the identity-based self-encryption is written purely in Rust, while the client application is written in Go. This creates a demand for a way to integrate Rust library into Go code. Among the solutions to tackle the problem are:

1. Use Go tools to assemble the Go code and compile Rust code into a static library. Then link compiled code using additional assembly "glue-code" [17].
2. Compile Rust to a static library and call it from the Go code using Go build-in pseudo-library C for interacting with native interfaces.
3. Compile Rust to WebAssembly (WASM) code and call it from Go using Wasmer library[4].

All of the methods have been successfully tried. The first two methods do not allow cross compilation, because both of them require compiling Rust to a static library, which is platform-specific. Additionally, the first methods requires the use of assembly language, which is different on different processor architectures and operating systems. The second method also uses C pseudo-library, which does not allow cross-compilation of the Go code. Overall, both methods are very *platform-specific*, which makes them less preferable choice.

The third method was chosen for connecting Rust library to Go code. Compiling Rust to WASM to use as a standalone application or a library, can be done using the following command:

```
$ cargo build —target =[chosen_target]
```

where *chosen_target* is a WebAssembly target that can be either wasm32-unknown-unknown or wasm32-wasi. The latter was used, because it compile using WASI API[5], which is a system API that provides access to multiple operating system functionalities, such as access to the file system.

The resulting WASM file is then placed in a hidden folder in the home directory of a user, so it can later be loaded by the Go code. As the WASM code is used within a virtual machine (VM), it's independent from the operating system it will run on, so requires compiling only for one target.

---

[3] https://github.com/ilyagrishkov/ib-self-encryption-rust.

[4] https://wasmer.io/.

[5] https://wasi.dev/.

Calling WASM from Go Using Wasmer. In order to call WASM code a VM needs to be used. Wasmer library provides such VM, that can also be initialized from within Go code. The process of calling WASM code from the Go application is demonstrated in the Fig. 3. This process consists of the following steps:

1. Loading WASM code into a Wasmer VM
   (a) A directory on the host operating system, that will be accessible in the VM, need to be specified
   (b) Optionally, standard output of the WASM library can be inherited.
2. Invoking a function by specifying its name and the return type and passing arguments to it

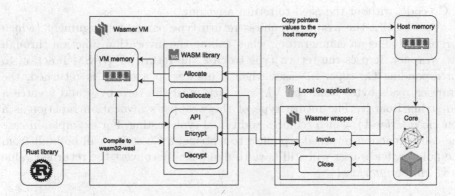

Fig. 3. Connection of the WASM encryption library to the client application via the Wasmer library and the developed wrapper

The communication between the Go code and WASM library and passing arguments for function invocation is happening using C types, which means that types like strings are not supported directly and need to be converted to corresponding C types. In case of a string being passed as an argument, it needs to be written to memory and end with a zero byte. The pointer to the first byte of this string is then passed to the invoked function as an argument.

As the host operating system memory is inaccessible for the VM, allocation and deallocation of memory need to happen within the VM itself. In order to facilitate the allocation and deallocation two dedicated Rust functions were developed as a part of id-based encryption library interface: allocate and deallocate.

In case the called function requires a string as an argument, the allocation needs to be performed before passing the pointer to that string. The allocate function has to be called to allocate memory inside the VM. The memory is then accessed from the Go code and each byte of the string argument is written to the newly allocated memory. The pointer to the memory and the length need to be preserved in order to deallocate the memory, before the program terminates. The pointer to the first memory cell containing the string argument is then passed as an argument to the function that is being called.

Wrapper Code for Wasmer Calls. A wrapper code has been written to simplify invocation of WASM functions. The major simplification that this code provides is the ability to pass Go native-type argument to the wrapper, which then performs all the necessary processing and allocation, if needed. The pointers to string or array types as well as their lengths are stored, so when the program terminates, the memory is getting deallocated.

Moreover, the developed wrapper code allows to pass simple numerical Go types (integers, floats, bytes, etc.) as pointers to the WASM library, so the changes that are happening to them when WASM functions run are also reflected in Go code, without the need to return anything.

Additionally, the wrapper requires return type parameter argument (which is represented as an enumerator), when calling the invocation function through the wrapper. It uses the return type to case the return of WASM function to corresponding Go type. In cases when a pointer to a string is returned, the wrapper reads bytes from the VM memory until the zero byte and creates a Go string from it. The return type of the wrapper's invocation function is a generic *interface{}*, which requires additional type casting. For example, in case the called function returned a pointer to a string, a Go string will be built from the pointer, but a user will still have to dynamically convert the returned value as it will be *interface{}*.

4.3 Smart Contract

The smart contract in Hyperledger Fabric allows to define assets that will be on the ledger. This paper defines an asset containing three fields: ID, Owner and CID. The code below shows the definition of an asset written in Go.

```go
type Asset struct {
        ID      string    `json:"ID"`
        Owner   string    `json:"Owner"`
        CID     []string  `json:"CID"`
}
```

Listing 1.1. The struct representing an asset on the Hyperledger Fabric ledger

The ID is a universally unique identifier (UUID) that is generated, when the new asset is created. The Owner is a string of hexadecimal numbers representing a public key of a user, who created the asset. The CID is an array if unique identifier that reference encrypted file chunks saved in IPFS. The references to the encrypted data chunks remain immutable, and can also be used for verifying if encrypted data chunks were manipulated (the hash of an encrypted data chunk is a unique value).

Additionally, the smart contract defines a list of functions for creating, deleting and updating assets. The implementation can be found on GitHub[6].

4.4 Self-encryption Work Flow in a Blockchain-IPFS Based Network

The encryption and decryption process as well as interactions with the IPFS and the Hyperledger Fabric are orchestrated by a local application, which is a command line interface (CLI) tool written in Go. The prototype of the tool is accessible from GitHub[7]

Execution of any command starts with creating a new instance of a WASM wrapper and loading of the encryption library. When the command requires interaction with the Hyperledger Fabric, presence of the wallet, containing identity (which is necessary to enable interaction with the smart contract), is being checked. If the wallet is missing it's getting populated based on the certificates and keys of a user. When this preparation is done, the execution of the command starts.

At the end of the program execution the wrapper iterates over all allocated memory pointers and individually deallocates them.

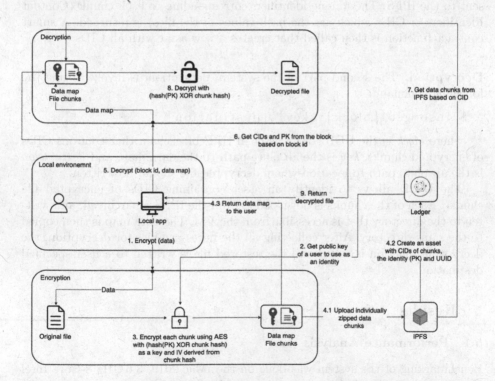

Fig. 4. Work flow in the blockchain-IPFS based network when using self-encryption

---

[6] https://github.com/ilyagrishkov/ib-self-encryption-smart-contract.
[7] https://github.com/ilyagrishkov/ib-self-encryption.

There are two major parts of the system - encryption and decryption. Figure 3 demonstrates the workflow of both of them.

Encryption. The first part, encryption, that deals with encrypting a file and uploading data to the Hyperledger Fabric starts when the following command is called:

```
$ ibse add [file] [key_output_path]
```

where *ibse* is the name of the local app, *file* is the absolute path to the file that needs to be encrypted, and *key_output_path* is the absolute path to location where the key will be stored.

The original file is getting uploaded to the directory that was mapped during the VM initialization. From there it can be read by the WASM code. The encryption function is then called and the output is written to a new directory inside the mapped one. The output consists of multiple encrypted file chunks and a data map. The data map is moved to the location specified by the user and can later be shared via a secure channel. Each encrypted file chunk is being put into a zip archive to preserve their names, when uploading to the IPFS, and sent to the IPFS. The unique identifier, corresponding to each chunk (Content Identifiers or CIDs which are the hash values of the files) is returned. A smart contract function is then called that creates a new asset with all CIDs.

Decryption. The second part of the system, decryption, is invoked using the following command:

```
$ ibse get [block] [key] [destination]
```

where *block* is the UUID of an asset in HLF blockchain that contains CIDs of encrypted chunks, *key* is the absolute path to the data map, and *destination* is the absolute path to location where decrypted file should be written.

The UUID allows to identify an asset containing CIDs of encrypted file chunks. Each of the chunks is downloaded from the IPFS, unarchived, and written to the directory that is accessible from the VM. The data map is then copied to the same directory. After collecting all the necessary files for decryption, the decryption function is called and the restored file is written to a user-specified destination.

5 Results

5.1 Performance Analysis

Benchmarking of the system was done on the iMac 2019, 3,6 GHz 8-Core Intel Core i9 with 32 GB of memory running on MacOS 12.3.1.

Benchmarking of the implemented id-based self-encryption scheme was done. As the encryption itself is not implemented in the same language as the rest of the project (the encryption is implemented in Rust and the rest of the project is in Go), the execution time can differ when Rust functions are called from Go compared to pure Rust execution time.

Files of sizes 100-, 250-, 500-, 750 kilobytes, 1 megabyte, 10-, 25-, 50-, 75-, and 100 megabytes were created for benchmarking both the pure Rust implementation as well as the WASM + Go implementations. Moreover, for this benchmark both the Rust code and the WASM library were optimized using maximum level of optimization provided by the Rust compiler.

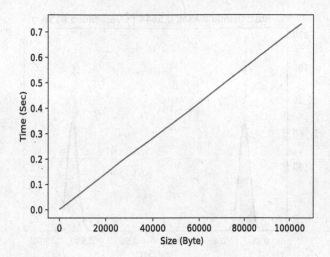

Fig. 5. Dependence of the execution time of id-based self-encryption algorithm in pure Rust from the file size

The initial benchmark was performed on the encryption function only and was measuring execution time of the pure Rust implementation. Figure 4 shows the results of the benchmarking.

The chart show near-linear dependence between the size of the file and the time it takes to encrypt it. This dependence can be explained by the fact that the most demanding computational is the AES 128 encryption process and with the increase of the file size, then number of chunks it is split to increases. Each chunk of the original file needs to be individually encrypted, hence the computation time grows linearly with the size of the file.

As the encryption function execution time grows linearly due to the computational demand of the AES 128 and the hashing algorithms, the decryption process will be identical, because it uses the same algorithms for decryption.

In order to achieve more objective benchmark results, file of each size has been encrypted 100 times and the average calculated. In order to visualize execution time a chart in Python using MatPlotLib[8] was created. The chart contains a 25-bin histogram, each representing density of a particular measurement. Following

---

[8] https://matplotlib.org/.

central limit theorem the distribution of the execution time measurements was assumed normal, so the mean and the standard deviation were calculated and the distribution plotted over the histogram. Figure 5 shows an example of combined charts for pure Rust and WASM + Go execution times, when encrypting 50 megabytes file. The blue histogram on the left-hand side shows results of the 100 measurements of the execution time of the Rust implementation; on the right-hand side - of the WASM + Go implementation.

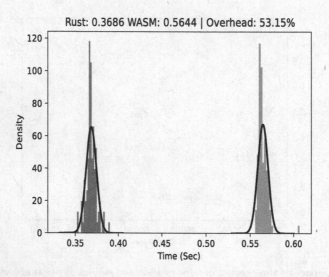

Fig. 6. Run time distribution for 50 MB file encryption using pure Rust and WebAssembly + Go implementations (Color figure online)

The results of execution time measurements have for various file sizes are summarized in Table 1. The execution time shown in the table is the average number of seconds it takes a corresponding implementation to encrypt a file of a corresponding size. In addition to the average execution time, the overhead of the WASM + Go implementation is calculated for every pair of measurements.

It is visible from the table that the overhead has a clear downwards trend (except the spike, when encrypting 250 KB file). When the execution time of a WASM + Go encryption implementation is less than 0.01 s, the overhead falls in the range between 70% and 85%. When the execution time is longer than 0.1 s, the overhead goes down to 50%–55% and stays in that range when the file size increases. Figure 6 demonstrates the overhead of WASM + Go encryption of file of different sizes.

Table 1. Average execution time and overhead when encrypting files of different sizes using id-based self-encryption

File size (Byte)	Average execution time (Sec)		Overhead (%)
	Rust	WASM + Go	
100 KB	0.0024	0.0042	75.89
250 KB	0.0038	0.007	84.51
500 KB	0.005	0.0088	75.48
750 KB	0.0069	0.0117	71.4
1 MB	0.0081	0.0139	71.29
10 MB	0.0747	0.117	56.55
25 MB	0.1885	0.2851	51.22
50 MB	0.3686	0.5644	53.15
75 MB	0.5492	0.8447	53.81
100 MB	0.7317	1.1201	53.08

Such decrease in the overhead, when the execution time becomes longer is explained by the presence of the Wasmer library invocation overhead, which occurs every time a call is made to the Wasmer VM. When execution time itself is less than 0.01 s the invocation overhead is significant compared to the execution time. At the same time, when the execution time becomes longer, the overhead from invocation becomes insignificant, and measurements start to approximate real WASM VM overhead, which is around 50%–55%.

5.2 Benefits Overview

The designed app has multiple surfaces of attack. The IPFS nodes, where the encrypted file chunks are stored can attacked. Also, an adversary can be gain unauthorized access to the ledger with references to file on the IPFS. Both of those possibilities are analyzed below.

The security of IPFS nodes (assuming the encrypted file chunks were stored individually on multiple nodes) can be compromised, in which case encrypted files will be leaked to the malicious user. As encrypted file chunks have been stored on different nodes, the probability that all of them being compromised is negligible and should not be considered. Additionally, individual files do not have any link to each other, so matching multiple encrypted chunks, that are needed for successful decryption, is not computationally feasible. The data map containing the keys for the decryption, was stored locally by the user, who encrypted the file. Without the original keys, the decryption of the self-encrypted data is computationally not feasible [9]. Moreover, as the proposed self-encryption is also related to the data owner or user identity, the decryption cannot be done until the identity is not provided. Thus the data ownership is also provided by the id-based implantation.

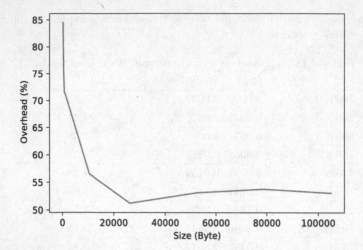

Fig. 7. WebAssembly + Go implementation overhead measurements over for files of different sizes compared to pure Rust implementation

6 Discussion

The results show high security guarantees of the id-based self-encryption scheme, when used for encrypting data, stored on the Hyperledger Fabric blockchain. This allows to use the implemented prototype as a secure medium for saving a retrieving information from the ledger.

In future works full Go implementation of self-encryption should be compared with the design proposed in this paper.

It was also beyond the scope of this study to create a standardized benchmarking for WASM and Rust libraries. It can be done by using multiple sample programs that test specific properties of the programming language (e.g. efficacy of memory allocation and deallocation) or very computationally intensive programs [6]. The objective could be running a containerized version of both libraries against a set of such programs and analyzing the run time.

Moreover, the study can be expanded by analyzing and comparing CPU and memory load of WASM and Rust libraries. Such benchmark could be also done using sample programs mentioned in the previous paragraph (Fig. 7).

7 Conclusion

In this study a new approach to storage of files on the Hyperledger Fabric blockchain was presented. The demonstrated approach allows for secure storage of data in a decentralized way, with ability to preserve the original file ownership and also information about the person, who encrypted it. This approach can be used where high security and trust in the integrity of data stored on the ledger is need. The prototype uses Rust implementation of id-based self-encryption that is compiled to WebAssembly and invoked from Go code.

Additionally, the study demonstrates the generic way of integrating ID-based self-encryption into the blockchain context with a relatively low overhead (the overhead is around 55%) and high performance level of WebAssembly library integration with the Go code base, compared to the pure Rust implementation. Relatively low overhead of WASM creates possibilities for developers to use WASM integration with Go and other languages that support Wasmer library as a cross-platform solution that allows to achieve high degrees of performance, while also being deterministic.

The wrapper proposed in this work can also be used in Golang-based backend applications that aim to use the cryptographic libraries deployed in Rust providing a more memory-safe execution.

Acknowledgements. This research is supported by European Union's Horizon 2020 researchand innovation programme under grant agreement No. 952697 (ASSURED), No. 101021727 (IRIS), and No. 101070052 (TANGO).

References

1. Buterin, V.: Ethereum: a next-generation smart contract and decentralized application platform (2014). https://github.com/ethereum/wiki/wiki/White-Paper. Accessed 22 Aug 2016
2. Chen, Y., Ku, W.S.: Self-encryption scheme for data security in mobile devices. In: 2009 6th IEEE Consumer Communications and Networking Conference, pp. 1–5. IEEE (2009)
3. Christian, C.: Architecture of the hyperledger blockchain fabric (2016). https://www.zurich.ibm.com/dccl/papers/cachin$_$/$dccl.pdf. Accessed 10 Aug 2016
4. Dabholkar, A., Saraswat, V.: Ripping the fabric: attacks and mitigations on hyperledger fabric. In: Shankar Sriram, V.S., Subramaniyaswamy, V., Sasikaladevi, N., Zhang, L., Batten, L., Li, G. (eds.) ATIS 2019. CCIS, vol. 1116, pp. 300–311. Springer, Singapore (2019). https://doi.org/10.1007/978-981-15-0871-4_24
5. Gerrits, L., Kromes, R., Verdier, F.: A true decentralized implementation based on IoT and blockchain: a vehicle accident use case. In: 2020 International Conference on Omni-Layer Intelligent Systems (COINS), pp. 1–6 (2020). https://doi.org/10.1109/COINS49042.2020.9191405
6. Gouy, I.: Toy benchmark programs. https://benchmarksgame-team.pages.debian.net/benchmarksgame/why-measure-toy-benchmark-programs.html
7. Huang, Y., Bian, Y., Li, R., Zhao, J.L., Shi, P.: Smart contract security: a software lifecycle perspective. IEEE Access 7, 150184–150202 (2019). https://doi.org/10.1109/ACCESS.2019.2946988
8. Hyperledger: Using the fabric test network (2020). https://hyperledger-fabric.readthedocs.io/en/release-2.2/test$_$network.html. Accessed 19 Mar 2022
9. Irvine, D.: Self encrypting data (2010). Unpublished Manuscript
10. Kromes, R., Gerrits, L., Verdier, F.: Adaptation of an embedded architecture to run hyperledger sawtooth application. In: 2019 IEEE 10th Annual Information Technology, Electronics and Mobile Communication Conference (IEMCON), pp. 0409–0415 (2019). https://doi.org/10.1109/IEMCON.2019.8936264
11. Maidsafe: self_encryption (2022). https://github.com/maidsafe/self$_$/$encryption

12. Nakamoto, S.: Bitcoin: a peer-to-peer electronic cash system (2008). https:// bitcoin.org/bitcoin.pdf. Accessed 01 July 2015
13. Park, C.: Using self-encryption to safeguard data security in fabric's smart contract. Bachelor's thesis (2022). https://repository.tudelft.nl/islandora/object/ uuid:15c5eee3-0be6-4d71-bf67-3ea5e576aa05?collection=education
14. Rahardjo, M.R.D., Shidik, G.F.: Design and implementation of self encryption method on file security. In: 2017 International Seminar on Application for Technology of Information and Communication (iSemantic), pp. 181–186. IEEE (2017)
15. Ray, P.P., Dash, D., Salah, K., Kumar, N.: Blockchain for IoT-based healthcare: background, consensus, platforms, and use cases. IEEE Syst. J. **15**(1), 85–94 (2021). https://doi.org/10.1109/JSYST.2020.2963840
16. Stamatellis, C., Papadopoulos, P., Pitropakis, N., Katsikas, S., Buchanan, W.J.: A privacy-preserving healthcare framework using hyperledger fabric. Sensors **20**(22), 6587 (2020)
17. Valsorda, F.: Rustgo: calling rust from go with near-zero overhead (2022). https:// words.filippo.io/rustgo/
18. Yamashita, K., Nomura, Y., Zhou, E., Pi, B., Jun, S.: Potential risks of hyperledger fabric smart contracts. In: 2019 IEEE International Workshop on Blockchain Oriented Software Engineering (IWBOSE), pp. 1–10. IEEE (2019)
19. Zibin, Z., Xie, S., Dai, H.N., Chen, X., Wang, H.: Blockchain challenges and opportunities: a survey. Int. J. Web Grid Serv. **4**, 352–375 (2018). https://doi.org/10. 1504/IJWGS.2018.095647

Scalable Smart Contracts for Linear Regression Algorithm

Syed Badruddoja$^{(\boxtimes)}$, Ram Dantu, Yanyan He, Abiola Salau,
and Kritagya Upadhyay

University of North Texas, Denton, TX 76207, USA
{syedbadruddoja,abiolasalau,kritagyaupadhyay}@my.unt.edu,
{ram.dantu,yanyan.he}@unt.edu

Abstract. Linear regression algorithms capture information from previous experiences and build a cognitive model to forecast the future. The information and the cognitive model representing the history of predicting future outputs must be reliable so that expected results are trusted. Furthermore, the algorithms must be explainable and traceable, making the learning process meaningful and trackable. Blockchain smart contracts boost information integrity, providing trust and the provenance of distributed ledger transactions that support such requirements. Smart contracts are traditionally developed to perform simple transactions with integer operations. However, developing learning algorithms such as linear regression with smart contracts mandates complex computation involving floating-point operations, which are not supported by smart contracts. Moreover, smart contract transactions are expensive and time-consuming. In this work, we propose a novel implementation of smart contracts for linear regression algorithms with fraction-based computation that can train and predict on the Ethereum blockchain. Our smart contract-based training and prediction technique with Solidity programming language produced a similar mean square error to the scikit-learn-based prediction model. Moreover, our design strategy saves training costs for linear regression algorithms through off-chain computations with an optimistic roll-up solution. The off-chain training and on-chain prediction strategy demonstrated in our work will help academic and industry researchers to develop cost-effective distributed AI applications in the future.

Keywords: Blockchain · dApp · Smart Contract · Artificial Intelligence · Multiple Linear Regression · Arbitrum · Ethereum

1 Introduction and Motivation

Fabricated Forecast: Artificial intelligence provides methods to make intelligent decisions for various applications [1]. The models are prepared with well-known algorithms proven to yield high accuracy with many modes of learning techniques. However, one of the crucial problems in recent development involves

© ICST Institute for Computer Sciences, Social Informatics and Telecommunications Engineering 2023
Published by Springer Nature Switzerland AG 2023. All Rights Reserved
W. Meng and W. Li (Eds.): BlockTEA 2022, LNICST 498, pp. 19–31, 2023.
https://doi.org/10.1007/978-3-031-31420-9_2

the trust of the data and model [2]. Data poisoning attacks wreak havoc in applications demanding predictive intelligence where input data, the training model, and output data can be questioned [3]. The training of tampered data fabricates the learning model. The manipulated model forecasts unreliable results. Moreover, the model of training and prediction results are also targets of attack. For example, if the training of the linear regression model is flawed using the tampered dataset in a weather forecast center, the forecast would produce a fake prediction. Therefore, a trusted machine learning model is mandatory to build confidence in the prediction system [5].

Explainable and Transparent AI: The machine learning models predominantly suffer from unclear training methods that make the learning process inexplicable [5]. For instance, in healthcare systems, the severity of diseases (a regression problem) requires investigation of multiple symptoms that mandates explainable features for a complete comprehension of the underlying illness [6]. However, the AI application does not explain the learning process. Moreover, the models also lack provenance to provide proof of learning [7]. Consequently, users sway away from trusting these applications due to low trust and confidence in AI applications. Moreover, AI applications raise ethical concerns about biased models on race, gender, ethnicity, and any feature relevant to the data set. A biased model can predict the wrong regression value and create more discrimination among application users [15].

Smart Contracts Scalability: Blockchain addresses trust, provenance, and explainability of AI [12] application through immutable distributed ledger and integrity feature. It works as a confidence machine for making a consensus-based transaction that is secure and intact. However, smart contracts in blockchain suffer from programming and scalability issues. The solidity programming language [23] in Ethereum blockchain (*one of the popular programming languages for developing DApps*) is a static programming language that denies floating-point computations. Therefore, cognitive smart contracts cannot produce accurate predictions. Moreover, the Ethereum blockchain also has scalability issues with transaction block limit, high computation cost, and delay in the finality of creation of block [9]. For instance, training a linear regression model with iterative optimization [10] requires thousands of iterations and function updates to optimize a model. The delay in the transaction time of the blockchain network deems the training unreasonable, and the higher cost of computations makes it unaffordable.

2   Problem Definition

A tampered linear regression model falsifies predictions, dissuading users from trusting AI applications. Hence, a trustable model is mandatory for reliable forecasts. A trustworthy model mandates untampered data, transparent learning, and explainable predictions. Blockchain smart contracts provide immutable, consensus-based, and tamper-proof transactions that can secure linear regression models for linear regression models. Moreover, a blockchain distributed ledger provides data provenance, which helps keep the system transparent. However, smart contract languages restrict such learning capabilities due to a lack of floating-point computations. Consequently, the accuracy of learning a multiple linear regression model is unreliable and does not produce the intended regression accuracy for the sake of predictions. Moreover, the scalability of blockchain smart contracts raises concerns about developing such models, as the training of models tends to be very expensive and time-consuming.

3   Our Contribution

- Despite the limitation of the Solidity programming language, we have trained the linear regression model with an iterative optimization method in the smart contract. See Sect. 5
- We have proposed a novel architecture to train linear regression model with layer two blockchain and predict using layer one blockchain. See **Sect. 5**
- We produced comparable training accuracy on blockchain concerning scikit-learn (python machine learning library) based training. See **Sect. 5**
- Our prediction results confirm that smart contracts can predict with high efficacy compared to scikit-learn prediction (Python machine learning library). **See Table 1, Fig. 3 and 4.**
- We have reduced the cost of training multiple linear regression on blockchain network by 100 times through layer two blockchain scalability solution. **See Table 2.**

4   Literature Review

Blockchain for AI: Blockchain provides enhanced data security for storing sensitive information in diskless environments [13]. The data in the blockchain is digitally signed, ensuring the security of data for AI and enhancing trust. In healthcare systems, for instance, blockchain helps AI with cryptographic security protocols that protect patient data and make a graph database of patient healthcare systems [14]. Ethical concerns and privacy of patient data are two of the main problems when an artificially intelligent application analyzes patient data [15]. Blockchain secures the privacy of the patient data with private key and public key combinations [16] that do not reveal the patient's identity. In addition, blockchain provides automation features that are missing in machine learning applications, eventually improving performance [17]. Such applications are used for fraud detection in financial transactions. Whenever data is exposed to a private authority, it is at risk of exposure depending on the organization's interest. Blockchain helps machine learning applications build a privacy-preserving model for its prediction technique [18]. However, protecting data for integrity and privacy does not guarantee trust in the training and prediction of machine learning models.

Blockchain Integrated AI Applications: *DeepBrainChain* [19] is one of the first frameworks in the industry to run artificial intelligence platforms with blockchain technology. The project reduces the cost of AI tasks with the help of distributed resources and shares the computing load with decentralization but fails to protect AI applications. *CortexAI* [20] is a decentralized AI platform that trains machine learning models offline and predicts online to incentivize the developers and providers of the service. However, online prediction does not use smart contracts and hence lacks trust. *Algorithmia* [21] developed a Danku project that allows anyone to post a dataset and ML model for evaluation and incentivize the model owners. When we train the model outside the blockchain, the data and model become vulnerable to threats and may not be trusted, thus making the platform susceptible to poisoning attacks. Liu et al. [13] discuss the advantage of collaboration between ML and blockchain technology that aids network and communication systems. In this work, blockchain facilitates training data and a sharing model for decentralized intelligence. ML applications can utilize blockchain in communication and networking systems to provide security, scalability, and privacy in intelligent smart contracts. Such promising integration requires the blockchain application to run machine learning algorithms for prediction or classification on distributed ledger platforms. However, the attempt to secure machine learning with blockchain remains unexplored.

Smart Contract Limitations: Solidity suffers from floating point arithmetic operations as they do not allow float division, signed exponents, and other float operations. Fixidity [24], ABDK [25], PrbMath [33], and Decimalmath [34] are some of the libraries trying to implement fixed-point equivalent outcomes, but these libraries increase the transaction cost of float operations along with the integer overflow problem which makes the libraries unreasonable for a training model.

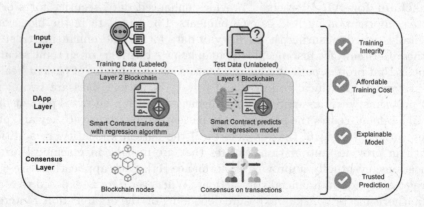

Fig. 1. Design of smart contract-based blockchain application for training multiple linear regression algorithm to optimize learning parameters for prediction purpose

5   Methodology

Design Approach: We developed a fraction-based numerical computation to train a linear regression model with smart contracts to assure integrity, provenance, and trust. We train the model with an optimistic roll-up approach (a layer two scalability method) and predict using the developed model on the blockchain (a layer one blockchain). The iterative optimization of the multiple linear regression method has a gradient descent-based learning approach that learns the parameter with a constant learning rate. The model trained with a smart contract on the Blockchain network produces consensus-based transactions which are highly trusted. Blockchain network and distributed file system together provide a provenance capability of tracing the model. Moreover, this approach also provides explainability of decisions made by the machine learning model that can be updated with a required correction. Figure 1 shows a high-level design of our proposed work. The input layer consists of the dataset. The DApp layer consists of smart contracts deployed on blockchain for training and prediction. The consensus layer computes transaction outputs with verified results.

Layer Two Blockchain for Training: Blockchain provides scalability solutions with an optimistic roll-up, zero-knowledge roll-up, sharding, and sidechains [8]. Although sharding and side chains are layer one scalability solutions of blockchain networks where the transaction delay is similar to the Ethereum network, they provide cheaper transactions. Zero-knowledge roll-up is a layer two blockchain scalability solution that produces complex cryptographic proofs that make the computations highly complex, resulting in inexplicable AI. On the other hand, optimistic roll-up (a layer two scalability solution) assumes that the miners are honest and will produce cheaper transactions with faster outputs, which is ideal for training machine learning algorithms. We chose optimistic roll-up as the blockchain network for training the linear regression algorithm and compared the performance with the Ethereum test network.

Optimistic Roll-up for Off-chain Training: Optimistic roll-ups execute transactions parallel to Ethereum main chain. After all the transactions are complete, the last state change is stored on the main chain [8]. This increases the speed of transactions from 10 to 100 times. "Optimistic" refers to the aggregate of bare minimum information required to be stored without proof, assuming no fraud is committed. Optimism and Arbitrum are two of the platform that implements optimistic roll-ups with layer two blockchain solutions. The proof is provided only when fraud is committed.

Multiple Linear Regression: Multiple linear regression involves learning multiple parameters to form a line of the equation that can best fit a model [10]. Equation 1 shows the prediction formula for linear regression where we have to learn and optimize weights and biases which are $W_1, W_2, ...Wn$ and c. The learning of parameters is performed through the iterative optimization method. The same equation is referred to as $\overline{y}$(referred to as $yhat$) for training purposes.

The $\overline{y}$ is computed repeatedly with updated weights and biases. Multiple linear regression implementation can be detailed at [10]. The next section details how we have implemented iterative optimization with smart contracts.

$$y = W_1 x_1 + W_2 x_2 + W_3 x_3 \ldots\ldots + W_n x_n + c \tag{1}$$

Event Flow: Figure 2 shows the event flow of our proposed model, where AI application developers access our smart contracts to train linear regression models on the blockchain network. Later, an AI user access the prediction smart contract to predict the desired outcome through the blockchain network.

Iterative Optimization: The iterative optimization model is implemented with a fraction-based computation to ensure that Solidity smart contract can execute those functions on the Ethereum Platform. Iterative optimization involves 3 steps. Step 1 is to compute $\overline{y}$ with random weight and bias parameters. From step 1, we get the mean square error between $\overline{y}$ and the actual y value. Step 2 involves the derivative computation of weights and biases annotated as *delta_weight* and *delta_bias* concerning the mean square error. Lastly, step 3 involves updating weights and biases with learning rate α [10].

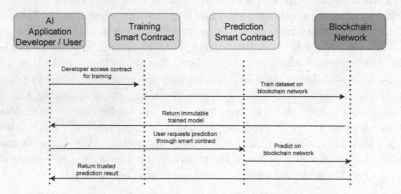

Fig. 2. Event flow of regression model development through smart contracts where training a model and prediction are computed on blockchain networks.

$$get\_y\_hat = \frac{\overline{y\_num}}{y\_den} = \frac{weight\_num}{weight\_den} * \frac{x\_num}{x\_den} + \frac{bias\_num}{bias\_den} \tag{2}$$

$$get\_y\_diff = \left(\frac{\overline{y\_num}}{y\_den} - \frac{y_i\_num}{y_i\_den} \right) \tag{3}$$

$$get\_delta\_weights = \frac{\delta w\_num}{\delta w\_den}$$
$$= \frac{1}{N} \sum_{i=0}^{n-1} 2 * \frac{x_i\_num}{x_i\_den} (get\_y\_diff) \tag{4}$$

$$get\_delta\_bias = \frac{\delta b\_num}{\delta b\_den} = \frac{1}{N}\sum_{i=0}^{n} 2 * (get\_y\_diff) \qquad (5)$$

$$\frac{weight\_num}{weight\_den} = \frac{weight\_num}{weight\_den} - \frac{\alpha\_num}{\alpha\_den} \cdot \frac{\delta w\_num}{\delta w\_den} \qquad (6)$$

$$\frac{bias\_num}{bias\_den} = \frac{bias\_num}{bias\_den} - \frac{\alpha\_num}{\alpha\_den} \cdot \frac{\delta b\_num}{\delta b\_den} \qquad (7)$$

Fraction Transformation for Multiple Linear Regression: We have obtained a fraction-based computational method from the standard iterative optimization method that transfers decimal numbers into a fraction for performing iterative optimization in the solidity smart contract. The Eq. 2 computes $\overline{y}$ values multiplies *weights* with *features* and adds biases. The $\overline{y}$ is represented with $\overline{y\_num}/y\_den$ (*numerator/denominator*). Equation 3 subtracts true y value from $\overline{y}$. The Eq. 4 computes the gradient descent derivative of *weights* concerning the difference between the true values of training data and $\overline{y}$ values that are computed with Eq. 2. Similarly, Eq. 5 provides the derivative of bias. After completing all the derivative computations the new parameters are updated with Eq. 6 and Eq. 7. All the parameters are computed in fractions with numerator and denominator terms.

6 Experimental Setup

We have considered two datasets for testing our hypothesis. The two datasets are "Diabetes progression" [28] and "Real state valuation" [35] with 442 and 414 samples. The "Diabetes Progression" dataset provides a quantitative measure of diabetes progression concerning age, sex, body mass index, average blood pressure, and six blood serum measurements for 442 diabetes patients. The "Real state valuation" dataset provides price estimates of real estate concerning transaction date, house age, distance to nearest meter station, number of nearby convenience stores, latitude, and longitude with geographical coordinates. These datasets have categorical and continuous variables. Data are pre-processed with label encoders to convert categorical values to continuous variables for smart contract inputs. Moreover, we have deployed the training smart contract on layer two blockchain network (Arbitrum) [27]. The prediction smart contract is deployed in the Ethereum Ropsten test network. To build a comparable analysis, we deployed a linear regression model with the scikit-learn library to record baseline performance accuracy. Scikit-learn [28] provides a set of python standard libraries for various AI algorithms.

7 Performance Evaluation

Prediction Accuracy: The Table 1 provides mean square errors in the prediction of all the datasets for smart-contract-based prediction and python-based prediction. The prediction error of diabetes and real-state cost are close for both smart contract and python deployment in Table 1, which ensures the reliability of training with smart contracts.

Table 1. Mean square error comparison between smart contract-based and python scikit-learn based prediction

Dataset	MSE in Smart Contract	MSE in Python
Diabetes Progression	2865	2900
Real State Cost	72.67	1.00

The Fig. 3 and 4 provide the comparison of ground truth, library prediction, and smart contract prediction values for the test datasets of diabetes progression and real state costs. The graph in Fig. 3 shows that the scikit-learn-based prediction and smart contract-based predictions are converging. The accuracy of prediction is approximately 95% to the python-library-based function. Furthermore, the graph in Fig. 4 provides another convincing prediction result close to the ground truth that confirms that the mean square error is low.

Cost of Smart Contracts Functions: The smart contract transaction cost for Ethereum Rospten test network follows the formula $transaction cost(Ethers) = gas\_used * (gasprice + basefee))/10^9 Gwei$ [8]. We have plotted the get_y_hat function (another name for $\overline{y}$) in Fig. 5 with y-axis showing rise of cost in GWei and x-axis as number of features. It is clear from the graph that the cost of computing $\overline{y}$ forms a linear relationship with a number of features and is predictable. The cost computations of the remaining functions are plotted in Fig. 6. The cost of transaction for $get_d elta\_w$, and get_y_diff similarly forms linear relationships

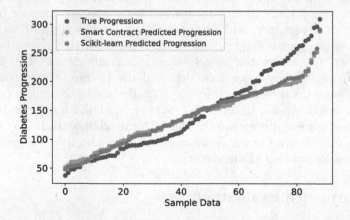

Fig. 3. Comparison of true sorted diabetes progression with predicted progression for scikit learn library and blockchain smart contracts. The scikit-learn and smart contracts produced similar progression estimates.

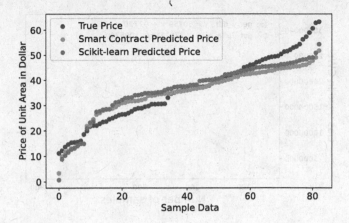

Fig. 4. Comparison of true sorted real state valuation (price) with predicted valuation (prices) for scikit learn library and blockchain smart contracts. The scikit-learn and smart contracts produced similar progression estimates.

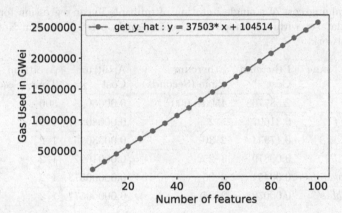

Fig. 5. Shows the cost of computing *get_y_hat* function on Ropsten test network for a rising number of data samples. The relationship is linear for the x-axis and y-axis, with a slope value of 37503.

with rising number of samples as shown in Fig. 6. The slope of get_delta_w is greater than get_y_diff due to the higher number of computations involved in calculating weight parameters.

The Table 2 provides the comparative analysis of the cost of training a single iteration for 353 samples on Rospten and Arbitrum networks. The cost of get_y_hat computation is the highest among all the functions for the Ethereum Ropsten network. It computes the $\bar{y}$ values for all the samples. The number of function execution is equivalent to the number of examples in the training dataset. Linear regression requires more than 1000 iterations to optimize weights with iterative optimization methods, and the cost of $\bar{y}$ function is 2587 ethers, US dollar equivalent to 50,590,801, which is drastically high. Conversely, the

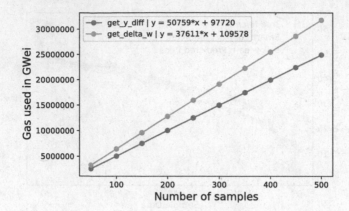

Fig. 6. Shows the cost of computing $get\_y\_diff, get\_delta\_weights, get\_delta\_bias$ and function on Ropsten test network. The slope of get_delta_w is greater than get_y_diff due to the higher number of computations involved in calculating weight parameters.

Table 2. Training cost of a single iteration of multiple linear regression for Diabetes progression dataset with 353 samples of training on Ropsten Ethereum Network and Arbitrum network.

Function Name	Ethereum Cost	Ethereum Time (Seconds)	Arbitrum Cost	Arbitrum Time (Seconds)
get_y_hat	2.587768	4500–6000	0.0066046	300
get_y_diff	0.31607	3–25	0.00080997	1–2
get_delta_w	0.17934	2–30	0.0033095	1–2
get_delta_b	0.00879	3–25	0.00016627	1–2
$get\_new\_weights$	0.00451	3–26	0.00000573	1–2
get_new_bias	0.00072	2–34	0.00000571	1–2

Arbitrum network seems to reduce the price more than 100 times and make the cost of training a model on a blockchain platform more affordable. The cost of training the model with 1000 iterations would be approximately 10.016 Arbitrum ethers, equivalent to 0.0033 USD (1 Arbitrum ether = 0.0002933 USD).

Table 3. Shows a rise in the number of operations for fraction-based computations for smart contract functions while compared with non-fraction-based computations.

Function	Decimal Flops	Fraction Flops
get_y_hat	2 nm	6 nm
get_delta_w	2 nm	6 nm
get_delta_b	n	4n

8   Computational Analysis

The number of lines of code and operations in blockchain smart contracts is crucial for the computational cost of functions defined underneath. We have analyzed the difference in the number of computations between fraction and non-fraction-based calculations. We have considered Watkins's "Fundamental of Matrix Computation" book [29] for the analysis of the number of operations involved in our application. Considering a training dataset of $m * n$ matrix, Table 3 shows that the number of computations will increase by approximately 3–4 times when calculations are performed with fractions compared to decimal counts. This rise in the count will impact the cost of smart contract functions.

9   Limitation and Challenges

Block Gas Limit: The gas limit for the Ethereum Ropsten transaction reached block capacity to compute a higher number of computations to develop a linear regression model with a smart contract. For Ropsten, the default gas limit is a hard limit of 4712388 GWei [30] as current information. Due to the number of iterations involved in computing the entire set of functions, the gas capacity could not be controlled. The main Ethereum network has a default block gas limit of 15,000,000 Gwei [31] and can be increased to 30,000,000 Gwei. We assume that the Ethereum main network will allow a higher number of computations due to the higher block gas limit.

10   Conclusion

Smart contracts do not allow floating-point computations for linear regression algorithms. This hinders the development of the AI model in blockchain networks. We have proposed a novel approach to develop a trustable machine learning model with the help of blockchain technology and make the artificially intelligent application more secure. Our work also shows that static smart contracts can be transformed into learning smart contracts by running machine learning algorithms inside the blockchain network. We have deployed a smart contract with a multiple linear regression mechanism to train our models on blockchain and achieved excellent training accuracy concerning mean square error computation. We have also achieved good prediction accuracy for the model learned on-chain. Moreover, our solution minimizes the cost of training linear regression algorithms using optimistic roll-up (layer two blockchain). We have analyzed the cost of training a machine learning model and showed that the optimistic roll-up saves the training cost by more than 100 times. In the future, we aim to develop more AI algorithms using smart contracts with further investigation and analysis.

References

1. Bangbit Technologies: Introduction to artificial intelligence (AI): a deep dive into machine learning & deep learning (2019). https://medium.com/@BangBitTech/introduction-to-artificial-intelligence-ai-a-deep-dive-into-machine-learning-deep-learning-4763e6985344
2. Bantis, A.C.: Is your ML model secure. https://medium.com/slalom-technology/is-your-ml-model-secure-fe10b8589b71. Accessed Sep 2021
3. Pitropakis, N., et al.: A taxonomy and survey of attacks against machine learning. Comput. Sci. Rev. **34**, 100199 (2019). https://doi.org/10.1016/j.cosrev.2019.100199
4. Liao, Q.V., et al.: Introduction to explainable AI. In: Extended Abstracts of the 2021 CHI Conference on Human Factors in Computing Systems, pp. 1–3 (2021)
5. Kale, A., et al.: Provenance documentation to enable explainable and trustworthy AI: a literature review. Data Intell. 1–41 (2022)
6. Pawar, U., O'Shea, D., Rea, S., O'Reilly, R.: Explainable AI in healthcare. In: 2020 International Conference on Cyber Situational Awareness, Data Analytics and Assessment (CyberSA), pp. 1–2 (2020). https://doi.org/10.1109/CyberSA49311.2020.9139655
7. Kastner, C.: Versioning, provenance, and reproducibility in production machine learning (2021). https://ckaestne.medium.com/versioning-provenance-and-reproducibility-in-production-machine-learning-355c48665005
8. Ethereum, W.: Ethereum whitepaper. Ethereum (2014). https://ethereum.org. Accessed 07 July 2020
9. Parizi, R.M., Dehghantanha, A.: Smart contract programming languages on blockchains: an empirical evaluation of usability and security. In: Chen, S., Wang, H., Zhang, L.J. (eds.) Blockchain (ICBC 2018). LNCS, vol. 10974, pp. 75–91. Springer, Cham (2018). https://doi.org/10.1007/978-3-319-94478-4_6
10. Neto, J.: Multiple linear regression from scratch using Python (2021). https://medium.com/analytics-vidhya/multiple-linear-regression-from-scratch-using-python-db9368859f
11. Shafiq, A.B.: Which methods should be used for solving linear regression? https://www.kdnuggets.com/2020/09/solving-linear-regression.html
12. Salah, K., et al.: Blockchain for AI: review and open research challenges. IEEE Access **7**, 10127–10149 (2019). https://doi.org/10.1109/ACCESS.2018.2890507
13. Liu, Y., et al.: Blockchain and machine learning for communications and networking systems. IEEE Commun. Surv. Tutor. **22**(2), 1392–1431 (2020). https://doi.org/10.1109/COMST.2020.2975911
14. Campbell, D.: Combining AI and blockchain to push frontiers in healthcare. https://www.macadamian.com/learn/combining-ai-and-blockchain-in-healthcare/
15. Bartoletti, I.: AI in healthcare: ethical and privacy challenges. In: Riaño, D., Wilk, S., ten Teije, A. (eds.) AIME 2019. LNCS (LNAI), vol. 11526, pp. 7–10. Springer, Cham (2019). https://doi.org/10.1007/978-3-030-21642-9_2
16. Kumar, R., Tripathi, R.: Secure healthcare framework using blockchain and public key cryptography (2020)
17. Wang, T.: A unified analytical framework for trustable machine learning and automation running with blockchain. IEEE Trans. Big Data **2018**, 4974–4983 (2018). https://doi.org/10.1109/BigData.2018.8622262

18. Kim, H., Kim, S., Hwang, J.Y., Seo, C.: Efficient privacy-preserving machine learning for blockchain network. IEEE Access **7**, 136481–136495 (2019). https://doi.org/10.1109/ACCESS.2019.2940052.27

19. Zou, J., et al.: DeepBrainChain: artificial intelligence computing platform driven by blockchain. White Paper. https://cryptorating.eu/whitepapers/DeepBrain-Chain/DeepBrainChainWhitepaper.pdf. Accessed Nov 2021

20. Chen, Z., Wang, W., Yan, X., Tian, J.: Cortex-AI on blockchain- the decentralized AI autonomous system. White Paper. https://cryptorating.EU/whitepapers/Cortex/Cortex_AI_on_Blockchain_EN.pdf. Accessed Nov 2021

21. Kurtulmus, A.B., Daniel, K.: Trustless machine learning contracts; evaluating and exchanging machine learning models on ethereum blockchain. https://arxiv.org/pdf/1802.10185.pdf

22. Harris, J.D., Waggoner, B.: Decentralized and collaborative AI on blockchain. IEEE Int. Conf. Blockchain **2019**, 368–375 (2019). https://doi.org/10.1109/Blockchain.2019.00057

23. Solidity Programming guide. https://docs.soliditylang.org/en/v0.8.9/. Accessed Sept 2021

24. Fixidity fixed point library for solidity. https://github.com/CementDAO/Fixidity. Accessed Nov 2021

25. ABDK library for solidity. https://github.com/abdk-consulting/abdk-libraries-solidity/blob/master/ABDKMath64x64.sol. Accessed Nov 2021

26. Ethereum white paper, "Scaling" (2022). https://ethereum.org/en/developers/docs/scaling/

27. Kalodner, H., Goldfeder, S., Chen, X., Weinberg, S.M., Felten, E.W.: Arbitron: scalable, private smart contracts. In: 27th USENIX Security Symposium (USENIX Security 2018), pp. 1353–1370 (2018)

28. Pedregosa, F., et al.: Scikit-learn: machine learning in Python. J. Mach. Learn. Res. **12**, 2825–2830 (2011)

29. Watkins: Fundamentals of matrix computations. https://davidtabora.files.wordpress.com/2015/01/david_s-_watkins_fundamentals_of_matrix_computat.pdf

30. Moriya, H.: How to get ethereum block gas limit. https://piyopiyo.medium.com/how-to-get-ethereum-block-gas-limit-eba2c8f32ce. Accessed Dec 2021

31. Notik, D.: Ethereum. https://ethereum.org/en/developers/docs/gas/. Accessed Dec 2021

32. Project Implementation: "Github Source". https://github.com/syber2020/LR-KNN-6950-FA21/tree/master/LR-Python-Web3/MLR

33. PRBMath library. https://github.com/paulrberg/prb-math. Accessed July 2022

34. Decimalmath. https://github.com/alcueca/DecimalMath. Accessed July 2022

35. Yeh, I.C., Hsu, T.K.: Building real estate valuation models with comparative approach through case-based reasoning. Appl. Soft Comput. **65**, 260–271 (2018)

Combining ID's, Attributes, and Policies in Hyperledger Fabric

Daan Gordijn[1], Roland Kromes[1(✉)], Thanassis Giannetsos[2], and Kaitai Liang[1]

[1] Cyber Security Group, Delft University of Technology, Delft, The Netherlands
`D.A.Gordijn@student.tudelft.nl`, {`R.G.Kromes,Kaitai.Liang`}`@tudelft.nl`
[2] Ubitech Ltd., Digital Security and Trusted Computing Group, Athens, Greece
`agiannetsos@ubitech.eu`

Abstract. This work aims to provide a more secure access control in Hyperledger Fabric blockchain by combining multiple IDs, attributes, and policies with the components that regulate access control. The access control system currently used by Hyperledger Fabric is first completely analyzed. Next, a new implementation is proposed that builds upon the existing solution but provides users and developers with easier ways to make access control decisions based on combinations of multiple ID's, attributes, and policies. Our proposed implementation encapsulates the Fabric CA client to facilitate attribute addition and simplify the process of registering and enrolling a newly created certificate (corresponding to a new user). This research, concludes that it is possible to combine multiple ID's, attributes, and policies with the help of Hyperledger Fabric's smart contract technology. Furthermore, it could be seen that the performance impact for real-world applications is negligible compared to the insecure case of always providing access to a resource without performing access control.

Keywords: Blockchain · IPFS · Privacy · Security

1 Introduction

Ever since the anonymous Satoshi Nakamoto published his Bitcoin white paper [21] in 2008, blockchain has become one of the most disruptive technologies in the computer science industry. In recent years, many other innovative blockchain technologies have been developed [20], which are becoming increasingly more popular.

While Bitcoin was created to provide a digital alternative to traditional, bank-controlled currencies [17], many of these newer blockchain technologies are designed to provide a platform for building and deploying decentralized applications through the use of smart contracts[1]. By implementing their business

---

[1] A digital contract written into code that is stored and automatically executed on the nodes of a distributed blockchain network [6].

© ICST Institute for Computer Sciences, Social Informatics and Telecommunications Engineering 2023
Published by Springer Nature Switzerland AG 2023. All Rights Reserved
W. Meng and W. Li (Eds.): BlockTEA 2022, LNICST 498, pp. 32–48, 2023.
https://doi.org/10.1007/978-3-031-31420-9_3

logic within these smart contracts, decentralized applications can automatically execute any transaction without human intervention, making them completely independent and decentralized [28]. Due to the many benefits of decentralized applications [2], the adoption of blockchain technologies has recently expanded to many non-financial applications such as "healthcare, supply chain management, market monitoring, smart energy, and copyright protection" [29].

Most of these traditional blockchain technologies, such as Bitcoin, Ethereum, and Cardano, are so-called "permissionless" blockchain technologies. This type of blockchain technology, however, has many privacy issues when it is being used in the context of enterprise-level applications, as described in [23]. Many alternative, so-called "permissioned" blockchain technologies have been proposed to solve the issues, the most promising of which is Hyperledger Fabric [9]. Through the use of innovative concepts such as channels, policies, identities, and Membership Service Providers, Hyperledger Fabric can determine the identity of participants, perform access control based on these identities, and ensure the privacy of transactions and smart contracts.

As with many technologies, the increase in popularity of blockchain technologies also drives an increase in security threats and attacks. One of the major issues that many blockchain technologies, including Hyperledger Fabric, currently have is providing secure access control to the distributed ledger and smart contracts. Hyperledger Fabric partially addresses this issue by only granting network access upon submission of a valid X.509 certificate [22], issued and approved by a trusted Certificate Authority. However, this type of ID-based access control is not scalable for larger organizations. This paper will therefore investigate how secure access control in Hyperledger Fabric can be improved, in particular by looking into solutions that can combine these ID's with attributes and policies.

The study also highlights the access control components that currently interact within Hyperledger Fabric. This work also provides a an implementation for combining multiple ID's, attributes, and policies be combined within Hyperledger Fabric, and analyzes the performance impact of ID-, attribute-, and policy-based access control.

This paper is structured in the following manner. First, Sect. 2 will provide a summary of the most relevant work that currently exists in literature. Next, Sect. 3 will provide an overview of the contributions made by this research. Then, Sect. 4 will provide a background on the current access control system of Hyperledger Fabric, while Sect. 5 will present the proposed system model that has been implemented as part of this research. Subsequently, Sect. 6 will provide an overview and analysis of the results that have been obtained during the research, while Sect. 7 will provide a brief discussion. Finally, Sect. 8 will present the main conclusions of this research.

2   Related Work

Research into secure access control in various blockchain technologies, including Hyperledger Fabric, has been conducted in multiple papers. Many of these studies are performed in the context of exploring the integration of blockchain technologies with the Internet of Things (IoT), as blockchain is currently seen as the most promising technique for providing secure access control to IoT devices [3].

In [24], a summary of the major problems of modern access control systems is presented, together with an explanation of how these problems can potentially be solved using blockchain technologies. Furthermore, this paper provides an overview of existing access control studies and describes the current challenges of blockchain-based access control.

In [3], an attribute-based access control scheme for Internet of Things devices is proposed by employing blockchain technology to keep track of the distribution of the attributes. Next, [26] proposes a different scheme that is built upon various smart contracts and so-called "functional modules", which are jointly responsible for managing attribute information and making access control decisions. Finally, [31] proposes yet another access control scheme which is implemented and deployed using the smart contract technology of the Ethereum blockchain network.

While the papers discussed so so far describe general blockchain-based access control systems, other papers make specific use of the Hyperledger Fabric blockchain technology. First, [13,30], and [16] explore basic access control scenarios for IoT devices in Hyperledger Fabric. Next, [32] combines the Hyperledger Fabric blockchain technology with the InterPlanetary File System (IPFS) [15], allowing IoT devices to easily store documents on a distributed file system and store the hashes of these documents on the blockchain ledger. Finally, [1] proposes a multi-layered and multi-model access control system in the context of an agricultural supply chain system that runs on Hyperledger Fabric.

While research into secure access control in Hyperledger Fabric and other blockchain technologies certainly exists, no study into combining multiple ID's, attributes, and policies during the decision-making process has been conducted. To fill in this gap, this paper will propose a new access control scheme that combines these ID's, attributes, and policies within a single smart contract deployed to a Hyperledger Fabric network. For consistency, this research paper will consider the scenario where an IoT device wants to store a document on IPFS and subsequently save the returned document hash on the blockchain network, as also used in [32].

3   Contribution

Using the existing literature from the previous phase, a new design was proposed to provide secure access control in Hyperledger Fabric. As stated in the research question, this design had to combine multiple ID's, attributes, and policies in the decision-making process. Subsequently, during the implementation phase, the design was implemented using a smart contract and deployed to a local Hyperledger Fabric test network, which was set up using the official tutorial [11].

Hyperledger Fabric currently supports three programming languages for the development of smart contracts and client applications: Go, Java, and NodeJS [12]. For each language, several SDK's are available [10] that help make the implementation of smart contracts and client applications easier. For this particular research project, NodeJS with TypeScript has been selected as the toolchain for the implementation phase, as this language is very easy to learn and understand.

The complete repository that contains a basic test network together with the smart contracts and sample applications that have been implemented during this research project is available on GitHub[2]. The README stored in this repository also includes a small tutorial, as well as a complete overview of the required tools and their recommended versions.

4   Background

This section discusses the current approach to secure access control in Hyperledger Fabric. This section begins with a brief introduction to Hyperledger Fabric and secure access control in general, and subsequently discusses the main components and methodologies that Hyperledger Fabric currently uses to provide secure access control.

4.1   Hyperledger Fabric

Hyperledger Fabric is an "open-source enterprise-grade permissioned distributed ledger technology (DLT) platform, designed for use in enterprise contexts" [12]. While many well-established blockchain platforms such as Bitcoin and Ethereum are currently being modified to be used in enterprise-grade applications, Hyperledger Fabric has been built around enterprise applications from the beginning. First, Hyperledger Fabric is highly modular, which allows core parts of the blockchain network to be customized. Second, Hyperledger Fabric has support for writing smart contracts in general-purpose languages, including Go, Java, and NodeJS, while most other blockchain technologies require developers to learn new languages, such as Vyper or Solidity in the case of Ethereum [5]. Finally, Hyperledger Fabric is permissioned, which means that the identity of all participants of the network is known and can therefore be verified using access control systems, allowing organizations to establish trust.

Each node in the network maintains a local Membership Service Provider (MSP). These service providers store all X.509 certificates that have been issued by the Certificate Authorities of their corresponding organizations, which are then used by network nodes to map X.509 identities to internal roles. Together with the Certificate Authorities, these providers are therefore responsible for providing the initial layer of identity-based access control.

---

[2] https://github.com/daangordijn/Fabric-Access-Control.

4.2   Secure Access Control

Access control is "a security technique that regulates who or what can view or use resources in a computing environment" [19]. Different types of access control exist, including Identity-Based Access Control (IBAC), Role-Based Access Control (RBAC), and Attribute-Based Access Control (ABAC) [4]. While older, established blockchain technologies such as Bitcoin and Ethereum are non-permissioned and therefore do not implement these types of access control systems, Hyperledger Fabric is a permissioned blockchain technology, which enforces it to perform access control.

Currently, Hyperledger Fabric employs multiple layers of access control to provide security and privacy within the blockchain network. First, at the most basic level, Hyperledger Fabric uses a simple identity-based access control system, which prevents unauthorized entities from accessing anything on the blockchain network. This layer is explained in more detail in Sects. 4.3 and 4.4 since the purpose of this paper is to extend this simple system to a more complex attribute-based access control system. Second, at an organizational level, Hyperledger Fabric can restrict access to smart contracts and the ledger through the use of channels, as described in Sect. 4.1. By only granting individual organizations access to the minimal required subset of channels, the privacy of smart contracts and ledger states can be preserved.

4.3   Certificate Authorities (CAs)

A Certificate Authority is an "organization that acts to validate the identities of entities and bind them to cryptographic keys through the issuance of electronic documents known as digital certificates" [27]. Hyperledger Fabric provides a special implementation, called the "Fabric Certificate Authority" or "Fabric CA" in short, which can be used to create and sign these digital certificates using the international X.509 standard [14]. Fabric CA consists of both a client-side and server-side command line interface (CLI), called `fabric-ca-client` and `fabric-ca-server`, respectively. Fabric CA provides many features including "registration of identities, issuance of enrollment certificates, and certificate renewal and revocation" [7].

When an administrator wants to enroll a new identity, Fabric CA will generate a key-value pair that consists of a private key and a public key. Together with the parameters provided by the administrator, a Certificate Signing Request (CSR) will be created, which is then processed by Fabric CA.

In Sect. 4.5, this process of registering and enrolling a new identity with the Fabric CA server is visualized. This section will also describe a new command line interface (CLI) that has been implemented as part of this study and makes the creation of new identities much easier.

4.4   Membership Service Providers (MSPs)

A Membership Service Provider is a component within Hyperledger Fabric that can be used by participants of the blockchain network to prove their identity to other participants of this network. When a user wants to start interacting with a Hyperledger Fabric blockchain network, it needs to create a key pair, which consists of a public key and a private key, which is needed to prove its identity to the rest of the network. Next, this public key must be included in a Certificate Signing Request (CSR), which is then submitted to a Certificate Authority and used to issue a new X.509 certificate. While X.509 certificates, including public keys, can be shared publicly, private keys must always be kept secret to comply with the principles of Public-Key Infrastructure (PKI) [18].

When a participant of the blockchain network now wants to submit a transaction, it needs to create a transaction proposal and sign this proposal using its private key. All nodes on the blockchain network are then able to verify this transaction proposal using the public X.509 certificate of this participant since it is stored inside the Membership Service Providers. Because of this, Membership Service Providers can establish trust on the permissioned blockchain network, without the need of sharing private keys.

4.5 Generating Certificates

In Fig. 1, a simplified version of the process of generating X.509 certificates using Fabric CA is visualized. As can be seen, the Fabric CA Client has to invoke the Fabric CA Server using two commands, `fabric-ca-client register` and `fabric-ca-client enroll` [7]. By doing this, the server will generate a private key, a public key, and a corresponding signed X.509 certificate. This certificate is then automatically stored in the Membership Service Providers that are located on various nodes inside the blockchain network.

While this process of generating X.509 certificates for Hyperledger Fabric is not overly complicated, it can become cumbersome to run multiple commands with many different flags to just create one certificate. Therefore, as part of this research paper, a wrapper around the `fabric-ca-client` was created. This tool, called `certgen`, is publicly available in the GitHub repository (see footnote 4), together with a small tutorial on how to interact with it. The `certgen` tool internally uses the `fabric-ca-client` commands and has the advantage that it can automatically populate a local file system wallet with the correct files which are required to connect a client application to the blockchain network. In addition, since this tool is highly interactive, it makes it much easier for administrators to add attributes to the certificate. More about the importance of setting attributes within X.509 certificates will be explained in Sect. 5.

5 Proposed Implementation

This section discusses the proposed implementation that improves the current implementation of secure access control in Hyperledger Fabric, introduced in Sect. 4. This section begins with a brief discussion of how to independently combine multiple ID's, attributes, and policies, and subsequently presents the final design incorporating these components.

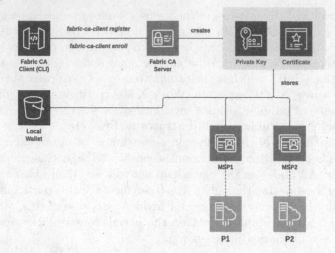

Fig. 1. Current process of enrolling a new identity within a Hyperledger Fabric network. The `fabric-ca-client` CLI is used to run the `register` and `enroll` commands, respectively. Then, the resulting X.509 certificate is stored on a set of peer nodes, while both the X.509 certificate and the corresponding private key are stored in the user's local file system wallet.

5.1 Combining Attributes

In Hyperledger Fabric, every X.509 certificate issued by Fabric CA [7] can have attributes. These attributes can be used during access control to determine whether a client should be given access, or not. To allow for more complex access control decisions, multiple attributes can be combined into so-called "policies", which are visualized in Fig. 2.

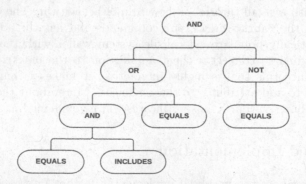

Fig. 2. Combining multiple attributes. The `EQUALS` and `INCLUDES` operators validate whether a specified attribute equals or includes a certain value, respectively. The `AND`, `OR`, and `NOT` boolean operators can be then be applied to combine or negate these individual attribute checks, allowing the client to create complex policies.

For this study, the following boolean operators have been selected that can be used for building access control policies:

- EQUALS: Checks whether an attribute is present on the certificate, and whether it is equal to the provided value.
- INCLUDES: Checks whether an attribute is present on the certificate, and whether it includes the provided value. This operator can be used when the specified attribute on the certificate has a comma-separated list of strings as its value, which must include a particular value.
- AND: Logical operator that combines two or more operator trees. This operator returns true if and only if all operator trees combined by this operator evaluate to true, and returns false otherwise.
- OR: Logical operator that combines two or more operator trees. This operator returns true if and only if at least one of the operator trees combined by this operator evaluates to true, and returns false otherwise.
- NOT: Logical operator that negates the output of another the given tree. This operator returns true if and only if the operator tree provided to this operator evaluates to false, and returns false otherwise.

Together, these operators can build complex policies that can later be evaluated to determine whether a client has access to a resource on the blockchain network, or not.

5.2   Combining Policies

As described in the previous subsection, an access policy is a rule that enforces an X.509 certificate to possess a particular combination of attributes and values. These access policies can be used in Hyperledger Fabric to verify whether an entity invoking a smart contract has sufficient permissions to invoke the endpoint. Figure 3 shows a simplified example of a client invoking three different operations on a smart contract: reading an asset, updating the asset, and deleting the asset.

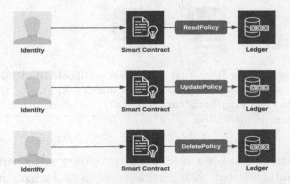

Fig. 3. Combining multiple policies. Each smart contract has a different purpose and might need different policies for different operations. Multiple policies can be defined in a single smart contract, and depending on the operation requested by the client, the correct validation policy will be selected and used for access control.

As can be seen in the image, the invoked smart contract has a different access policy for each of the three supported operations. For example, a client might be able to satisfy the `ReadPolicy` with its X.509 certificate, but might not be able to satisfy the `UpdatePolicy` and `DeletePolicy`. Therefore, this client will only be allowed to read the asset and will be denied access when it tries to update or delete the asset.

5.3   Combining ID's

In Hyperledger Fabric, IDs are composed of X.509 certificates [22], issued by Certificate Authorities and managed by Membership Service Providers. Research into combining multiple such X.509 certificates has not been published to the date of writing. In fact, X.509 certificates cannot be combined by a simple merge, since the X.509 standard [14] does not allow this. Therefore, for this study, alternative ways of combining multiple X.509 certificates had to be found.

The solution proposed in this study can integrate one X.509 certificate, referred to as the "parent", into another X.509 certificate. The process by which this integration can be realized is visualized in Fig. 4 and described below.

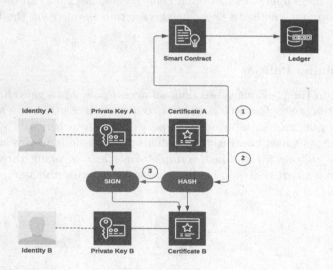

Fig. 4. Combining multiple ID's. First, the X.509 certificate of identity A is hashed. Next, this hash is signed with the private key of identity A. Finally, these two values, `hash(certificate)` and `sign(hash(certificate))`, are added to the X.509 certificate of identity B as custom attributes.

- First, the member invokes a special smart contract using certificate A (the member is authenticated with certificate A to blockchain network). This smart contract then extracts the certificate from the request, and subsequently stores it into a hashmap on the distributed blockchain ledger;
- Second, the member creates the SHA-256 hash of certificate A.

- Third, the member signs the obtained SHA-256 hash using private key corresponding to certificate A.
- Fourth, the member provides the previously performed hash value and signature to an admin using the *certgen* tool. These arguments allows the *certgen* tool to set the `hfa.ParentHash` and `hfa.ParentSignature` attributes of the child certificate (e.g., certificate B).

Whenever a client now invokes a smart contract on the blockchain network using identity B, this smart contract can verify that this client also owns identity A, since it needed access to private key A in step (3) to calculate the `hfa.ParentSignature` attribute. If the client would not have access to this private key, the signature provided in this attribute cannot be valid. Since certificate A was previously stored on the ledger in step (1), the invoked smart contract has access to the public key of identity A, and could therefore easily establish that the provided signature was forged, thus denying access to the network.

Having established that the client invoking the smart contract with identity B also owns identity A, the smart contract can retrieve the certificate of identity A from the hashmap stored on the distributed ledger, and use it to make access control decisions. The proposed smart contract has been implemented and made available in the GitHub repository[3]. This implementation currently supports one parent certificate to be set in the `hfa.ParentHash` and `hfa.ParentSignature` attributes, although it can easily be extended to support multiple parents or recursive ancestor lookups in the future.

The proposed solution to combine multiple ID's can be particularly useful for decentralized applications and IoT-device applications, where the device or application belongs to a specific owner. In these cases, the identity and access rights of the applications can easily be identified by setting the owner's certificate as the parent certificate within the X.509 certificate of each application. Furthermore, it guarantees that if an application belongs to user B, and therefore contains the hash of user's B identity in its X.509 certificate, it will not be able to access data related to user A.

5.4   Workflow in a Blockchain-IPFS-Based Network

In the previous subsections, the proposed methods of combining multiple ID's, attributes, and policies have been discussed on an individual basis. This subsection will explain how these three concepts will fit together, and how this combined design has been implemented using Hyperledger Fabric. Figure 5 shows a simplified version of the final system architecture[4].

The final system design consists of four main components, which will be described below.

---

[3] https://github.com/daangordijn/Fabric-Access-Control/tree/master/access-chaincode.

[4] More detailed version available at https://github.com/daangordijn/Fabric-Access-Control/blob/master/images.

Fabric CA Server. A Fabric CA Server instance will be used to issue certificates to various nodes and clients within a particular organization. Fabric CA plays a key role when combining multiple ID's, as it is responsible for creating the basic X.509 certificates and their corresponding private keys, as well as setting the `hfa.ParentHash` and `hfa.ParentSignature` attributes if applicable.

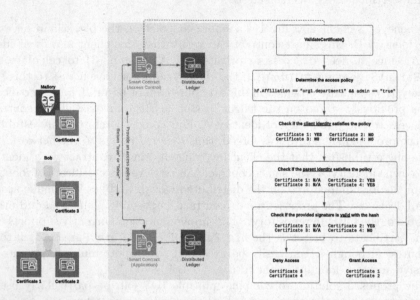

Fig. 5. Final system design, combining all discussed concepts. Certificate 1 is granted access to the resource since it satisfies the defined access policy. Certificate 2 is granted access to the resource since it contains the `hfa.ParentHash` and `hfa.ParentSignature` attributes, which connects it to certificate 1. Certificate 3 is denied access since it does not satisfy the access policy, while certificate 4 is denied access since it contains an invalid hash signature.

Security Smart Contract. The security smart contract is a custom-made smart contract that has two responsibilities.

- First, this smart contract is responsible for maintaining the "parent" X.509 certificates stored on the ledger, as described in Sect. 5.1. Clients that want to combine two identities, e.g., identity A and identity B, have to invoke this smart contract with identity A. The smart contract will then calculate the SHA-256 hash of the provided certificate, store it in the hashmap on the ledger, and return the hash to the client. Now, the client can calculate the signature and set the required attributes.
- Second, this smart contract can be invoked by other smart contracts that live on the blockchain network to determine whether a client satisfies a particular access policy. Smart contracts can make use of the `ctx.stub.invokeChaincode()` method to invoke this security smart contract, provide the access policy that has to be validated, and will then be returned a boolean

value indicating whether the client certificate satisfies the specified policy. The internal logic of this smart contract method is visualized on the right side in Fig. 5.

Client Smart Contract(s). The client smart contracts are basic smart contracts that allow clients of the blockchain network to interact with the ledger. Examples of such smart contracts are the `asset-transfer` or `commercial-paper` chaincodes provided in the `fabric-samples` repository[5]. While previously, these smart contracts had to implement their business logic to validate whether a client has access to the requested resource, developers are now able to simply invoke the security smart contract using the `ctx.stub.invokeChaincode()` method of the Hyperledger Fabric SDK, and use the returned boolean to allow or deny the client from accessing the requested resource.

Client Application(s). The client applications are basic applications that allow clients of the blockchain network to more easily interact with smart contracts, instead of having to use the peer CLI. Examples of such client applications are the `asset-transfer` or `commercial-paper` applications provided in the `fabric-samples` repository. To client applications, changes made to the proposed solution are not visible, except for the fact that some X.509 certificates containing valid `hfa.ParentHash` and `hfa.ParentSignature` attributes will now be granted access, while they would previously have been denied access from the network.

In summary, this section has presented a solution for combining multiple ID's, attributes, and policies in Hyperledger Fabric. Since this solution can be fully implemented using a single smart contract, the core components of the Hyperledger Fabric blockchain can remain unchanged. In the next section, a performance analysis will be presented, which analyses the increase in runtime due to the invocation and execution of the security smart contract.

6   Results

One of the most important considerations when proposing a new implementation is to minimize the latency and maximize the transaction throughput. To objectively analyze these performance indicators, two benchmarks of the implemented smart contract were performed with the help of the Hyperledger Caliper [8] blockchain benchmarking tool:

– **Basic:** This benchmark analyzes the average latency and throughput when the entity that submits the transaction proposal can satisfy the access policy with its own X.509 attributes; and
– **Parent:** This benchmark analyzes the average latency and throughput when the entity that submits the transaction proposal can only satisfy the access policy with a parent certificate.

---

[5] Available at https://github.com/hyperledger/fabric-samples.

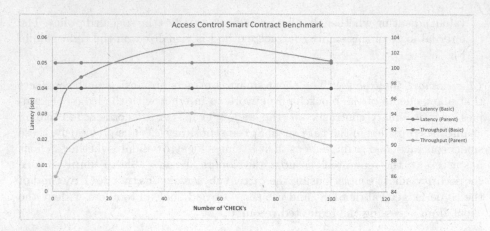

Fig. 6. Average latency and throughput of the access control smart contract, measured using the Hyperledger Caliper benchmarking tool. The blue and grey lines respectively show the average latency and throughput that corresponds to the case where the submitting entity satisfies the access policy with its own attributes, while the orange and yellow lines show the case where the access policy had to be satisfied with the parent X.509 certificate, i.e., using the `hfa.ParentHash` and `hfa.ParentSignature` attributes. (Color figure online)

The exact configuration files that have been used to perform these two benchmarks can be found in the `caliper` directory of the public GitHub repository[6].

During this study, all benchmarks were performed on a virtual machine running Ubuntu 20.04 LTS, with a total RAM memory of 8 GiB. The results that have been obtained are listed in Table 1 and visualized in Fig. 6. All reports generated by Hyperledger Caliper can be found in the previously mentioned GitHub repository.

Table 1. Average latency and throughput of the access control smart contract, measured using the Hyperledger Caliper benchmarking tool. Each row reports the measured latency and throughput associated with validating the submitted X.509 certificate on the defined access policy, which consists of n attribute checks.

Checks (n)	Latency (Basic)	Latency (Parent)	Throughput (Basic)	Throughput (Parent)
1	0.04 s	0.05 s	93.3 tx/s	85.9 tx/s
10	0.04 s	0.05 s	98.8 tx/s	90.7 tx/s
50	0.04 s	0.05 s	103.0 tx/s	94.1 tx/s
100	0.04 s	0.05 s	100.9 tx/s	89.9 tx/s

---

[6] Caliper configs: https://github.com/daangordijn/Fabric-Access-Control/tree/master/caliper.

As can be seen in the image, the average latency increases linearly with the number of attribute checks that have to be performed by the smart contract. On the contrary, the average throughput decreases exponentially with this same number of attribute checks. In addition, as can be seen in the image, the performance corresponding to satisfying the access policy with a parent X.509 certificate is slightly worse compared to satisfying this same access policy with its own attributes.

Finally, to objectively quantify these benchmark results, a base case was created and benchmarked using the same Hyperledger Caliper configuration. The smart contract method invoked during this base case benchmark immediately returned a Boolean value, without running any additional code. Hyperledger Caliper reported the average latency of this benchmark to be 0.04 s, and the average throughput to be 102.1 transactions per second. Comparing these values with the values listed in Table 1, it can be concluded that the increase in latency and decrease in throughput is very small. When keeping the number of attribute checks below 100, which is considered to be sufficient in most real-world applications, the decrease in performance can be disregarded.

7 Discussion

While this paper provides a working solution to solve the identified problem within Hyperledger Fabric, some improvements can be explored in future research. First, although the benchmarks performed by Hyperledger Caliper indicate that the performance impact caused by the proposed implementation is minor, research could be done into ways of improving the algorithms used to validate access policies within the smart contract. Second, the proposed implementation currently only allows users to set one certificate as their parent certificate using the `hfa.ParentHash` and `hfa.ParentSignature` attributes. Future research could be done to study whether multiple such parent certificates can be set, for example by allowing array-typed values for these two attributes. Third, since the proposed implementation only allows users to define complex access policies by combining one or more `EQUALS` or `INCLUDES` operators using the `AND`, `OR`, and `NOT` operators, research could be done into ways of allowing users to define even richer access policies. Finally, clients must currently store their private key data using file system wallets, which are considered insecure [25]. Future research could be done to allow users to store their private key data in Hardware Security Modules (HSM) to improve the security of this data.

8 Conclusions

One of the major problems of Hyperledger Fabric is that its current access control mechanism is not flexible enough for business scenarios. This study aimed to solve this issue by combining multiple ID's, attributes, and policies with the components that regulate access control.

First, to combine multiple ID's within Hyperledger Fabric, a technique has been proposed that hashes and signs one certificate, referred to as the parent certificate, and adds this hash and signature as attributes to another certificate. A smart contract has been implemented that verifies the ownership of this parent certificate.

Second, to combine multiple attributes, a flexible logic within a smart contract has been proposed that allows access policies to be defined using policy checks combined with Boolean operators. Finally, to combine multiple policies, a technique has been proposed that maintains multiple policy definitions on the distributed ledger, which can dynamically be selected as the validating policy depending on the method invoked with the transaction proposal.

Finally, in terms of performance, it has been established that for real-world applications the performance impact is negligible. For access policies with less than 100 attributes to check, the increase in average latency is below 0.01 s compared to the base case of always allowing access. However, an increase in average latency of 0.01 s has been measured when comparing the case where the access policy is satisfied with a member's own attributes with the case where the access policy is satisfied with a member's parent certificate.

Acknowledgements. This research is supported by European Unions Horizon 2020 researchand innovation programme under grant agreement No. 952697 (ASSURED), No. 101021727 (IRIS), and No. 101070052 (TANGO).

References

1. Bandara, H.D., Chen, S., Staples, M., Sai, Y.: Modeling multi-layer access control policies of a hyperledger-fabric-based agriculture supply chain. In: 2021 Third IEEE International Conference on Trust, Privacy and Security in Intelligent Systems and Applications (TPS-ISA), pp. 355–364 (2021). https://doi.org/10.1109/TPSISA52974.2021.00039
2. Cai, W., Hong, Z., Wang, Z., Feng, C.: Decentralized applications: the blockchain-empowered software system. IEEE Access (2018). https://www.researchgate.net/publication/327711685_Decentralized_Applications_The_Blockchain-Empowered_Software_System
3. Ding, S., Cao, J., Li, C., Fan, K., Li, H.: A novel attribute-based access control scheme using blockchain for IoT. IEEE Access **7**, 38431–38441 (2019). https://doi.org/10.1109/ACCESS.2019.2905846, https://ieeexplore.ieee.org/document/8668769
4. Ed-Daibouni, M., Lebbat, A., Tallal, S., Medromi, H.: Toward a new extension of the access control model ABAC for cloud computing. In: Sabir, E., Medromi, H., Sadik, M. (eds.) Advances in Ubiquitous Networking. LNEE, vol. 366, pp. 79–89. Springer, Singapore (2016). https://doi.org/10.1007/978-981-287-990-5_7
5. Ethereum: Smart Contract Languages. https://ethereum.org/en/developers/docs/smart-contracts/languages/
6. Frankenfield, J.: Smart Contracts. https://www.investopedia.com/terms/s/smart-contracts.asp
7. Hyperledger: Fabric CA User's Guide. https://hyperledger-fabric-ca.readthedocs.io/en/release-1.4/users-guide.html

8. Hyperledger: Hyperledger Caliper. https://hyperledger.github.io/caliper/v0.5.0/getting-started/
9. Hyperledger: Hyperledger Fabric Documentation. https://hyperledger-fabric.readthedocs.io/en/release-2.2/
10. Hyperledger: Hyperledger Fabric SDKs. https://hyperledger-fabric.readthedocs.io/en/release-2.2/fabric-sdks.html
11. Hyperledger: Using the Fabric Test Network. https://hyperledger-fabric.readthedocs.io/en/release-2.2/test_network.html
12. Hyperledger: What is Hyperledger Fabric? https://hyperledger-fabric.readthedocs.io/en/release-2.2/whatis.html
13. Iftekhar, A., Cui, X., Tao, Q., Zheng, C.: Hyperledger fabric access control system for internet of things layer in blockchain-based applications. Entropy 23(8) (2021). https://doi.org/10.3390/e23081054, https://www.mdpi.com/1099-4300/23/8/1054
14. International Telecommunication Union: Public-Key and Attribute Certificate Frameworks. https://www.itu.int/rec/T-REC-X.509-201910-I/en
15. IPFS: IPFS Documentation. https://docs.ipfs.io/
16. Islam, M.A., Madria, S.: A permissioned blockchain based access control system for IOT. In: 2019 IEEE International Conference on Blockchain (Blockchain), pp. 469–476 (2019). https://doi.org/10.1109/Blockchain.2019.00071
17. Kelleher, J.: Why do bitcoins have value? https://www.investopedia.com/ask/answers/100314/why-do-bitcoins-have-value.asp
18. KeyFactor: What is PKI and How Does it Work? https://www.keyfactor.com/resources/what-is-pki/
19. Lutkevich, B.: What is access control? https://www.techtarget.com/searchsecurity/definition/access-control0
20. McGovern, T.: How many blockchains are there in 2022? https://earthweb.com/how-many-blockchains-are-there/
21. Nakamoto, S.: Bitcoin: a peer-to-peer electronic cash system. Bitcoin.org (2008). https://bitcoin.org/bitcoin.pdf
22. National Institute of Standards and Technology: X.509 Public Key Certificate. https://csrc.nist.gov/glossary/term/x_509_public_key_certificate
23. Peng, L., Feng, W., Yan, Z., Li, Y., Zhou, X., Shimizu, S.: Privacy preservation in permissionless blockchain: a survey. Digit. Commun. Netw. (2020). https://www.researchgate.net/publication/342455474_Privacy_preservation_in_permissionless_blockchain_A_survey
24. Rouhani, S., Deters, R.: Blockchain based access control systems: state of the art and challenges. In: IEEE/WIC/ACM International Conference on Web Intelligence, WI 2019, pp. 423–428. Association for Computing Machinery, New York (2019). https://doi.org/10.1145/3350546.3352561
25. Solana: Command Line Wallets. https://docs.solana.com/wallet-guide/cli
26. Song, L., Li, M., Zhu, Z., Yuan, P., He, Y.: Attribute-based access control using smart contracts for the internet of things. Proc. Comput. Sci. 174, 231–242 (2020). https://doi.org/10.1016/j.procs.2020.06.079, https://www.sciencedirect.com/science/article/pii/S1877050920315933. 2019 International Conference on Identification, Information and Knowledge in the Internet of Things
27. SSL.com: What is a certificate authority? https://www.ssl.com/faqs/what-is-a-certificate-authority/
28. Tapscott, D., Tapscott, A.: The blockchain revolution: how the technology behind bitcoin is changing money, business, and the world (2016)

29. Xu, M., Chen, X., Kou, G.: A systematic review of blockchain. Financial Innovation (2019). https://jfin-swufe.springeropen.com/articles/10.1186/s40854-019-0147-z
30. Yang, Z., Shao, D., Qu, L., Zhang, M.: Internet of things access control system based on hyperledger. J. Phys.: Conf. Ser. **1748**(4), 042031 (2021). https://doi.org/10.1088/1742-6596/1748/4/042031
31. Yutaka, M., Zhang, Y., Sasabe, M., Kasahara, S.: Using ethereum blockchain for distributed attribute-based access control in the internet of things. In: 2019 IEEE Global Communications Conference (GLOBECOM), pp. 1–6 (2019). https://doi.org/10.1109/GLOBECOM38437.2019.9014155
32. Zhao, X., Wang, S., Zhang, Y., Wang, Y.: Attribute-based access control scheme for data sharing on hyperledger fabric. J. Inf. Secur. Appl. **67**, 103182 (2022). https://doi.org/10.1016/j.jisa.2022.103182, https://www.sciencedirect.com/science/article/pii/S2214212622000643

A Secure Microgrid Power Transaction Scheme Based on Hyperledger Fabric

Shuihai Zhang[1], Haoyi Sun[1], Bei Pei[2], and Chunli Lv[1(✉)]

[1] College of Information and Electrical Engineering, China Agricultural University, Beijing, China
lvcl@cau.edu.cn
[2] The 3rd Research Institute of the Ministry of Public Security, Shanghai, China

Abstract. As part of the smart grid, distributed power trading based on clean energy generation has attracted a lot of attention and investment in recent years. This paper adopts the Hyperledger Fabric blockchain as the underlying framework, combined with key technologies such as smart contracts, blockchain oracles, bilateral auction mechanisms, and multi-signatures, and proposes a secure microgrid power transaction scheme based on Hyperledger Fabric. Different from the existing schemes, this paper considers the security and integrity issues that may arise in the transaction process. In terms of power trading, this scheme proposes two trading modes that can be carried out simultaneously and don't affect each other, that is, trading based on predicted power and trading based on reserved power. In terms of transaction protection, the user credit and proof of work algorithm are introduced into the continuous double auction mechanism to solve the possible malicious bidding problem. In addition, the multi-signed address wallet is used to ensure the transaction security of users without a trusted center. Finally, the security and feasibility analysis of the paper proves the effectiveness of the scheme.

Keywords: Blockchain · Power Trading · Smart Grid · Smart Contract · Multiple Signature

1 Introduction

Energy is an important material basis for the national economy, and the future destiny of a country depends on the development and effective utilization of energy. In recent years, clean energy, led by solar energy, wind energy, and nuclear energy, has accounted for an increasing proportion of power generation. In Beijing, clean energy has replaced coal as the main energy source in this international metropolis, accounting for 46.7% of the city's energy consumption. Furthermore, as more and more people choose to install solar panels in their homes, the current energy structure is also characterized by a tendency

This work was supported by the Key Laboratory of Information and Network Security, Ministry of Public Security, the Third Research Institute of the Ministry of Public Security (C19605).

W. Meng and W. Li (Eds.): BlockTEA 2022, LNICST 498, pp. 49–65, 2023.
https://doi.org/10.1007/978-3-031-31420-9_4

to be decentralized. The distributed trend is conducive to solving the problem of energy loss due to the long physical distance of power transmission through the community-level microgrid [1]. Prosumers of clean power are allowed to trade power with others or to sell it to higher-level grids for subsidies in the microgrid. However, in the past, the transactions between prosumers were characterized by a large number of orders, small scale and fragmentation. Therefore, how to build a suitable trading platform and supervision mechanism is the focus of the current electric power research.

1.1 Related Works

Thanks to features of decentralization, tamper resistance, trustworthiness, and anonymity [2], blockchain technology is widely used in energy transactions in microgrids. Blockchains are shared and distributed ledgers of data that securely store digital transactions without the use of centralized nodes [3]. In recent years, the combination of blockchain technology and community-level microgrid power trading has been widely researched and applied pilots [4]. The Brooklyn Microgrid is the first energy blockchain project in the world to be put into practice. It adopts P2P direct energy trading without going through a third-party power supplier. The project is deployed on the Ethereum blockchain platform, and integrates the smart contract function of the Ethereum blockchain at the bottom of the smart meter for data collection. However, the experimental scale of this project is small, limited to 10 participating users, and further verification is required for larger-scale project implementation. Nonetheless, The Brooklyn Microgrid has served as a good example for energy blockchain projects around the world, driving the development of related P2P distributed electricity transactions [5].

In the academic field, there has also been a lot of discussion about energy blockchain in recent years. One of the first systematic reviews in this field was made by Andoni et al. [6]. By analyzing the existing use cases of energy blockchain, it discusses the advantages and limitations of blockchain applications in this field. Mengelkamp et al. analyze seven market components that may be required to build a blockchain microgrid energy market and analyzed and discussed the world's first energy blockchain project, the Brooklyn Microgrid [5]. Lüth et al. analyze the value of batteries in local peer-to-peer energy trading schemes and market designs for battery systems at the customer level and community level, respectively [7]. Zhao et al. designed a blockchain-based multi-microgrid energy transaction double-layer framework, which considers transactions between multiple microgrids in addition to transactions within microgrids [8]. In addition, some researchers focus on the use of cryptography to realize the protection of user privacy and transaction security in the microgrid energy trading market. Aitzhan et al. use blockchain technology, multi-signature, and anonymous encrypted information flow respectively to realize the security verification of the decentralized energy trading system [9]. Gai et al. focus on how to prevent attackers from exploiting data mining algorithms to obtain user privacy from transaction data stored in the blockchain [10]. Yao et al. introduce the lightweight WireGuard VPN technology that has been widely used in recent years based on the blockchain platform to protect users' communication privacy [11]. Furthermore, Wang H et al. [12] and Wang H.Z et al. [13] focus on research on accurate forecasting techniques for renewable energy generation to ensure a reliable environment for electricity trading.

1.2 Contribution

Most of the existing distributed energy trading schemes have the following three problems. First, most current energy blockchain designs are based on public chains such as Ethereum. However, the confidentiality of transaction information is one of the important attributes for electricity transactions in smart grids. As a consortium chain, Hyperledger Fabric can better meet privacy and permission requirements than public chains. Second, most schemes fail to consider the potential attacker's damage to the transaction process, and cannot well meet the security requirements of the system. Finally, due to the volatility and other characteristics of clean energy power generation, the corresponding transaction methods are based on the predicted energy and based on reserve energy. But many studies have considered only one of them.

This paper proposes a distributed power trading system based on Hyperledger Fabric, which fully considers the security and integrity issues that may arise in the trading process. The main contributions of this paper are described as follows:

1) In view of the possible electricity trading situations in reality, we have designed two trading models based on predicted power and based on reserve power.
2) In order to curb the malicious bidding behavior of users and encourage the honest behavior of participants, we designed a bilateral continuous bidding mechanism based on credit behavior and proof of work algorithm.
3) We use multi-signature technology to protect the smooth delivery of funds during the transaction process without a trusted center.

The remainder of this paper is organized as follows. We introduce the main technologies used in the distributed power trading system in Sect. 2. The user model, framework design, and core components of the scheme are elaborated in Sect. 3. In Sect. 4, We describe the process of distributed electricity trading in detail. In Sect. 5, we analyze the effectiveness of this scheme from two aspects of safety and feasibility. Finally, we summarize the overall work in Sect. 6.

2 Preliminary

2.1 Hyperledger Fabric

Blockchain, also known as distributed ledger technology, is essentially a decentralized distributed ledger database [14]. Cryptography and consensus algorithms enable multiple peer nodes in a blockchain network to replicate, synchronize and share the same ledger. They ensure the consistency of ledger data, and also make the blockchain have the characteristics of decentralization, tamper-proof, trustworthiness, and traceability [15]. Depending on the way users of the network participate, blockchains can be divided into permissionless and permissioned. In permissionless blockchains, such as Bitcoin and Ethereum, nodes are free to participate without any permission, and transactions are completely transparent. Anyone can access the data. Correspondingly, permissioned blockchains only allow authorized users to join the network and have the ability to control data access. Furthermore, transactions on permissioned blockchains are not transparent.

Permissioned blockchains can be further divided into consortium blockchains and private blockchains. Different from the private blockchain, each node of the consortium blockchain usually has a corresponding entity organization, which can only join and exit the network after authorization. Various institutions and organizations form stake-related alliances to jointly maintain the healthy operation of the blockchain.

Hyperledger Fabric is a type of consortium blockchain, launched by the Linux Foundation in 2015 for developing applications or solutions with a modular architecture. Compared with public blockchain platforms. The biggest differences in Fabric compared to Bitcoin and Ethereum are privacy attributes and permission attributes. Fabric registers and records all members through the member management module, and gives them corresponding access rights. The Fabric architecture is shown in Fig. 1, and its modular and versatile design can satisfy a wide range of industrial use cases.

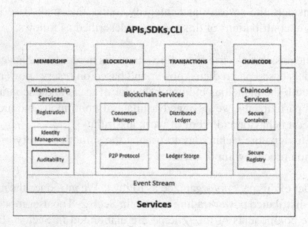

Fig. 1. The Architecture of Hyperledger Fabric.

2.2 Blockchain Oracle

A major limitation of blockchain technology is that it can't interact with the "outside world", only by manipulating the data on the blockchain to calculate and reach a consensus on the calculation results [16]. In addition, smart contracts usually require relevant information from the outside world as input (or meet certain conditions) in order to execute the agreement [17]. Therefore, how to realize the interaction between smart contracts and external resources is a practical problem that must be faced by the scheme design. The blockchain oracle is a consensus mechanism that incorporates external data into the blockchain [18]. It is a trusted entity that can collect, verify and transmit data from external sources [19]. Oracles need to provide reliable and valid information to ensure the consistency and validity of smart contract execution [20].

2.3 Proof of Work

As a consensus algorithm, Proof of Work (PoW) is widely used in most public chains and virtual currencies to ensure the consistency of distributed ledgers [21]. The effectiveness of this algorithm has been extensively demonstrated. Its process can be summarized as: by searching for a suitable random number *nonce*, the Hash value of the content obtained after the data x is spliced with the *nonce* is less than or equal to the target hash value T. The hash value T is determined by the difficulty value n. The probability of finding a suitable nonce for a given target T is given by the following formula.

$$P(Hash(x||nonce) \leq T) = T / \left(2^{256}\right) \qquad (1)$$

In this scheme, the broadcast of each quotation of a trader needs to meet the requirements of the PoW algorithm. That is, the appropriate *nonce* is calculated so that the transaction data x satisfies $Hash(x||nonce) \leq T$. In a transaction cycle, the difficulty value n of the PoW algorithm is the smallest at the beginning and increases with the increase of the number of quotations. In addition, the initial value of n is related to the user's credit value, and well-behaved users will likely have more bidding opportunities.

3   Smart Microgrid Power Trading System Based on Consortium Blockchain

In Hyperledger Fabric, the channel is a very important concept. It's a private atomic broadcast channel divided and managed by ordering nodes [22]. Its function is to isolate the information in the channel so that users outside the channel can't access the distributed ledger in the channel. The transaction in the channel satisfies privacy. To meet the practical needs of the two transaction modes proposed in this paper, namely forecast energy transaction and real-time reserve energy transaction, we have established two sets of application channels to ensure that they can be performed simultaneously without affecting each other. The design of channels and tissues in this protocol is shown in Table 1. Channel 1 is used to predict power trading, and Channel 2 is used to Stored power trading.

Table 1. Channel and organizational design in the scheme.

Channel	Channel 1	Channel 2
Organization 1	Prosumers	Prosumers with battery
Organization 2	Consumers	Consumers
Organization 3	Grid Operators	Grid Operators

In the microgrid power transaction based on predicted power, there may be three roles based on whether the power generation capacity is available. They are prosumers, consumers, and upper-level grid operators. Prosumers refer to community users who own clean energy output devices such as solar photovoltaic panels or wind turbines, and they can buy and sell power. Consumers refer to traditional electricity users who can't generate power. Since it is difficult to achieve a complete balance between the generation and consumption of microgrids, the upper-level grid operators will participate in microgrid market transactions to regulate power.

In the microgrid power transaction based on reserve power, there may also be three roles: prosumers with energy storage devices, consumers, and upper-level grid operators. They are divided by whether they have the ability to store energy. Users in the microgrid can freely choose to purchase clean energy or fossil energy. They can also buy fossil fuels to meet demands when clean energy production is insufficient. Likewise, the prosumer can also sell the power he produces to the grid operator. The overall frame diagram of the system is shown in Fig. 2.

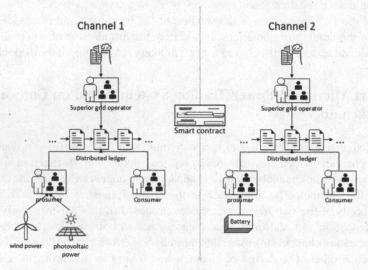

Fig. 2. The overall frame diagram of the system.

3.1 User and Node Definitions

Certificates are the basis of authority management in Fabric, and any entity or organization has its own unique identity certificate. The scheme adopts the asymmetric encryption algorithm based on ECDSA to generate the public key and private key, and the certificate format adopts the X.509 specification. When community users join the network for the first time, they need to verify the authenticity of their identities, and then the Fabric CA project will generate corresponding certificates for them. In addition, for the need of confidential communication outside the network, the ECDSA algorithm will additionally generate a pair of public key and private key for the user. The public-private key pair used to prove identity is denoted as pk, sk, and the public-private key pair used for secure communication is denoted as pk', sk'. In addition, credit should be used as an important indicator to evaluate users, which reflects whether users comply with the rules of network operation. Record the user's credit level as c. In this scheme, tokens are used to conduct virtual electricity transactions in the network. However, it is not a virtual currency like Bitcoin, but is regarded as a kind of points obtained by exchanging or recharging legal currency. The user's token balance is recorded as a. The increase in the token balance can only be done in two ways: transaction or fiat currency exchange. The basic attributes of the node account A_i of user i in this scheme can be expressed as:

$$A_i = <pk_i, sk_i, pk_i', sk_i', c_i, a_i> \tag{2}$$

In fact, the above information of the node account is not completely public. For privacy reasons, the token balance recorded in the distributed ledger will be encrypted by pk_i, and the encrypted token balance will be recorded as a_i', as shown in the following formula.

$$a_i' = ENG_{pk_i}(a_i) \tag{3}$$

The encrypted token balance a_i' can only be unlocked by the private key sk_i. Therefore, all users in the network have no right to view the number of other users' tokens. This effectively protects the privacy of users. Build a structure for storing accounts in smart contracts. Record the mapping of node account A_i in the ledger as A_i'. Its structure is shown in the following formula.

$$A_i' = <pk_i, pk_i', c_i, a_i'> \tag{4}$$

Smart meter is an intelligent meter with microprocessor application and network communication technology as the core, and has the capabilities of automatic metering/measurement, data processing, two-way communication and function expansion. In this scheme, the smart contracts in Fabric will be highly integrated with the smart meter, and will be installed and executed on the smart meter. Users participating in the transaction need to install smart meters with integrated smart contracts. Smart meters can statistically analyze users' power consumption or generation in real time, and make predictions and preparations for users to participate in power transactions in the network. For prosumers, power analysis helps them master power consumption and generation. Excess power can be sold for profit under the premise of meeting their own availability. For consumers, mastering power consumption is conducive to purchasing the right amount of energy during the transaction phase, without causing excess or shortage of energy. We assume that the smart meter is sealed and tamper-proof. In addition, all smart meters installed by users participating in the microgrid in the community have the same model and computing power.

3.2 Smart Contract and Blockchain Oracle Design

In blockchain, smart contracts automate the process of transactions. The smart contract is a self-validating, self-executing, tamper-proof program executed on blockchain platform. It is defined as a program that digitally facilitates, verifies, and executes a contract between two or more participants on blockchain. Smart contracts are event-driven, which means they can be activated when predefined conditions are met [23]. In Fabric, smart contracts are called chaincodes, which are programs that can run independently in docker

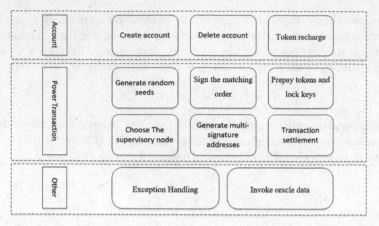

Fig. 3. Smart Contracts Design of Distributed Electricity Trading System.

containers. The main interfaces and functions of the smart contract designed in this scheme are shown in Fig. 3.

In this scheme, the oracle is designed to transmit local power generation and consumption data to the blockchain. Additionally, oracles complete transactions by interacting with smart contracts. Blockchain oracles will collect data from the physical world, including user electricity consumption information recorded in electricity meters and the power generation of clean energy power generation equipment under different conditions. The oracle will be installed in the smart meter along with the smart contract, and the smart meter is sealed and immutable.

The collection and upload of oracle data is designed in a *"Request − Response"* mode. This is because the user's data is too large to be completely stored in the blockchain. In addition, the smart contract only needs a part of the data per operation. *"Request − Response"* mode will initiate requests for oracle data by smart contracts on the blockchain. The off-blockchain infrastructure (the smart meter) will be used to monitor requests and retrieve data.

3.3 PCDA Algorithm

In transactions with multiple sellers and buyers, such as electricity transactions, the continuous double auction (CDA) mechanism is widely used [24]. When the auction starts, both buyers and sellers can make multiple bids. The transaction is completed when the prices of both parties match [25]. However, unrestricted offers from users can lead to increased processing burden on the system and even lead to DDoS attacks. In order to prevent traders from making multiple bids maliciously, this scheme introduces a credit-based PoW algorithm on the basis of CDA. c is the user's credit value, and x is the quotation order. *num* is the number of bids in the current trading cycle, and *nonce* is a random number that satisfies the PoW algorithm. The process of Algorithm PCDA $(x, c, num, t) \rightarrow nonce$ is as follows.

1) At the beginning of the transaction phase, the user executes smart contracts to obtain the random seed t of the transaction period. The content of t is shared by all nodes in the network and is only valid within this period;
2) Calculate the required hash value $T \leftarrow f(c, num)$;
3) Traverse to find the random number *nonce* to satisfy $Hash(x||t||nonce) < T$;
4) Output target *nonce*.

Correspondingly, each quotation order will be checked whether the nonce meets the requirements of the PCDA algorithm, such as formula 5.

$$Hash(x||t||nonce) < T \leftarrow f(c, num) \tag{5}$$

Any cheating behavior of the user will make the bid verification fail, and the calculation used to find the nonce of the random number will be in vain, which will further increase the difficulty of bidding. Therefore, it can be concluded that honest and curious nodes will consciously abide by the PCDA algorithm when bidding transactions. Malicious multiple bidding will not occur.

4 Distributed Power Transaction Process

This paper uses the concept of channels in Fabric to design two different power trading modes for forecast power and reserve power, respectively. This section will describe their detailed designs and processes.

In the distributed power transaction based on predicted power, namely channel 1, time is divided into time periods of length T in days. Due to the strong dependence of photovoltaic power generation on the environment and climate, the power generation in different cycles has great differences. Therefore, the division of cycles is necessary. Trade matching for predicted power will only take place at a fixed time before the start of a cycle, while trade settlement will take place at the end of the cycle. The difference is that in the distributed transaction based on reserve power, namely channel 2, the transaction is no longer divided into time periods or stipulated transaction time. Traders will be allowed to publish orders and trade at any time. The specific process of distributed power transaction is shown in Fig. 4.

The distributed power transaction processes are as follows:

Step 1: The smart meter statistically analyzes the user's electricity consumption and power generation in each cycle, and provides a reference for the user's quotation;
Step 2: Entering the trading stage, users generate eligible quotation orders and broadcast them through the p2p network. Nodes participating in the transaction establish a distributed order matching database locally to match the orders of buyers and sellers;
Step 3: Users can quote multiple times by executing the PCDA algorithm, and the successfully matched quote orders are submitted to the smart contract;
Step 4: The two parties of the successfully matched order will further confirm and sign the contract through the smart contract;
Step 5: After the contract is signed, the buyer prepays tokens and the seller delivers the electricity usage rights. The transaction result is written to the blockchain.

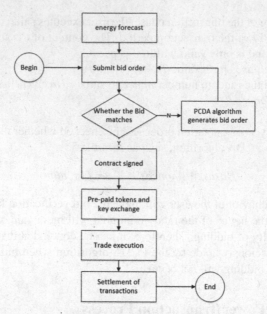

Fig. 4. The specific process of distributed power transaction.

Step 6: At the end of the order execution cycle, the smart contract reads the meter data of the transaction party and settles the transaction.

4.1 Publish Bid Order

In distributed electricity transactions, both prosumers and sellers have the right to issue orders. However, any prosumers who want to sell power will need to prove to the smart contract its ownership of the declared pre-sale power before publishing bid order. Take prosumer b as an example, generate b_α and b_β and store them in blockchain.

$$b_\alpha = Hash(pk_b||E_b||Time) \qquad (6)$$

$$b_\beta = Hash(b_\alpha||RandomNumber) \qquad (7)$$

E_b is the pre-sold electricity of prosumer b, and pk_b is its identity public key. b_α represents the ownership of the sellable power E_b by the prosumer b, and b_β is used for locking to prevent double payment for the power E_b. If b_β is not locked during the transaction, then b may sell the same power multiple times to other consumers.

For power trading based on forecasted power, quoting and matching of orders is only allowed during the order-issuing phase. The content of quotation order M^1 in channel 1 is shown in Eq. 8.

$$M^1 = <pk, S, E, P, c, num, nonce, Time> \qquad (8)$$

Among them, pk represents the identity public key of the publisher, and S represents the type of quotation order issued (selling power or purchasing power). E is the amount of electricity the bidder wants to trade. P is the unit price of power. c represents the credit rating of the publisher. *Time* is the order generation time. *num* represents the number of bids, and the initial value is 0. *nonce* is a random number that satisfies the condition calculated by the publisher through the *PCDA*. In addition, in order to prevent malicious attackers from forging or tampering with communication information, the publisher will use the communication private key sk' to sign the content M and broadcast it together.

For channel 2, bid orders to buy energy or sell energy are allowed to be issued at any time. Bid orders are recorded as M^2. Compared with M^1, M^2 adds transaction execution time t. This is because the transaction in channel 1 has the regulation of the transaction cycle, while channel 2 needs to manually set the duration and end time of the transaction. Similarly, the publisher will use sk' to sign the content M^2 and publish it.

$$M^2 = <pk, S, E, P, t, c, num, nonce, Time> \qquad (9)$$

When nodes in the network receive the broadcasted bid order, the verification algorithm will be executed to verify whether the order is legal. Denote the signature of M as M'. The algorithm $BidVerify(M, M') \rightarrow True/False$ process are as follows.

1) Verify the authenticity of order M and its signature M';
2) If M is a power sale order, verify whether there are matching power ownership certificates b_α and b_β in blockchain;
3) Verify whether the order meets the requirements of the PCDA algorithm according to *num* and c;
4) Returns *True* if the content is correct, otherwise returns *False*.

4.2 Bid Matching and Contract Signing

The bid matching stage will generate a large amount of intermediate data, which lacks the necessity of long-term storage. The blockchain has the characteristics that data cannot be tampered with and deleted. If the intermediate data of the transaction is stored in blockchain, it will inevitably cause a lot of waste of resources in the long run. Therefore, the system temporarily stores these data on all nodes in the network that participate in the transaction at this stage, which is achieved by establishing a temporary distributed order matching database locally on the node. The content of the order matching database is based on the broadcast order information. Since the predicted power transaction and the reserve power transaction are in two channels of Fabric, their transaction data and order matching database are independent of each other.

In the temporary order matching database, orders for energy sales will be ranked from lowest to highest in price, and orders for energy purchases will be ranked from highest to lowest in price. If the bid is the same, credit value and bid time will be used as the ranking basis. If $P_{buy} \geq P_{sell}$, both orders are deemed to have been matched and the energy price will be settled at P_{buy}. Both parties with successful order matching will further confirm and sign the contract through smart contracts. N is denoted as a trading contract. The processes of contract signing algorithm $Signcontract(M_{sell}, M_{buy}) \rightarrow N$ are as follows:

1) Smart contracts send trade proposals to both parties;

2) Both parties further confirm whether the transaction is executed, and sign the proposal separately if they agree;
3) Smart contracts send proposals with signatures to endorsement nodes in each organization according to endorsement policies;
4) The endorsement node verifies whether M_{sell} and M_{buy} match the quoted order of both parties, and agrees to endorse if they match;
5) Smart contracts use a random generation algorithm to select a transaction supervisor from the set of nodes participating in the endorsement;
6) Smart contracts generate the transaction contract N and writes it into blockchain by the accounting node.

The trading contract N^1 in channel 1 is shown in Eq. 11. *Value* Represents the total transaction price. *Time* Represents the time when the contract was signed. pk_{sup} Indicates the identity public key of the supervisory node of the transaction.

$$N^1 = <pk_{sell}, pk_{buy}, pk_{sup}, E_{buy}, P_{buy}, Value, Time> \qquad (10)$$

$$Value = E_{buy} * P_{buy} \qquad (11)$$

The transaction contract N^2 in channel 2 is shown in Eq. 12. T_{sell} represents the transaction settlement time.

$$N^2 = <pk_{sell}, pk_{buy}, pk_{sup}, E_{buy}, P_{buy}, Value, T_{sell}, Time> \qquad (12)$$

Before power transmission starts, the consumer needs to prepay tokens, and the prosumers needs to lock the power ownership keys b_α and b_β stored in the blockchain. The specific algorithm $Protrade\left(pk_{sell}, pk_{buy}, pk_{sup}\right) \rightarrow RScript$ processes are as follows.

1) The smart contract sends a request for the prepaid token *Value* to the consumer.
2) After the consumer agrees to the request, the smart contract generates a (2, 3) multi-signature address *RScript*.

$$RScript = OP\_2||pk_{sell}||pk_{buy}||pk_{sup}||OP\_3||OP\_CHECKMULTISIG$$

3) The consumer hashes the *RScript* to generate a *P2SH* signature address and transfers the token worth *Value* to the corresponding address.
4) After verifying the token balance in the address, the prosumer locks the power ownership keys b_α and b_β stored in the blockchain through smart contracts.
5) After the completion of the locked key and prepaid token, the transaction will enter the physical transmission stage of power.

(2, 3) Multi-signed address wallet *RScript* means that at least 2 private keys are involved in order to use the prepaid tokens in it. Even if the consumer refuses to pay the token after the transaction is settled, the prosumer and the supervisor can also use the private key to ensure the smooth delivery of the token. Accordingly, if the prosumer refuses to process *RScript* due to violations in the physical transmission process of power, the existence of supervisor can still ensure the safety of consumers' funds.

It is important to note that if $E_{sell} > E_{buy}$, one order to sell power may be able to meet the needs of many orders to buy power. Conversely, a single order to buy power may require multiple orders to sell power to meet demand. Therefore, successful bid matching does not necessarily mean the end of the bid order, and it can continue to participate in the transaction after splitting the successfully matched electricity E. Accordingly, the power ownership key b_α will be split into multiple parts as the case may be, as shown in Formula 13.

$$b_{\alpha+1} = Hash(b_\alpha || E_{buy}/E_{sell}) \tag{13}$$

Similarly, in the fourth step of the above algorithm, the locked key is only the key $b_{\alpha+1}$ corresponding to the power E_{buy} for the transaction.

4.3 Transaction Settlement

After the transaction, the smart contract will settle the transaction based on the transaction contract N and the power (generation and consumption) data in the smart meters of both parties.

The actual power generation during the transaction or the power in the storage device is recorded as E_1'. The actual power consumption is E_2'. The power agreed in contract N is E_{buy}. c_{sell} is the credit value of the prosumer, and c_{buy} is the credit value of the consumer.

1) $E_1' < E_2', E_1' \leq E_{buy}$

   The actual generating power of the prosumer during the transaction period didn't reach the agreed amount of power. Prepaid tokens of the consumer were not fully used. Consumers will suffer financial losses due to the need to purchase additional power from higher grids. The smart contract will pay $Value'$ to the prosumers according to the ratio of E_1' and E_{buy}. The remaining prepaid funds will be returned to the consumer's account.

2) $E_2' \leq E_1', E_2' \leq E_{buy}$

   The consumer's power consumption during the transaction time doesn't reach the purchased power, and the consumer's prepaid funds are not fully used. There may be a certain amount of power waste in the microgrid. The smart contract will pay $Value'$ to the prosumers according to the ratio of E_1' and E_{buy}. The remaining prepaid funds will be returned to the consumer's account.

5   System Analysis

5.1   System Security Analysis

The main goal of this section is to evaluate and analyze the security of the proposed distributed microgrid power trading system. First of all, compared with the traditional centralized power trading system, this system doesn't have the problem of user data loss that may be caused by a single point of failure. In addition, for malicious attacks such as double-spending attacks and witch attacks that the blockchain system may suffer from, the response and description of this system are as follows.

Double-Spending Attack. There are two possible scenarios for a double-spend attack in an energy trading platform, one for power and one for tokens [26]. The power double-spend attack refers to the fact that prosumers legally sell more power in the system than they produce. For the power double-spending attack, the system requires the prosumer to upload the ownership certificates b_α and b_β of the energy E before they issue the energy sale order. The data stored in the blockchain is immutable, so it can be considered that prosumers don't have the ability to modify the data they upload. After the two parties of the transaction reach an agreement, smart contracts will lock the b_α and b_β of the prosumer stored in the blockchain. Before offer matching and contract signing, the system checks the existence and status of the power ownership proof key. Therefore, we believe that the system is resistant to power double-spend attacks.

The token double-spend attack is that consumers legitimately spend more tokens than they have in their accounts. For token double-spending attacks, consumers need to prepay tokens declared in the bid order to the multi-signature address after the transaction is successfully matched and before the power transmission starts. The prepayment behavior must require sufficient balance in the consumer's account, so the token double-spending attack is also impossible.

Sybil Attack. Sybil attack means that the attacker injecting a huge number of fake puppet nodes needs to build a private sub-network that sieges and isolates victim nodes from the rest network and can perform malicious activities on victim nodes [9]. The system is based on the Hyperledger Fabric blockchain design and has the characteristics of privacy and access permission [27]. New users will need to authenticate when joining organizations and networks, as well as check or install appropriate smart metering devices. Therefore, we believe that the system is resistant to Sybil attack.

Distributed Denial of Service Attack. In the design of previous blockchain-based distributed electricity trading schemes, most schemes did not take into account the possible DDOS attacks during the trading process. For example, during bilateral continuous bidding, one or more malicious actors may block or even destroy the system through a large number of meaningless bid orders. In this scheme, PCDA algorithm makes participants pay a certain amount of computing power for each bid, and the cost is related to the number of bids and historical credit. Any cheating behavior by the user will make the bid verification fail and further increase the difficulty of bidding. In addition, the consistency of smart meter devices owned by users ensures a fair bidding process. Therefore, it can be determined that this system can effectively reduce the possibility of DDOS attacks.

5.2   System Feasibility Analysis

This scheme designs and proposes the PCDA algorithm, and the number of users' bids within the specified time will be limited by the credit rating and computing power. Users are not able to bid unlimitedly without control. To verify the feasibility of the algorithm in practical applications, we simulate the user's behavior in the bid stage in MATLAB. The simulation results are shown in Fig. 5.

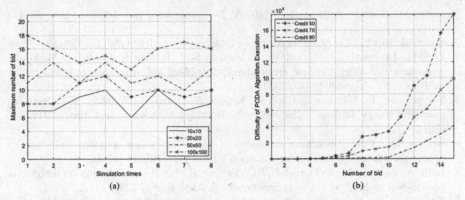

Fig. 5. Simulation of user bidding behavior, where: (a) shows the relationship between transaction size and number of quotations. (b) shows the relationship between the number of bids and the calculation cost under different user credit levels.

Firstly, we simulate the number of bids required by participants to reach a consensus on a deal under different deal sizes. The result is shown in Fig. 5a. Next, we simulate the relationship between the number of bids and the calculation cost under different credit levels. The results are shown in Fig. 5b. It can be seen that the computational cost required for bidding by users with high credit values is much smaller than that of users with low credit values. The advantage of high credit value becomes more and more obvious as the number of bids increases. We believe that the PCDA algorithm can incentivize users to participate in transactions legally while limiting malicious bids. In addition, the further deployment of the system in the future, the PCDA algorithm will also support dynamic adjustment of the computational cost.

6 Conclusions

This paper designs a transaction security microgrid power transaction scheme based on Hyperledger fabric. Compared with most schemes that only have the function of predictive power trading, we design two trading modes, predictive power trading and reserve power trading, which are carried out simultaneously through different channels of Fabric. In addition, this paper proposes the PCDA algorithm by introducing the user credit and proof of work algorithms into the bilateral bidding mechanism. We simulate and prove the effectiveness of the PCDA algorithm in eliminating malicious bidding behaviors, as well as the incentives for users to participate in transactions with integrity. In terms of transaction security, this paper uses the multi-signature address wallet to ensure the user's transaction security without the trusted center.

References

1. Silvente, J., Kopanos, G.M., Pistikopoulos, E.N., Espuña, A.: A rolling horizon optimization framework for the simultaneous energy supply and demand planning in microgrids. Appl. Energy **155**, 485 (2015)

2. Nofer, M., Gomber, P., Hinz, O., Schiereck, D.: Blockchain. Bus. Inf. Syst. Eng. **59**, 183 (2017)
3. Swan, M.: Blockchain: Blueprint for a New Economy. O'Reilly Media, Inc. (2015)
4. Zia, M.F., Benbouzid, M., Elbouchikhi, E., Muyeen, S.M., Techato, K., Guerrero, J.M.: Microgrid transactive energy: review, architectures, distributed ledger technologies, and market analysis. IEEE Access **8**, 19410 (2020)
5. Mengelkamp, E., Gärttner, J., Rock, K., Kessler, S., Orsini, L., Weinhardt, C.: Designing microgrid energy markets: a case study: the Brooklyn Microgrid. Appl. Energy **210**, 870 (2018)
6. Andoni, M., et al.: Blockchain technology in the energy sector: a systematic review of challenges and opportunities. Renew. Sustain. Energy Rev. **100**, 143 (2019)
7. Lüth, A., Zepter, J.M., Del Granado, P.C., Egging, R.: Local electricity market designs for peer-to-peer trading: the role of battery flexibility. Appl. Energy **229**, 1233 (2018)
8. Zhao, Z., et al.: Energy transaction for multi-microgrids and internal microgrid based on blockchain. IEEE Access. **8**, 144362 (2020)
9. Aitzhan, N.Z., Svetinovic, D.: Security and privacy in decentralized energy trading through multi-signatures, blockchain and anonymous messaging streams. IEEE Trans. Dependable Secure Comput. **15**, 840 (2016)
10. Gai, K., Wu, Y., Zhu, L., Qiu, M., Shen, M.: Privacy-preserving energy trading using consortium blockchain in smart grid. IEEE Trans. Ind. Inform. **15**, 3548 (2019)
11. Yao, S., Tian, X., Chen, J., Xiong, Y.: Privacy preserving distributed smart grid system based on hyperledger fabric and wireguard. Int. J. Netw. Manage. e2193 (2021)
12. Wang, H., et al.: Taxonomy research of artificial intelligence for deterministic solar power forecasting. Energy Convers. Manage. **214**, 112909 (2020)
13. Wang, H.Z., Wang, G.B., Li, G.Q., Peng, J.C., Liu, Y.T.: Deep belief network based deterministic and probabilistic wind speed forecasting approach. Appl. Energy **182**, 80 (2016)
14. Nakamoto, S.: Bitcoin: a peer-to-peer electronic cash system. Decent. Bus. Rev. 21260 (2008)
15. Wattenhofer, R.: The Science of the Blockchain. Inverted Forest Publishing (2016)
16. Berryhill, R., Veneris, A.: ASTRAEA: a decentralized blockchain oracle. IEEE Blockchain Tech. Briefs (2019)
17. Beniiche, A.: A study of blockchain oracles. arXiv preprint arXiv:2004.07140 (2020)
18. Al-Breiki, H., Rehman, M.H.U., Salah, K., Svetinovic, D.: Trustworthy blockchain oracles: review, comparison, and open research challenges. IEEE Access **8**, 85675 (2020)
19. Ahn, J.: EdenChain: the programmable economy platform. Eden, Singapore, White Paper, vol. 1 (2018)
20. Mammadzada, K., Iqbal, M., Milani, F., García-Bañuelos, L., Matulevičius, R.: Blockchain oracles: a framework for blockchain-based applications. In: Asatiani, A., et al. (eds.) BPM 2020. LNBIP, vol. 393, pp. 19–34. Springer, Cham (2020). https://doi.org/10.1007/978-3-030-58779-6_2
21. Vashchuk, O., Shuwar, R.: Pros and cons of consensus algorithm proof of stake. Difference in the network safety in proof of work and proof of stake. Electron. Inf. Technol. **9**, 106 (2018)
22. Baliga, A., Solanki, N., Verekar, S., Pednekar, A., Kamat, P., Chatterjee, S.: Performance characterization of hyperledger fabric. In: 2018 Crypto Valley Conference on Blockchain Technology (CVCBT), vol. 65. IEEE (2018)
23. Pan, J., Wang, J., Hester, A., Alqerm, I., Liu, Y., Zhao, Y.: EdgeChain: an edge-IoT framework and prototype based on blockchain and smart contracts. IEEE Internet Things J. **6**, 4719 (2018)
24. Zhang, S., Pu, M., Wang, B., Dong, B.: A privacy protection scheme of microgrid direct electricity transaction based on consortium blockchain and continuous double auction. IEEE Access **7**, 151746 (2019)
25. Zhong, W., Xie, K., Liu, Y., Yang, C., Xie, S.: Auction mechanisms for energy trading in multi-energy systems. IEEE Trans. Ind. Inform. **14**, 1511 (2017)

26. Zhang, S., Lee, J.: Double-spending with a sybil attack in the bitcoin decentralized network. IEEE Trans. Ind. Inform. **15**, 5715 (2019)
27. Dabholkar, A., Saraswat, V.: Ripping the fabric: attacks and mitigations on hyperledger fabric. In: Shankar Sriram, V.S., Subramaniyaswamy, V., Sasikaladevi, N., Zhang, L., Batten, L., Li, G. (eds.) ATIS 2019. CCIS, vol. 1116, pp. 300–311. Springer, Singapore (2019). https://doi.org/10.1007/978-981-15-0871-4_24

Privacy Protection

An Outsourced Multi-authority Attribute-Based Encryption for Privacy Protection with Dynamicity and Audit

Zhifa Deng[1] and Jiageng Chen[1,2]([✉])

[1] School of Computer Science, Central China Normal University, Wuhan, China
jiageng.chen@ccnu.edu.cn
[2] Wollongong Joint Institute, Central China Normal University, Wuhan, China

Abstract. Attribute-based Encryption (ABE) realizes a novel and practical many-to-many encryption paradigm, in which the encryptor can appoint someone to decrypt it, and the decryptor does not know who the encryptor is. Therefore, the ABE has better privacy preserving to a certain extent for both participants to a certain degree. The original attribute-based encryption scheme usually has only one trusted authority, and the state of the system is not flexible enough to meet various dynamic needs of users, which become the bottleneck of the system. In addition, the computational overhead of the decryption is not cheap. In order to reduce the cost of decryption, a series of schemes such as encryption/decryption outsourcing have been proposed. However, those solutions simply outsource the process independently without any in-depth investigation into the trustworthiness issues. Hence, we construct an outsourced multi-authority attribute-based encryption with dynamicity and auditing (OMADA-ABE), which makes the system more practical and more flexible. Our solution can support the dynamic changes of the system as well as the auditing of outsourced decryption information to solve the above-mentioned related problems, so as to meet the potential requirements related to the real-world system. What's more, we prove that the proposed scheme is secure against selective chosen-ciphertext attacks without random oracles, and it also achieves the collusion resistance. Finally, we compare our scheme with related researches and showed our advantage regarding the performance and other aspects.

Keywords: Multi-authority ABE · Dynamicity · Outsourcing decryption · Audit · Collusion resistance · Privacy protection

1 Introduction

Cloud computing is an emerging and popular business model, more and more data is stored in the cloud rather than in local data centers, which can also reduce the loss of system maintenance. Traditionally, data cloud servers are considered to be trusted to guarantee privacy security and confidentiality of data, and to enforce access control policies correctly. However, in the current era of big data, since the cloud service

W. Meng and W. Li (Eds.): BlockTEA 2022, LNICST 498, pp. 69–88, 2023.
https://doi.org/10.1007/978-3-031-31420-9_5

provider (CSP) and the double-end user are not in the same trusted domain, the storage platform is not directly controlled by the data owner, and the CSP may not be fully trusted, so the technology inevitably has some risks and it is no longer applicable. Therefore, protecting the privacy and security in the process of interacting with others is particularly important. In order to reduce users' concerns about data privacy, a common solution is to store data in the form of ciphertext, which can still ensure the security of user data even if the data server or storage device is corrupted. However, encrypted data also needs to be shared, and public key encryption or symmetric encryption lacks flexible access control. Therefore, a better way is attribute-based encryption (ABE), which was first proposed by Sahai and Waters [1] to protect the confidentiality of sensitive data. Attribute-based encryption is divided into ciphertext policy attribute-based encryption (CP-ABE) and key policy attribute-based encryption (KP-ABE), both of which can prevent unauthorized users from accessing data [2], even if users store data in untrusted servers.

Moreover, the expensive decryption overhead of CP-ABE is a serious drawback of the attribute-based encryption system, which may essentially prevent its widespread deployment (especially on some small devices or platforms). How to effectively solve this bottleneck is also a problem worth exploring. In addition, the complexity of access policy in ABE system will also increase the computational cost to a certain extent, making the pairing computation cost higher, so it is a very serious challenge to balance the policy complexity and reduce the computational cost. An effective method to reduce the user's decryption overhead is outsourcing decryption, which can outsource a large number of complex decryption operations to a third-party cloud server (CSP), so as to reduce the local overhead. However, CSP is considered untrustworthy third party, so how to check the correctness of outsourced decryption is a very challenging problem. Therefore, none of the above-mentioned research have focused on combining dynamicity and auditable mechanisms with the multi-authority setting.

1.1 Our Contribution

In our work, we studied the above interesting issues and further propose an OMADA-ABE (Outsourced Multi-Authority attribute-based encryption with Dynamicity and Audit) system scheme, which incorporates dynamicity into multi-authority ABE, provides both outsourcing and auditing while protecting user privacy.

The main contributions of this work can be summarized as follows:

- **Dynamic management in the multi-authority setting.** We realize a series of dynamic operations, such as free registration of AAs, free joining, leaving and updating of users under the setting of multiple authorities. The attribute authority (AA) is responsible for the management of attributes, and the CA manages each AA, so as to ensure the stability of the system while taking into account of the dynamic performance. The existence of multi-authorities will make the above operations more smoothly.
- **Self-Auditability (by AA and CA).** Different from the verifiable methods introduced in [3,4], our auditable method does not require any extra parameters to be

added to the ciphertext of our system, and it will not bring any additional computing cost to users. At the same time, there is no need to introduce the cost of third-party auditors, and the audit role is jointly undertaken by the AAs and the CA. Our scheme only needs to perform one inversion and decryption operation to check the correctness of cloud decryption, so this also makes our scheme more efficient and applicable.

1.2 Paper Organization

The overall organizational framework of this paper is as follows. In Sect. 2, we review a series of related works of attribute-based encryption, compare and analyze several types of attribute encryption with different features. In Sect. 3 and 4, we give the preliminaries including the related definitions and present the system security assumptions. In Sect. 5, we give the concrete scheme construction, and the security analysis of our scheme is presented in Sect. 6. In Sect. 7, an evaluation and comparison of relevant performance is provided. Finally, we conclude our work in Sect. 8.

2 Related Work

In a single-authority ABE, both attribute management and key distribution are handled by a single authority. However, in most practical scenarios, users have more than one attribute, so a multi-authority attribute-based encryption system is proposed. Under a multi-authority ABE system, different attribute authorities manage different attribute sets and distribute corresponding attribute keys. In 2007, Chase implemented the Multi-authority Attribute-Based Encryption (MA-ABE) scheme for the first time [5]. In [5], the AA (Attribute Authority) are independent of each other and do not need to exchange information, but it needs a fully trusted CA (Central Authority) to manage all private information. What's more, it achieves collusion resistance by assigning a unique Global Identifier (GID) to each user. In 2008 Lin et al. [6] proposed an MA-ABE scheme that does not require a central authority. Later, Lewko and Waters [7] proposed a new MA-ABE scheme called decentralizing CP-ABE (DCP-ABE) scheme, in which the authority center CA is removed, and any party can become an authority.

Also, Green et al. [8] introduced outsourced decryption in the ABE system, so complex operations in the decryption phase can be outsourced to the ODCSP, and users can recover plaintext only by performing a power operation. Although complex operations are entrusted to the ODCSP, they do not consider the correctness and security of the cloud returned results, only obtain the decryption results. In order to solve the above problems, Ren et al. [9] proposed a mutually verifiable data audit method. Later, Lai et al. [10] introduced the verifiability of ABE to further verify the outsourcing results. Lin et al. [11] reviewed the verifiable outsourcing ABE and proposed a more effective construction method. In 2020 Sethi et al. [12] outsources expensive decryption operations to more powerful computing resources, reduces the overall cost and constrains third-party computing resources to be trusted.

Moreover, after the multi-authority attribute encryption is proposed, a series of functional features are also derived, such as policy updating or hiding [13], attribute revocation [14], searchable ABE [8], attribute-based encryption on lattices [15], online or offline combined computing [16], large universe mechanisms [14], traceability scheme [12], verifiable scheme [3], and so on. However, only some papers are aimed at member management or auditing or outsourcing [9,11,17], just pay attention to one aspect, they cannot use multi-authority decentralized management while ensuring dynamicity. None of the above-mentioned research have focused on combining dynamicity and auditable mechanisms with multi-authority.

3 Preliminaries

3.1 Access Structures

Definition 1 (*Access Structure* [18]). *Let* $\{P_1, P_2, ..., P_n\}$ *be a set of parties. A collection* $A \subseteq 2^{\{P_1, P_2, ..., P_n\}}$ *is monotone if* $\forall$ *B,C: if* $B \in A$ *and* $B \subseteq C$ *then* $C \subseteq A$. *An access structure (respectively, monotone access structure) is a collection (respectively, monotone collection) A of non-empty subsets of* $\{P_1, P_2, ..., P_n\}$, *i.e.,* $A \subseteq 2^{\{P_1, P_2, ..., P_n\}} \setminus \{\emptyset\}$. *The sets in A are called the authorized sets, and the sets not in A are called the unauthorized sets.*

3.2 Lagrange Interpolation

According to [18,19], a Lagrange interpolating polynomial is a polynomial of degree not greater than $(n-1)$ that passes through n points $(x_i, y_i), ..., (x_n, y_n)$, and is given by,

$$p(x) = \sum_{j=1}^{n} p_j(x) \tag{1}$$

where

$$p_j(x) = y_j \prod_{k=i,...,n, k \neq j} \frac{x - x_k}{x_j - x_k} \tag{2}$$

For $i \in Z$ and $S \subseteq Z$, the Lagrange coefficient $\triangle_{i,s}(x)$ is defined as

$$\triangle_{i,s}(x) = \prod_{\forall j \in S, j \neq j} \frac{x - j}{i - j} \tag{3}$$

3.3 Bilinear Pairings

Let G and G_T be two multiplicative cyclic groups of prime order p. Let g be a generator of G and $e : G \times G \to G_T$ be a bilinear map with the properties:

- Bilinearity: $e(A^x, B^y) = e(A, B)^{xy}$ for all $A, B \in G$ and $x, y \in Z_p$.
- Non-degeneracy: $\exists A \in G_1, B \in G_2, e(A, B) \neq 1$, where 1 is the identity of G_T.
- Efficient computability: there exits an algorithm that can efficiently compute $e(A, B)$ for all $A \in G_1, B \in G_2$.

3.4 The Decisional Bilinear Diffie-Hellman Problem (DBDH)

Let G_1, G_2 and G_T be three cyclic groups of prime order q, P and Q be arbitrarily-chosen generators of G_1 and G_2, respectively, and $e : G_1 \times G_2 \to G_T$ be a bilinear mapping. Given $(P, Q, aP, bP, cP, aQ, bQ, cQ, Z)$ for some $a, b, c \in Z_q^*$ and $Z \in G_T$, decide if $Z = e(P, Q)^{abc}$.

An algorithm B that outputs $b' \in \{0, 1\}$ has advantage ϵ in solving the DBDH problem if

$$
\begin{aligned}
&|Pr[B(P, Q, aP, bP, cP, aQ, bQ, cQ, e(P, Q)^{abc})] \\
&- Pr[B(P, Q, aP, bP, cP, aQ, bQ, cQ, Z)]| \geq \epsilon
\end{aligned}
\tag{4}
$$

Definition 2 *(The decisional-BDH Assumption [20]). We say that the decisional BDH assumption holds if no polynomial-time adversary has non-negligible advantage in solving the decisional BDH problem.*

3.5 Trapdoor Function

We say a trapdoor is a secret that allows one to efficiently invert the function; however, if one do not know the trapdoor, it's still difficult to reverse the function.

Definition 3 *(The trapdoor function scheme [21]). Let X and Y be finite sets. A trapdoor function scheme T, define over(X, Y), is a triple of algorithm(G, F, I), where*

1. *G is a probabilistic key generation algorithm that is invoked as $(pk, sk) \xleftarrow{R} G()$, where pk is called a public key and sk is called a secret key.*
2. *F is a deterministic algorithm that is invoked as $y \leftarrow F(pk, x)$, where pk is a public key (as output by G) and x lies in X. The output y is an element of Y.*
3. *I is a deterministic algorithm that is invoked as $x \leftarrow I(sk, y)$, where sk is a secret key (as output by G) and y lies in Y. The output x is an element of X.*

Also, when we know the trapdoor, we can easily calculate the secret value.

4 Syntax and Security

4.1 Security Assumptions

In our scheme, we make some security assumptions as follows:

- The Central Authority (CA) must be fully credible and not collude with any other authority.
- The Attribute Authority (AA) is trusted, but it is not completely trusted, and it may be corrupted by other malicious adversary.
- The Data User (DU) is honest but curious, is likely to be under the profit-driven to collude with other users, thereby gaining unauthorized data access control.
- The CSP and OD-CSP are honest but curious, just like DU. They will faithfully perform their duties, but they may also have some curiosity about data.

4.2 Security Model

Here, we describe a selectively ciphertext policy and chosen-ciphertext attack (sCP-IND-CCA) model for the OMADA-CPABE scheme, played by a game between a challenger and an adversary. Let A denote the adversary who attempts to attack the scheme, C denote the challenger who encrypt the challenge ciphertext. Formally, this is represented by the following game interaction between A and C [22,23].

- **Init**: The adversary A chooses a challenge access control policy T^* that he wants to attack and sends it to the challenger C.
- **Setup**: The challenger runs $CASetup()$ algorithm to output CA_{pk} and invokes $AASetup()$ algorithm to generate the required keys for corrupt and honest AA respectively. The adversary selects the corrupted authorities among all the AA, i.e. $S'_{AA} \subset S_{AA}$. Then the challenger gets public key AA_{pk} and secret key AA_{sk} for all AAs in S_{AA} by running $AASetup()$ algorithm. For all non-corrupted attribute authorities in $\tilde{S} : (S_{AA} - S'_{AA})$, only its public key AA_{pk} will be issued to A; Otherwise, the public/private key pairs AA_{pk} and AA_{sk} of the remaining corrupted AAs in S'_{AA} should be sent to the adversary A.
- **Query Phase 1**: In phase 1, the adversary A makes the following queries to challenger C as follows.
  1. Private key query. The adversary is allowed to request the private keys $SK_{u_{id}}$ corresponding to his/her desired attribute sets $S_1, ..., S_q$ from AAs and extract the private key $SK_{u_{id}}$. (However, there is a restriction that there must be at least one non-corrupted attribute authority AA in order to prevent the adversary from obtaining a sufficient number of secret keys). Finally, $SK_{u_{id}}$ will be recorded in a set L_{SK}.
  2. Decryption query. The adversary is also allowed to query the decryption of the given ciphertext CT and output the message M corresponding to the CT. If the ciphertext is not correctly constructed, then outputs $\perp$.
- **Challenge**: The adversary A submits (M_0, M_1, T^*) to the challenger, of which M_0 and M_1 is two messages of equal length and T^* is an access tree structure, and all the sets $S_1, ..., S_q$ in Phase 1 do not meet this access structure. Now the challenger randomly selects $b \in \{0, 1\}$ and $K \in G_T$, then computes the encryption result $E_K(M_b)$ of the message M_b and encrypts the symmetric key K under the access tree T^*, and finally generates the matching CT^*. Once there exits $SK_i \in L_{SK}$ that can decrypt $CT*$, then the challenge will be terminated. Otherwise, the ciphertext CT^* proceeds normally and is sent to the adversary.
- **Query Phase 2**: Repeat phase 1, more secret key queries can be made by the adversary when he satisfies the requirement given previously, but the only limitation is that decryption queries cannot be made again.
- **Guess**: Finally, the adversary has to guess which message the challenger encrypted, then outputs a guess b' of b. If $b' = b$, we say the adversary wins the game.

We now define the advantage of the adversary in the above game as follows,

$$Adv^{CCA}_{OMADA}(A) = |\Pr(b' = b) - 1/2| \tag{5}$$

Definition 4. *An Outsourced Multi-Authority Attribute-Based Encryption with Dynamicity and Audit scheme is said to be selectively ciphertext policy and chosen-ciphertext attack (sCP-IND-CCA secure) if for any polynomial-time adversary A, the advantage $Adv_{OMADA-ABE}^{CCA}(A)$ is negligible.*

5 Our Construction

Table 1. Notations

Notation	Meaning
S_{AA}	the set of all attribute authorities (AA)
S_{A_i}	the set of attributes maintained by AA_i
$S_{u_{id}}$	the set of attributes owned by user u_{id}
λ	the security parameter
U	the set of registered users
E_K	the symmetric encryption function with key K
D_K	the symmetric decryption function with key K
N_L	the set of all leaf nodes of access tree T
k_N	the threshold value associated with node N
d_N	the degree of the polynomial of node N
$parent_{(N)}$	the parent node of node N
$index_{(N)}$	the index associated with node N
$Attr(N)$	the attribute associated with node N
$val(N)$	the attribute value associated with node N

First, some symbol notations in this chapter are described in Table 1, and then the system design details of this paper are described in the following parts.

5.1 System Initialization

1. $CASetup(1^\lambda) \rightarrow ((CA_{sk}, CA_{pk}), (CA_{sig}, CA_{verify}))$. The CA takes the security parameter λ as input, and then generates a bilinear mapping $e : G_1 \times G_2 \rightarrow G_T$, where G_T is a multiplicative group, G_1 and G_2 are two additive groups. Then the public parameters $PP = \{G_1, G_2, G_T, g, h, e(g, h)\}$ are obtained, where $g \in G_1$ and $h \in G_2$ respectively, and G_1, G_2, G_T are groups with prime order q. The CA perform the steps as follows:

– Step 1: Choose two random elements α, β from Z_q^*.
– Step 2: Selects two one-way collision-resistance hash functions, named H_1 and H_2:
$H_1 : \{0, 1\}^* \rightarrow Z_q^*$
$H_2 : \{0, 1\}^* \rightarrow \{0, 1\}^{l_\lambda}$ (where l_λ represents the string length.)
– Step 3: The algorithm generates (CA_{sk}, CA_{pk}) as follows:
$CA_{sk} = \{\alpha, \beta\}$,
$CA_{pk} = \{PP, e(g, h)^{\alpha\beta}, f = e(g, h)^{\alpha(\beta-1)}, g^\alpha, H_1, H_2\}$

– Step 4: Next, the CA exploits cryptography algorithm to generate a pair of signature verification key (CA_{sig}, CA_{verify}), and assists AA to verify the user's identity after the keys are generated.

After the subsequent AASetup phase is deployed, the CA still needs to initialize some parameter settings in the systems. For details, see the AAsetup phase.

2. $AAEnroll(CA_{sk}, CA_{pk}, AA_{info}) \rightarrow (AA_i, CA_{verify}, CA_{sk})$. Each authority sends a request to CA to register to the system. The CA runs the algorithm and generates a global unique identity for each legitimate authority in the system, and sends its private key CA_{sk} and verify key CA_{verify} to every legal AAs. Therefore, the AA has the ability to use the authentication key Ca_{verify} to check whether the user is valid. The AA will cooperate with the user to complete the verification once they have relevant requirements.

3. $AASetup(CA_{sk}, AA_i) \rightarrow (AA_{i,sk}, AA_{i,pk})$. Every AA runs the algorithm with CA_{sk} as input, and then outputs a pair of public and secret keys as follows:

– Step 1: The AA_i picks a random $c_i \in Z_q$ and computes x_i, y_i as follows:

$$x_i = g^{c_i}, y_i = h^{c_i}$$

– Step 2: Then generates $AA_{i,sk}$ and $AA_{i,pk}$ as:

$$AA_{i,sk} = c_i, AA_{i,pk} = \{x_i, y_i\}$$

– Step 3: When the attribute authority is set, the CA then sets two default users in this step to be used as the credential information to bind the user and AA together. The default user generation process is as follows:

(1) First, set $U = \{0, 1\}$ and randomly select some values $\{v_{u_{id},j}\}_{\forall u_{id} \in U, j \in S_{A_i}}$ and $\{\sigma_i\}_{\forall i \in S_{AA}}$ in Z_q^*.

(2) Then, we get

$$\begin{cases} \left\{ V_j = (\prod_{\forall j \in S_{A_i}} v_{u_{id},j})h \right\} \\ \left\{ \bar{v}_{u_{id},j} = \sigma_i \prod_{\forall k \neq u_{id}, k \in U} v_{k,j}^{-1} + v_{u_{id},j} \mod q \right\}_{\forall j \in S_{A_i}} \end{cases} \quad (6)$$

Finally, the public key of CA is newly changed. The PK contains the information about $\{V_j, \{\bar{v}_{u_{id},j}\}_{\forall j \in S_{AA}}\}$, which is used for subsequent operations. Also, we can view this part as some kind of credential information in the process of system dynamic change. The newly changed PK as follows:

$CA_{pk} = \{PP, e(g, h)^{\alpha\beta}, f = e(g, h)^{\alpha(\beta-1)}, g^\alpha, H_1, H_2, \{V_j, \{\bar{v}_{u_{id},j}\}_{\forall j \in S_{A_i}}\}\}$.

4. $UserEnroll(CA_{sk}, CA_{pk}, u_{info}) \rightarrow (u_{id}, cert(u_{id}), u_{sk}, u_{pk})$. The algorithm randomly picks a $t_{u_{id}} \in Z_p$, then outputs the public and secret key pair of the user $\{u_{pk}, u_{sk}\}$ as follows:

$$u_{sk} = \{t_{u_{id}}\}, u_{pk} = \{h^{t_{u_{id}}}\}$$

Meanwhile, it also generates user certificates $cert(u_{id})$ where

$$cert(u_{id}) = \{sign_{\{CA_{sign}\}}(u_{id}, h^{t_{u_{id}}})\}$$

Thus one person can prove that he/she is a legal user in the system by using the certificate $cert(u_{id})$ received from CA. Then we randomly pick $\{\sigma_i, v_{u_{id},j}\}_{\forall j \in S_{A_i}}$ in Z_q^*, set $\{V_j, \{\bar{v}_{u_{id},j}\}_{\forall j \in S_{A_i}}\}$ (We can view this part as some kind of credential information in the process of system dynamic change).

$$\begin{cases} \left\{V_j = (\prod_{\forall j \in S_{A_i}} v_{u_{id},j})g\right\} \\ \left\{\bar{v}_{u_{id},j} = \sigma_i \prod_{\forall k \neq u_{id}, k \in U} v_{k,j}^{-1} + v_{u_{id},j} \bmod q\right\}_{\forall j \in S_{A_i}} \end{cases} \tag{7}$$

After a user is registered to the system, then set $U = U \vee \{u_{id}\}$ and update $\{V_j, \{\bar{v}_{u_{id},j}\}_{\forall j \in S_{A_i}}\}$.

5.2 Execution

1. $KeyGen(CA_{pk}, AA_{i,sk}, u_{id}, S_{u_{id}}) \to (SK_{u_{id}})$. Each user registered to the system has its own global identity. They request the decryption key from the AA bound to their own attributes.

– Step 1: Randomly pick some elements $\{h_{u_{id},j}, \{\rho_i, \sigma_i\}_{\forall i \in S_{AA}}, \{v_{u_{id},j}\}_{\forall j \in S_{u_{id}} \cap S_{A_i}},$ $\{r_{i,j}\}_{\forall i \in S_{AA} \forall j \in S_{u_{id}} \cap S_{A_i}}\}$ in Z_q^*.
– Step 2: Compute

$$\begin{cases} \left\{V_j = v_{u_{id},j} V_j\right\}_{\forall j \in S_{u_{id}} \cap S_{A_i}} \\ \{\bar{v}_{u_{id},j} = \sigma_i \prod_{\forall k \neq u_{id}, k \in U} v_{k,j}^{-1} + v_{u_{id},j} \bmod q\} \quad {}^{\forall i \in S_{AA},}_{\forall j \in S_{u_{id}} \cap S_{A_i}} \\ \{\bar{v}_{k,j} = (\bar{v}_{k,j} - v_{k,j}) v_{u_{id},j}^{-1} + v_{k,j} \bmod q\} \quad {}^{\forall k \neq u_{id}, k \in U,}_{\forall j \in S_{u_{id}} \cap S_{A_i}} \end{cases} \tag{8}$$

– Step 3: According to the relevant information about user u_{id} and then compute his/her decryption key as follows:

$$\begin{cases} D_{u_{id}} = (\alpha h + \rho_i \sigma_i c_i H_1(u_{id})h)_{\forall i \in S_{AA}} \\ \{D_{u_{id},j} = v_{u_{id},j}^{-1}(\rho_i + r_{i,j}) \cdot H_1(u_{id})\}_{\forall i \in S_{AA}, \forall j \in S_{u_{id}} \cap S_{A_i}} \\ \{D'_{u_{id},j} = r_{i,j} g \cdot H_1(u_{id})\}_{\forall i \in S_{AA}, \forall j \in S_{u_{id}} \cap S_{A_i}} \\ \{D''_{u_{id},j} = \sigma_i c_i r_{i,j} g + \rho_i c_i g v_j\}_{\forall i \in S_{AA}, \forall j \in S_{u_{id}} \cap S_{A_i}} \end{cases} \tag{9}$$

– Step 4: It outputs the secret key $SK_{u_{id}, j \in S} = \{D_{u_{id}}, D_{u_{id},j}, \quad D'_{u_{id},j},$ $D''_{u_{id},j}\}_{\forall j \in S_{u_{id}} \cap S_{A_i}}$

2. $Update(u_{id}, j, m'_{u_{id},j}) \rightarrow (SK_{u_{id},j})$. With the dynamic changes of users' identities, roles, capabilities and other requirements in the system, their attributes are constantly changing. Therefore, users can update their corresponding attribute values according to the current actual scenario, such as updating their j^{th} attribute value to $m'_{u_{id},j}$ to meet the needs of the new environment. The algorithm performs the following operations:

- Step 1: Firstly, randomly select some elements, ρ_i', $v'_{u_{id},j}$, and $r'_{i,j}$ in Z_q^*
- Step 2: Next, compute $h'_{u_{id},j} = H_2(m'_{u_{id},j})$
- Step 3: Then, give

$$\begin{cases} D_{u_{id}} = (\alpha h + \rho_i' \sigma_i c_i H_1(u_{id})h)_{\forall i \in S_{AA}, \forall j \in S_{A_i}} \\ \{D_{u_{id},j} = v'^{-1}_{u_{id},j}(\rho'_i + r'_{i,j}h_{u_{id},j}) \cdot H_1(u_{id})\}_{\forall i \in S_{AA}, \forall j \in S_{A_i}} \\ \{D_{u_{id},k'} = v^{-1}_{u_{id},k'}(\rho'_i + r'_{i,k}h_{u_{id},k'}) \cdot H_1(u_{id})\}_{\substack{\forall i \in S_{AA}, \\ \forall k' \in S_{A_i}\backslash\{j\}}} \\ \{D'_{u_{id},j} = r'_{i,j}gH_1(u_{id})\}_{\forall i \in S_{AA}, \forall j \in S_{A_i}} \\ \{D''_{u_{id},j} = h'_{u_{id},j}(r'_{i,j}\sigma_i c_i g + \rho'_i c_i g v_j)\}_{\forall i \in S_{AA}, \forall j \in S_{A_i}} \\ \{D''_{u_{id},k'} = h'_{u_{id},k'}(r'_{i,k'}\sigma_i c_i g + \rho'_i c_i g v_j)\}_{\substack{\forall i \in S_{AA}, \\ \forall k' \in S_{A_i}\backslash\{j\}}} \end{cases} \quad (10)$$

to user u_{id}.

- Step 4: Lastly, update $\{V_j, \{\bar{v}_{u_{id},j}\}_{\forall j \in S_{A_i}}\}$

$$\begin{cases} \{V_j = v^{-1}_{u_{id},j}v'_{u_{id},j}V_j\}_{\forall j \in S_{A_i}} \\ \{\bar{v}_{u_{id},j} = (\bar{v}_{u_{id},j} - v_{k,j}) + v^{-1}_{u_{id},j} \bmod q\}_{\substack{\forall k \neq u_{id}, \\ k \in U, \forall j \in S_{A_i}}} \\ \{\bar{v}_{k,j} = (\bar{v}_{k,j} - v_{k,j})v_{u_{id},j}v^{-1}_{u_{id},j} + v_{k,j} \bmod q\}_{\substack{\forall k \in U\backslash\{u_{id}\}, \\ \forall j \in S_{A_i}}} \end{cases} \quad (11)$$

3. $Revoke(u_{id})$. It is guaranteed that the leaving user cannot legally exist in the system, both the certificate and the private key are revoked. What's more, the credentials of system will also be modified, and his/her all related information will be removed. The algorithm update $\{V_j, \{\bar{v}_{u_{id},j}\}_{\forall j \in S_{A_j}}\}$ as follows:

$$\begin{cases} \{V_j = v^{-1}_{u_{id},j}V_j\}_{\forall j \in S_{A_i}} \\ \{\bar{v}_{k,j} = (\bar{v}_{k,j} - v_{k,j})v_{u_{id},j} + v_{k,j} \bmod q\}_{\substack{\forall k \in U\backslash\{u_{id}\}, \\ \forall j \in S_{A_i}}} \end{cases} \quad (12)$$

And then, set $U = U\backslash\{u_{id}\}$ and delete $\{\bar{v}_{u_{id},j}\}_{\forall j \in S_{A_i}}$ in PK.

5.3 Encryption and Decryption

1. $Encrypt(CA_{pk}, AA_{i,pk}, T, K, M) \rightarrow (CT)$. In our study, due to the encryption algorithm is operated under the tree access structure T [24], the generating process of ciphertext is divided into two parts: leaf node and internal node.

a) **Access tree structure construction** [25]: Let T represent an access structure tree. For a given tree T, start from the root node R and select a polynomial q_x for each node (including leaves) of T in a top-down manner. For each node x in the tree, set $d_x = k_x - 1$. The detailed process is described as follows:

- For the root node R: Randomly chooses an element $s \in Z_q^*$ and sets $q_R(0) = r$, where k_R is the threshold value of the root node R, and the process starts from the root node R. Then assign a unique index number x for each child of the root node R, randomly chooses d_R other points of the polynomial q_R to fully define it.

- For each non-leaf node N other than R: Randomly pick a polynomial q_N of degree $d_N = k_N - 1$ with $q_N(0) = q_{parent(N)}(index(N))$, where k_N is the threshold value of node N. Then assign a unique index number x for each child of the node N, randomly chooses d_N other points of the polynomial q_N randomly to fully define it.

- For each leaf node N_L: Randomly choose a polynomial q_{N_L} of degree 0 with $q_{N_L}(0) = q_{parent(N_L)}(index(N_L))$

b) **Ciphertext generation:** Randomly select a session key $K \in G_T$ and K is randomly divided into K_1 and K_2. The K_2 is saved by user and K_1 is used in ciphertext construction. Then pick a one-way trapdoor function F, which is a deterministic algorithm, and its inverse can be calculated when the trapdoor is known.

Then the generated ciphertext is below:

$$
\begin{aligned}
CT = \{&T, \tilde{C} = e(g, h)^{\alpha\beta r} K_1, C = rg, C' = f^r, \\
&\bar{M} = E_K(M), C_F = F(x_i, K_1 \oplus \bar{M}) \\
&\{C_N = q_N(0)V_{Att(N)}x_i, \\
&C'_N = q_N(0)H_2(val(N))y_i, \\
&C''_N = q_N(0)H_2(val(N))h \\
&\{\bar{v}_{u_{id}, Att(N)}\}_{\forall u_{id} \in U}\}_{\forall N \in N_L}\}
\end{aligned}
\tag{13}
$$

where $V_{Att(N)}$ are the credential information of current attribute node N, $H_2(val(N))$ are the hash value of the attribute information corresponding to the current node N.

2. $Decrypt_{ODCSP}(CT, SK_{u_{id}}) \rightarrow (K_1)$. After the user gets the ciphertext CT from the CSP, since there is a certain exponential operation for ciphertext decryption, our scheme is tend to transpose the overhead operation to the outsourcing decryption CSP.

If N is a leaf node: Then we let $j = Att(N)$ and $H_2(val(N)) = v_j$. If $j \in S_{A_i}$, then:

$$DecryptNode(CT, SK_{u_{id}}, N)$$

$$= \frac{e(D_{u_{id},j}, \bar{v}_{u_{id},j} \cdot C_N)}{e(D'_{u_{id},j}, C'_N)e(D''_{u_{id},j}, C''_N)}$$

$$= \frac{e(v_{u_{id},j}^{-1}(\rho_N + r_{N,j}) \cdot H_1(u_{id}), (\sigma_N v_j^{-1} v_{u_{id},j} + v_{u_{id},j})q_N(0)v_j h g^{c_N})}{e(r_{N,j}g H_1(u_{id}), q_N(0)H_2(val(N))h^{c_N})e(\sigma_N c_N r_{N,j}g \cdot H_1(u_{id}) + \rho_N c_N g v_j \cdot H_1(u_{id}), q_N(0)h)}$$

$$= \frac{e(\rho_N \cdot H_1(u_{id}) + r_{N,j} \cdot H_1(u_{id}), \sigma_N q_N(0)h g^{c_N})e(\rho_N \cdot H_1(u_{id}) + r_{N,j} \cdot H_1(u_{id}), q_N(0)v_j h g^{c_N})}{e(r_{N,j}h \cdot H_1(u_{id}), q_N(0)v_j g^{c_N})e(\sigma_N r_{N,j}g \cdot H_1(u_{id}), q_N(0)hc_N)e(\rho_N g v_j \cdot H_1(u_{id}), q_N(0)hc_N)}$$

$$= e(\rho_N h \cdot H_1(u_{id}), \sigma_N q_N(0)g^{c_N})$$

$$= e(g, h)^{\rho_N \sigma_N q_N(0)c_N \cdot H_1(u_{id})}$$

$$\tag{14}$$

If $j \notin S_{A_i}$, then we define

$$DecryptNode(CT, SK_{u_{id}}, N) = \bot. \tag{15}$$

If N is an internal node: It invokes the algorithm $DecryptNode(CT, SK_{u_{id}}, N_c)$ and stores its output results as F_{N_c}, where nodes N_c are children of N. Let S_N be an arbitrary k_n-sized set of child nodes N_c such that $F_{N_c} \neq \bot$. If there is no such set then the node does not meet the requirements, and the function returns $\bot$.

Otherwise, we get

$$F_N = \prod_{N_c \in S_N} F_{N_c}^{\Delta_{n,S'_N}(0)}$$

$$= \prod_{N_c \in S_N} \left(\omega^{\rho_N \sigma_N c_N H_1(u_{id}) \cdot q_{N_c}(0)}\right)^{\Delta_{n,S'_N}(0)}$$

$$= \prod_{N_c \in S_N} \left(\omega^{\rho_N \sigma_N c_N H_1(u_{id}) \cdot q_{parent(N_c)}(index(N_c))}\right)^{\Delta_{n,S'_N}(0)} \tag{16}$$

$$= \prod_{N_c \in S_N} \omega^{\rho_N \sigma_N c_N H_1(u_{id}) \cdot q_N(n) \cdot \Delta_{n,S'_N}(0)}$$

$$= \omega^{\rho_N \sigma_N c_N H_1(u_{id}) \cdot q_N(0)} (\textit{using polynomial interpolation})$$

where $\omega = e(g, h)$, $n = index(N_c)$, $S'_N = \{index(N_c) : N_c \in S_N\}$.

Then, the algorithm calls the function on the root node R of the tree T. If the set S satisfies the access tree, we set $A = DecryptNode(CT, SK_{u_{id}}, R)$, and then returns

$$A = DecryptNode(CT, SK_{u_{id}}, R)$$

$$= e(g, h)^{\rho_R \sigma_R c_R H_1(u_{id}) \cdot q_R(0)} \tag{17}$$

$$= e(g, h)^{\rho_R \sigma_R c_R H_1(u_{id}) \cdot q_R(0)}$$

Finally, the partial session key K_1 can be calculated from the formula $\tilde{C} \cdot A/(e(C, D_{u_{id}}) \cdot C')$ where

$$
\begin{aligned}
\frac{\tilde{C} \cdot A}{e(C, D_{u_{id}}) \cdot C'} \\
&= \frac{e(g, h)^{\alpha\beta r} K_1 \cdot e(g, h)^{\rho_R \sigma_R c_R H_1(u_{id}) \cdot r}}{e(rg, \alpha h + \rho_R \sigma_R c_R H_1(u_{id})h) e(g, h)^{\alpha(\beta-1)r}} \\
&= \frac{e(g, h)^{\alpha\beta r} K_1 \cdot e(g, h)^{\rho_N \sigma_N c_N H_1(u_{id}) \cdot r}}{e(g, h)^{\alpha r + \rho_N \sigma_N c_N H_1(u_{id})r} e(g, h)^{\alpha(\beta-1)r}} \\
&= \frac{e(g, h)^{\rho_N \sigma_N c_N H_1(u_{id}) \cdot r} \cdot e(g, h)^{\alpha\beta r} K_1}{e(g, h)^{\rho_N \sigma_N c_N H_1(u_{id})r} e(g, h)^{\alpha\beta r}} \\
&= K_1
\end{aligned}
\tag{18}
$$

5.4 Audit

1. $Audit_{AA}(AA_{i,sk}, CT, Decrypt_{ODCSP}(CT, SK_{u_{id}})) \rightarrow (1/0)$. AA calculates the one-way trapdoor function by using its private key to obtains the XOR result of the function value and the partial session key K_1. If $F^{-1}(c_i, C_F) \oplus K_1 = \bar{M}$, then it means that the decryption result of the outsourced decryption CSP is correct temporarily, and the values of the K_1 and $\bar{M}$ are consistent and unified, so the preliminary audit correct and then the algorithm returns 1; Otherwise, it indicates that the outsourced decryption CSP has an error and returns 0. Finally, the AA cannot decrypt a plaintext message even if it retains part of the session key K_1.

2. $Audit_{CA}(Audit_{AA}(*) == 1, CA_{pk}, CT, K, M) \rightarrow (1/0)$. The algorithm will judges the result returned by the $Audit_{AA}$, if it returns 1, the algorithm can be successfully executed; otherwise, it will fall back to the previous step. If $E_K(M) = \bar{M}$, that is, the value of $\bar{M}$ and M are kept unified. Tracing back to the source shows that both the outsourcing decryption CSP and the AA are calculated correctly, then the algorithm returns 1; otherwise, it indicates that there is collusion between the outsourcing decryption CSP and AA, or at least one party has calculation error.

5.5 Decryption by User

$Decrypt_{DU}(Audit_{CA}(*) == 1, cert(u_{id}), CT, K_1, K_2) \rightarrow (M/\perp)$. The algorithm will judges the result returned by the $Audit_{CA}$, when the algorithm $Audit_{CA}$ outputs 1, then user u_{id} submits his partial session key K_2 and own identity certificate. After the verification is passed, he will receive the correct partial session key K_1 jointly audited by AA and CA, then recover the complete session key according to the two partial session keys, and finally the plaintext M can be recovered by using the symmetric decryption algorithm, that is $E_K(\bar{M}) = M$.

6   Security Analysis

Theorem 1. *The OMADA-ABE scheme is sCP-IND-CCA secure under the DBDH assumption.*

Proof. Assuming that there exits an adversary in polynomial probability time that can break our algorithm, then there will be a challenger that can break the DBDH assumption by using the adversary. Suppose we have an adversary A, which has a non-negligible advantage $\epsilon = AdvA$ in the selective security game against our scheme. Here, we assume that the challenger has been given relevant parameters. If the challenger wants to break the DBDH assumption, he needs at least $\frac{1}{2} + \varepsilon$ probability to determine whether $Z = e(g, h)^{abc}$ or not. We now build a simulator B_e that plays DBDH problem. The details as follows.

Init: Specify a DBDH instance $(G_1, G_2, G_T, q, g, h, e, ag, bg, cg, ah, bh, ch, Z)$, the challenger generates the system default user list $U = \{0, 1\}$ and $\{V_j, \{\bar{v}_{u_{id},j}\}_{\forall j \in S_{A_i}}\}$ according to the $AASetup()$ algorithm in Sect. 5.1 initially. In addition, challenger publishes $PK = \{G_1, G_2, G_T, e, H, g, h, f = e(\alpha g, \beta h - h), e(\alpha g, \beta h), \{V_j, \{\bar{v}_{u_{id},j}\}_{\forall j \in S_{A_i}}\}\}$ and set the secret key $SK = \{\alpha, \beta\}$. The simulator B_e receives the above DBDH instance generated by the challenger and other relevant parameters, the simulator is ready now. Since this paper assumes the model as selective, the adversary can adaptively choose a challenge access policy tree T^* and send it to the simulator. The simulator builds a list L_{SK}, and starts to simulate the oracles in Phase 1.

Setup: The challenger runs $CASetup()$, $AAEnroll()$ and $AASetup()$ algorithm. For all corrupted AAs ($A_k \in C_A$): The simulator B_e picks $c_k \leftarrow Z_q$ and sets $X_k = g^{c_k}, Y_k = h^{c_k}$. Therefore, the public/secret key pairs for $A_k \in C_A$ is given as $\{(c_k), (X_k = g^{c_k}, Y_k = h^{c_k})\}$. Then the simulator B_e sends the public key of the corrupted authority together with the private key to the adversary. Now the adversary A can get the $SK_{u_{id},k}(D_{u_{id}}, D_{u_{id},k}, D'_{u_{id},k}, D''_{u_{id},k})$ alone for u_{id}. For the remaining AAs that are not corrupted, only the public key is given to the adversary.

Phase 1: The simulator B_e generates private keys for system default users $SK_{u_{id}}$ with complete set and satisfying access policy by following $KeyGen()$ algorithm. Then the adversary A queries for the private key of the ith authority corresponding to a user u_{id} that he wants to query, then the B_e return $SK_{u_{id},i}$ and store $SK_{u_{id},i}$ in L_{SK}. Upon receiving a decryption request from the adversary, simulator B_e will judge whether it's a correctly constructed ciphertext, and if not, the output will be $\perp$. Otherwise, the simulator B_e will check whether a private key $SK_{u_{id},i}$ used to decrypt CT exists in L_{SK}. If there exists key in L_{SK} that can decrypt, B_e decrypts CT exploiting $SK_{u_{id},i}$ and then returns the final result to A. If not, then the simulator B_e will create a pseudo user w and make full use of the user $w's$ private key to decrypt. Details are as follows.

1. Randomly select the following elements which are

$$\begin{cases} \{\rho_i, \sigma_i\}_{\exists i \in S_{AA}} \in Z_q^* \\ \{v_{w,j}, r_{i,j}\}_{\exists i \in S_{AA}, j \in S_{u_{id}} \cap S_{A_i}} \in Z_q^* \end{cases}$$

2. Compute

$$
\begin{cases}
\left\{ C_N = v_{w,att(N)} C_N \right\}_{\forall N \in N_L} \\
\left\{ \bar{v}_{w,j} = \sigma_w \prod_{\forall k \in U} v_{k,j}^{-1} + v_{w,j} \bmod q \right\}_{j \in S_{u_{id}} \cap S_{A_i}}
\end{cases}
\tag{19}
$$

where C_N is retrieved from CT and refreshed the credential information for pseudo-users w in this step.

3. Calculate the private key SK_{u_w} of pseudo user w as follows:

$$
SK_{u_w} =
\begin{cases}
D_{u_w} = \alpha h + \rho_i \sigma_i c_i H_1(u_w) h \\
\left\{ D_{u_w,j} = v_{w,j}^{-1}(\rho_i + r_{i,j}) \cdot H_1(u_w) \right\}_{\forall j \in S_{u_{id}} \cap S_{A_i}} \\
\left\{ D'_{u_w,j} = r_{i,j} g \cdot H_2(h^{t_{u_w}}) \right\}_{\forall j \in S_{u_{id}} \cap S_{A_i}} \\
\left\{ D''_{u_{id},j} = \sigma_i c_i r_{i,j} g + \rho_i c_i g v_j \right\}_{\forall j \in S_{u_{id}} \cap S_{A_i}}
\end{cases}
\tag{20}
$$

4. Take user w's private key SK_{u_w} to operate the CT and return the final result to adversary.

Challenge: At the beginning of the challenge, the adversary selects two messages of equal length M_0 and M_1 in advance, and sends them to the simulator as soon as he receives all the messages from the simulator. After receiving the (M_0, M_1, T^*), the simulator B_e creates a set list L_C to store the values of the nodes in the subsequent access tree. Meanwhile, let R be the root node of the received access policy tree T^*. Then set $m = val(N)$, $j = att(N)$, and get $C_N = v_{att(N)} C_{0\forall N \in N_L}$, $C'_N = q_N(0) H_2(val(N))$, $C''_N = H_2(val(N)) v_{att(N)}$. Now we store some values of the challenged node $\{C_N, C'_N, C''_N\}_{N \in N_L}$ in the list L_C. The B_e randomly picks a $b \in \{0,1\}$ and $K' \in G_T$, here we treat the selected message as M_b, and the b takes the value 0 or 1. After multiple operations above, we calculate the ciphertext $CT^* = \{T^*, \tilde{C} = Z K_1, C = \gamma g, C' = \frac{Z}{e(\alpha g, \gamma h)}, \bar{M}_b = E_{K'}(M_b), C_F = F(x_i, K_1 \oplus \bar{M}_b), \{C_N, C'_N, C''_N, \{\bar{v}_{u_{id},Att(N)}\}_{\forall u_{id} \in U}\}_{N \in N_L}\}$, where the encrypted value of the node is retrieved from the encrypted list L_C. In addition, we emphasize that CT^* is regarded as a valid encryption information for M_b when $Z = e(g,h)^{abc}$; Otherwise, the CT^* is just a random value. The challenge will be terminated if the key $SK_{u_{id},k} \in L_{SK}$ is found that can be used to decrypt the CT. If not, the B_e returns the result(CT^*) to A.

Phase 2: The adversary continues to follow phase 1 to make selective queries as he did, except for all decryption queries.

Guess: Finally, after several rounds of interaction, the adversary A gets his guess b'. The B_e outputs 1 and guess that $Z = e(g,h)^{abc}$(a valid BDH-tuple) if $b' = b$. Otherwise, the adversary is wrong and B_e outputs 0 denote that the Z is not a valid combination of elements but a random value in G_T. Therefore, if a polynomial time adversary can break our scheme with non-negligible advantage at least ε, which means that a challenger has non-negligible ε' to break the DBDH assumption where $\varepsilon' \geq \varepsilon - \delta$ and δ is a negligible advantage. Also, we can obtain

$\Pr[B_e(g, h, ag, bg, cg, ah, bh, ch, e(g, h)^{abc}) = 1] = \Pr[b' = b]$ if $Z = e(g, h)^{abc}$, where $\left| \Pr[b' = b] - \frac{1}{2} \right| \geq \varepsilon$. Otherwise(the Z is chosen at random in G_T), we have $\Pr[B_e(g, h, ag, bg, cg, ah, bh, ch, Z) = 1] = \Pr[b' = b]$, where $\left| \Pr[b' = b] - \frac{1}{2} \right| \leq \delta$ (δ is one probability that guarantees semantic security under symmetric encryption E_K). Finally, we have

$$
\begin{aligned}
&| \Pr[B_e(g, h, ag, bg, cg, ah, bh, ch, e(g, h)^{abc}) = 1] \\
&- \Pr[B_e(g, h, ag, bg, cg, ah, bh, ch, Z) = 1]| \\
&\geq \left| \left(\frac{1}{2} \pm \varepsilon \right) - \left(\frac{1}{2} \pm \delta \right) \right| \\
&\geq \varepsilon - \delta
\end{aligned}
\tag{21}
$$

7 Comparisons

In this section, we mainly compare the function and performance analysis of previous research schemes.

Table 2. Comparison of security and functionality

Schemes	CA	MA	OD	AU	DN	CR	PP	GID	MC	Hardness	Model
[23]	×	√	×	×	×	√	√	Privacy	CPA	DBDH	ROM
[19]	√	×	√	×	√	√	√	privacy	CPA	DBDH	ROM
[26]	×	√	×	×	×	×	√	Public	CPA	q-PBDHE q-SDH	ROM
[27]	√	×	×	×	√	×	×	Public	CPA	q-BDHE	ROM
[28]	×	√	×	×	×	√	√	Privacy	CPA	DBDH	ROM
[13]	√	×	×	×	√	×	√	Privacy	CCA	DBDH	Standard
[29]	√	√	×	×	×	√	√	Public	CPA	q-PBDHE	ROM
[30]	√	×	√	×	×	√	√	Private	CPA	q-BDHI	ROM
Our scheme	√	√	√	√	√	√	√	Privacy	CCA	DBDH	Standard

Abbreviated symbol description: **MA** = Multi-Authority, **OD** = Outsourced Decryption, **AU** = Auditability, **DN** = Dynamicity, **CR** = Collusion Resistance, **PP** = Privacy Protection, **GID** = Global Identity, **MC** = Message Confidentiality.

7.1 Feature and Security Comparisons

A detailed comparison of some relevant features between the proposed scheme and part of the existing schemes is given in Table 2. Obviously, some challenging features like traceable, policy updating and data access limited have been addressed in schemes [19,29]. But we have also addressed the perfect combination of dynamicity and multi-authorities, making the system practical while maintaining flexibility. In addition, we apply the auditing feature to solve the verification of outsourcing decryption to ensure the correctness for decrypted ciphertext by ODCSP.

7.2 Computational Analysis

In order to unify the measurement scale, this study divides the above schemes listed in the comparison into two categories according to the number of attribute authority: multi-authority schemes and non-multi-authority(single CA), and makes a horizontal comparison.

We give a description of the relevant symbols involved in the comparison process in Table 3. Among them, Table 4 represents the comparison of schemes without multi-authority, and Table 5 represents another.

Table 3. Notations used in performance evaluation.

Notation	Meaning
t_p	the time of one pairing operation
t_e	the time of one exponentiation operation
n_u	the number of users attributes
n_a	the number of attribute authorities
n_τ	the number of attributes in the access tree
n_c	the number of attributes associated to a ciphertext
n_{nl}	the number of non-leaf nodes in the access tree
$|U|$	the number of universal attributes
$|G_*|$	the number of the elements in G_*
l	the number of rows of the matrix in LSSS scheme

As the results shown in Table 4, the key generation cost of our scheme is lower than other series schemes, which is also better than Fan et al. [13], because our scheme requires fewer times of exponentiation operations. In Table 5, the DU in our scheme does not require any exponentiation or pairing operations in the decryption operation, which greatly reduces the decryption cost of client, and the user only needs to complete a symmetric decryption once. We also find that the client-side decryption overhead is much better than schemes with outsourced decryption, such as [19] and [30]. In this study, the decryption cost of DU is outsourced to the ODCSP, and the computational cost of this part is $(3n_\tau + 4)t_p + n_{nl}t_e$. Therefore, the total decryption cost can be calculated by combining the two results. Compared with other outsourced schemes [19, 30], our OMADA-CPABE scheme requires less computation time. In Table 4, it is not difficult for us to find that the computation overhead in all these schemes increases linearly with the increase of the number of members and attributes.

Table 4. Comparisons of computation overhead(a)

Schemes	Key Generation	Encryption	Decryption(user)	Outsourced Decryption
[23]	$(n_a^2+1)t_e$	$(n_\tau+2)t_e$	$(n_a+3)t_p+t_e$	-
[26]	$10n_a t_e$	$(n_a+3)t_e+n_c t_p$	$(4n_u+2l)t_p$	-
[28]	$5n_c t_e$	$2n_c t_e+n_c t_p$	$(n_c+n_a+1)t_p$	-
[29]	$2n_u t_e$	$(n_c+1)t_p+3n_c t_e$	$5n_c(t_p+t_e)$	-
Our scheme	1	$(n_c+1)t_e+t_p$	1	$(3n_\tau+4)t_p+n_{nl}t_e$

Table 5. Comparisons of computation overhead(b)

Schemes	Key Generation	Encryption	Decryption(user)	Outsourced Decryption
[19]	$(n_u+3)t_e$	$(n_\tau+2)t_e$	t_e	$(n_u+2)t_p+n_{nl}t_e$
[27]	$(3+n_u)t_e+2t_H$	$(n_c+1)t_e+t_p$	$(2n_u+1)t_p$	-
[13]	1	$(2n_c+1)t_e+t_p$	$(n_u+1)t_p+n_{nl}t_e$	-
[30]	$(n_u+5)t_e$	$(5n_\tau+2)t_e$	t_e	$(3n_\tau+3)t_p+lt_e$
Our scheme	1	$(n_c+1)t_e+t_p$	1	$(3n_\tau+4)t_p+n_{nl}t_e$

7.3 Storage Overhead

In this part, we only consider the storage overhead of public parameters, private keys, and ciphertext. The Table 6 combines several kinds of attribute-based encryption schemes in the past and gives a comparison of the storage required. For the cost storage of public parameters, the proposed scheme is consistent with the storage cost of [13] and [23]. Also, it can be clearly seen from Table 6 that the private key storage size of our scheme is slightly lower than that of other schemes, which can benefit the storage space to some extent. However, the ciphertext size in our work still has room for further optimization. How to balance the storage cost and security efficiency is also a problem that needs to be weighed and considered to ensure the high efficiency and security of the whole system.

Table 6. Comparisons of Storage

Schemes	Size of Public Parameters	Size of Private Key	Size of Ciphertext
[23]	$|G_1|+|G_2|+|G_T|$	$(n_u+1)|G|$	$(n_c+2)|G|$
[19]	$|G|+|G_t|$	$(n_u+3)|G|$	$(n_c+1)|G|+|G_t|$
[26]	$2|G|+|G_T|$	$6n_u|G|+|G_T|$	$(2l+3)|G|+|G_T|$
[27]	$2|G|$	$(n_u+2)|G|$	$(l^2+2)|G|$
[28]	$2|G_1|+|G_2|$	$3n_u|G_1|$	$(2n_c+1)|G_1|+|G_2|$
[13]	$|G_0|+|G_1|+|G_T|$	$3n_u|G_0|+|G_1|$	$2|G_0|+(3n_c+1)|G_T|$
[29]	$3|G|+|G_T|$	$(4n_u+1)|G|$	$(5l+1)|G|+|G_T|$
[30]	$2|G_T|$	$(2n_u+4)|G_T|$	$(3l+1)|G_T|$
Our scheme	$|G_1|+|G_2|+|G_T|$	$3|G_1|+n_u|G_2|$	$n_c|G_2|+|G_T|$

8   Conclusion

The scheme in the study realizes an instance of the combination of dynamicity and multi-authority, then adds dynamic management and outsourcing decryption method with auditing under multi-authority, which optimizes the performance bottleneck of encryption and decryption, making attribute-based encryption more practical and flexible. In this study, the high linear pairing cost generated in the decryption process is outsourced to the cloud server, and the content decrypted by the server is audited twice to ensure the integrity and correctness of the information and the security of the system. All of the above advantages make ABE more efficient and flexible in practical application. However, to be honest, our work doesn't consider the size of the ciphertext, only focus on security and encryption efficiency of the whole system. Therefore, in the subsequent research, the ciphertext size is compressed to optimize the overall performance and further enhance the robustness of the system while ensuring user privacy protection and security.

Acknowledgement. This work has been partly supported by the Fundamentral Research Funds for the Central Universities (No. 30106220482).

References

1. Sahai, A., Waters, B.: Fuzzy identity-based encryption. In: Cramer, R. (ed.) EUROCRYPT 2005. LNCS, vol. 3494, pp. 457–473. Springer, Heidelberg (2005). https://doi.org/10.1007/11426639_27
2. Bethencourt, J., Sahai, A., Waters, B.: Ciphertext-policy attribute-based encryption. In: IEEE Symposium on Security & Privacy (2007)
3. Qin, B., Deng, R.H., Liu, S., Ma, S.: Attribute-based encryption with efficient verifiable outsourced decryption. IEEE Trans. Inf. Forensics Secur. **10**, 1384–1393 (2015)
4. Hui, M., Rui, Z., Wan, Z., Yao, L., Lin, S.: Verifiable and exculpable outsourced attribute-based encryption for access control in cloud computing. IEEE Trans. Dependable Secure Comput. **14**(6), 679–692 (2017)
5. Chase, M.: Multi-authority attribute based encryption. In: Vadhan, S.P. (ed.) TCC 2007. LNCS, vol. 4392, pp. 515–534. Springer, Heidelberg (2007). https://doi.org/10.1007/978-3-540-70936-7_28
6. Huang, L., Cao, Z., Liang, X., Shao, J.: Secure threshold multi authority attribute based encryption without a central authority. In: International Conference on Cryptology in India: Progress in Cryptology, pp. 2618–2632 (2008)
7. Lewko, A., Waters, B.: Decentralizing attribute-based encryption. In: Paterson, K.G. (ed.) EUROCRYPT 2011. LNCS, vol. 6632, pp. 568–588. Springer, Heidelberg (2011). https://doi.org/10.1007/978-3-642-20465-4_31
8. Green, M., Hohenberger, S., Waters, B.: Outsourcing the decryption of ABE ciphertexts. In: Proceedings of the 20th USENIX Conference on Security (2011)
9. Ren, Y.J., Jian, S., Jin, W., Jin, H., Lee, S.Y.: Mutual verifiable provable data auditing in public cloud storage. éè · è **16**(2), 317–323 (2015)
10. Lai, J., Deng, R.H., Guan, C., Weng, J.: Attribute-based encryption with verifiable outsourced decryption. IEEE Trans. Inf. Forensics and Secur. **8**, 1343–1354 (2013)
11. Lin, S., Zhang, R., Ma, H., Wang, M.: Revisiting attribute-based encryption with verifiable outsourced decryption. IEEE Trans. Inf. Forensics Secur. **10**(10), 2119–2130 (2015)

12. Sethi, K., Pradhan, A., Bera, P.: Practical traceable multi-authority CP-ABE with outsourcing decryption and access policy updation. J. Inf. Secur. Appl. **51** (2020)
13. Fan, C.I., Huang, S.M., Ruan, H.M.: Arbitrary-state attribute-based encryption with dynamic membership. IEEE Trans. Comput. **63**(8), 1951–1961 (2014)
14. Lian, H., Wang, Q., Wang, G.: Large universe ciphertext-policy attribute-based encryption with attribute level user revocation in cloud storage. Int. Arab J. Inf. Technol. **17**(1), 107–117 (2019)
15. Liu, L., Wang, S., Yan, Q.: A multi-authority key-policy ABE scheme from lattices in mobile ad hoc networks. Ad-hoc Sens. Wirel. Netw. **37**(1–4), 117–143 (2017)
16. Hohenberger, S., Waters, B.: Online/offline attribute-based encryption. In: Krawczyk, H. (ed.) PKC 2014. LNCS, vol. 8383, pp. 293–310. Springer, Heidelberg (2014). https://doi.org/10.1007/978-3-642-54631-0_17
17. Yu, S., Wang, C., Ren, K., Lou, W.: Attribute based data sharing with attribute revocation. In: International Symposium on ACM Symposium on Information, p. 261 (2010)
18. Xu, X., Zhou, J., Wang, X., Zhang, Y.: Multi-authority proxy re-encryption based on CPABE for cloud storage systems. J. Syst. Eng. Electron. **27**, 211–223 (2016)
19. Premkamal, P.K., Pasupuleti, S.K., Alphonse, P.: Dynamic traceable CP-ABE with revocation for outsourced big data in cloud storage. Int. J. Commun. Syst. (6), e4351 (2020)
20. Boneh, D., Franklin, M.: Identity-based encryption from the Weil pairing. In: Kilian, J. (ed.) CRYPTO 2001. LNCS, vol. 2139, pp. 213–229. Springer, Heidelberg (2001). https://doi.org/10.1007/3-540-44647-8_13
21. Boneh, D., Shoup, V.: A graduate course in applied cryptography. Draft 0.5 (2020)
22. Kan, Y., Jia, X.: Attributed-based access control for multi-authority systems in cloud storage. In: IEEE International Conference on Distributed Computing Systems (2012)
23. Chase, M., Chow, S.S.M.: Improving privacy and security in multi-authority attribute-based encryption. In: Proceedings of the 2009 ACM Conference on Computer and Communications Security, CCS 2009, Chicago, Illinois, USA, 9–13 November 2009 (2009)
24. Sarma, R., Kumar, C., Barbhuiya, F.A.: MACFI: a multi-authority access control scheme with efficient ciphertext and secret key size for fog-enhanced IoT (2021)
25. Goyal, V., Pandey, O., Sahai, A., Waters, B.: Attribute-based encryption for fine-grained access control of encrypted data. ACM (2006)
26. Han, J., Susilo, W., Mu, Y., Zhou, J., Au, M.: Improving privacy and security in decentralized ciphertext-policy attribute-based encryption (2015)
27. Deng, Y.Q.: Dynamic attribute-based encryption scheme. Comput. Eng. Sci. (2014)
28. Rahulamathavan, Y., Veluru, S., Han, J., Fei, L., Rajarajan, M., Lu, R.: User collusion avoidance scheme for privacy-preserving decentralized key-policy attribute-based encryption. IEEE Trans. Comput. **65**(9), 2939–2946 (2016)
29. Ling, J., Chen, J., Chen, J., Gan, W.: Multiauthority attribute-based encryption with traceable and dynamic policy updating. Secur. Commun. Netw. **2021**(6), 1–13 (2021)
30. Ning, J., Cao, Z., Dong, X., Liang, K., Ma, H., Wei, L.: Auditable σ-time outsourced attribute-based encryption for access control in cloud computing. IEEE Trans. Inf. Forensics Secur. **13**(1), 94–105 (2017)

A Privacy-Preserving and Auditable Scheme for Interfacing Public Blockchain with Consortium Blockchain

Zejun Lu[1] and Jiageng Chen[1,2(✉)]

[1] Wollongong Joint Institute, Central China Normal University, Wuhan, China
jiageng.chen@ccnu.edu.cn
[2] School of Computer Science, Central China Normal University, Wuhan, China

Abstract. With the development of blockchain technology, consortium blockchain is being applied in various scenarios. However, data and related assets are restricted to the closed consortium blockchain environment, and the end-users who do not belong to the consortium are difficult to gain access without extra authentication. Thus, architectures concerning cross-chain interaction appear, while most solutions have only limited functionalities. Moreover, few solutions have considered privacy from multiple perspectives, including the privacy of end-users, consortium members, or the data itself. This paper proposes a privacy-preserving and auditable architecture scheme for interfacing consortium blockchain members with end-users of the public blockchain. Our scheme enables end-users to communicate with the inner consortium in a verifiable, privacy-preserving, and auditable manner. More specifically, we improve the existing cross-chain network architectures to further protect the consortium members' privacy. Also, the communication and the transactions of the cross-chain interaction are protected and auditable. Concrete protocols are proposed, and security models and corresponding analyses are investigated.

Keywords: Blockchain · Cross-chain · Consortium · Privacy · Auditability

1 Introduction

Distributed ledger with globally agreed and immutable transaction history is made available through the invention of blockchain technology [28]. Blockchain-based smart contracts further expanded the flexibility of the blockchain with Ethereum [34] being one of the well-known examples.

New architectures of blockchains were designed to adapt to different scenarios, while decentralized applications based on blockchains have become a growing family. To facilitate the development of decentralized applications, many high-level programming languages used to implement smart contracts were developed,

© ICST Institute for Computer Sciences, Social Informatics and Telecommunications Engineering 2023
Published by Springer Nature Switzerland AG 2023. All Rights Reserved
W. Meng and W. Li (Eds.): BlockTEA 2022, LNICST 498, pp. 89–105, 2023.
https://doi.org/10.1007/978-3-031-31420-9_6

such as Solidity [31]. As a result, it has become much easier to implement complex functions on the blockchain. With the prevalence of the blockchain in various fields like medical [4], supply chain [36], cloud [40], financial [14], and many others, the fact that data flowing in the blockchain is transparent gives rise to the possibility of leaking sensitive data, which makes the systems vulnerable to many attacks [12]. Researchers have proposed many schemes to defend against those attacks. However, it is not enough because blockchain application scenarios are becoming more complex, and architectures with only public or consortium blockchains cannot meet sophisticated requirements in different environments. Therefore, cross-chain architectures are developed.

Cross-Chain Scenarios. For example, Virtuozzo [27] has a cloud federation platform consisting of many cloud service providers (CSPs), and the platform aims to provide cloud services to customers. The customers post their requests in a public network, and the request data flows from the public user network to the consortium network, which consists of the CSPs. Upon incoming a request from outside, CSPs in the closed network decide how to respond collaboratively, and then the response flows from the closed network to the public user network. Another example is the supply chain, products are produced by a collaboration of companies along the manufacturing chain that form a consortium network, and customers form a public network. Customers post their requests to trace the manufacturing process of a product in the public network, and then the requests are transferred to the closed network. The counterpart companies respond to the request, and the consortium authenticates the response before it is transferred to the public network and read by the corresponding user. Both public and consortium networks can be implemented by blockchain architectures, with a cross-chain data transfer mechanism to interface two networks. In this way, cross-chain communication can obtain good properties such as traceability and immutability, and the whole system can be decentralized. A regular cross-chain workflow generalized from application scenarios like cloud federation, supply chain, etc., consists of transactions, each of which can be summarized as follows:

1. An end-user U initiates a transaction by posting a request in the public blockchain.
2. The request is transferred from the public to the consortium blockchain.
3. The request is handled, and the consortium authenticates the response.
4. The response is transferred from the consortium to the public blockchain.
5. U reads the response with its authentication from the public blockchain.

Except for the transactions, the consortium may release some official announcements, the process of which is similar to steps 3 to 5.

Existing solutions have developed protocols to interface public and consortium blockchains, but their schemes either barely considered privacy or lack generality.

1.1 Related Work

Privacy-Preserving Schemes. In the financial field, assorted cryptographical tools are introduced and integrated into blockchain architectures to fulfill its strong requirement for privacy. Several cryptocurrencies featuring strong privacy attributes are developed as discussed follows. Earlier versions of Monero called CryptoNote [33] achieve its privacy by using Schnorr-style multilayered linkable spontaneous anonymous group signatures to authenticate the inputs of transactions, using Pedersen commitments to conceal the amounts, and using Bulletproofs [9] to prove the range is legitimate. Later versions eliminated trusted third parties (Group Manager) at the expense of anonymity revocation by using ring signatures. Ideas from mainly [32] and [3,24,25] construct the Monero running today. At the same time, [23,35,37] pay their attention on the privacy in consortium blockchain architectures. The privilege of the consortium auditor is used to develop auditing possibility, a feature essential in the real world to combat illegal practices such as money laundering. [18,22,29,38] investigates the future of the privacy-preserving cryptocurrencies. Cryptographical tools like anonymous credentials, homomorphic encryption, zero-knowledge range proof, etc., are used to realize their visions of privacy. The idea of threshold signature [6] plays an important role in the investigation history of privacy-preserving cryptocurrencies to cover the identity of users, and it will be introduced in our work as well.

Although privacy has been comprehensively studied, few schemes are extended to cross-chain architectures for public and consortium blockchains. A new scheme is needed because public blockchain architectures are not suitable for many scenarios, while consortium architectures barely provide a verifiable service to end-users outside the consortium.

Cross-Chain Schemes. Most papers conduct their research in the context of single blockchain architecture. While [2,21] favor developing the shards of blockchains, they have developed how to deal with transactions between different shards of blockchain. Recently, [17] has made progress in reducing the number of cross-shard transactions. [1] shows their interest in crossing two consortium blockchains by designing a transfer protocol with verifiability. [39] is concerned about how to communicate across distributed ledgers, while [5,26] focuses on the transfer of tokens and assets between public blockchains. Cross-chain schemes like [10] tried to share data safely by adding a higher layer to the blockchain, while [16] has further developed the cross-chain architecture by providing an interface between public and consortium blockchains, through which the data can be transferred safely, users can interact with another blockchain in a soundness manner.

However, the protocols in those schemes either lack interoperability and mobility of data between the consortium and public blockchains or barely consider the privacy of consortium members and end-users.

1.2   Our Contribution: Cross-Chain with Privacy and Auditability

This article proposes a generic privacy-preserving and auditable cross-chain scheme with the following properties.

- **Generality**: Our scheme can be implemented by an almost arbitrary combination of consortium blockchain and public blockchain, as long as they have robust consensus algorithms like *Proof of Work (PoW)* and supports smart contracts.
- **Privacy-Preserving**: The request and response in the transaction are concealed from other end-users, and the identity of consortium members is concealed from their peers when running protocols in our scheme.
- **Auditability**: The consortium auditor can audit suspicious transactions by revealing the response process and authentication process in the consortium.
- **Cross-chain Safeness**: Consortium members agree on the same order and set of incoming requests, while these requests can be traced in the public blockchain. The responses posted in the public blockchain can also be traced in the consortium blockchain.

2   Preliminaries

2.1   Mathematical Backgrounds

Our scheme demands three groups G_U, G_1 and G_2 to implement the cryptographical tools. G_U is a prime-order group used for a public key encryption algorithm. (G_{T1}, G_{T2}) are a (τ, t, ε)-bilinear group pair as defined in Definition 2.1 and we summarised it below:

Computational co-Diffie-Hellman(co-CDH) on (G_1, G_2). Given $g_2, g_2^x \in G_2$ and $h \in G_1$ as input, compute $h^x \in G_1$.

Decision co-Diffie-Hellman(co-DDH) on (G_1, G_2). Given $g_2, g_2^x \in G_2$ and $h, h^y \in G_1$ as input, output **yes** if $x = y$ and **no**, otherwise. (g_2, g_2^x, h, h^a) is called a co-Diffie-Hellman tuple when the answer is **yes**.

(τ, t, ε)-co-GDH group pair. Two groups (G_1, G_2) are a (τ, t, ε)-co-GDH group pair if the following properties are satisfied.

- The group operation on both G_1 and G_2 and the isomorphism map ψ from G_2 to G_1 can be computed in time at most τ.
- The co-DDH problem on (G_1, G_2) can be solved in time at most τ.
- No algorithm (t, ε) breaks co-CDH on (G_1, G_2).

Given a group pairs (G_1, G_2) as defined above and another group G_T s.t. $|G_1| = |G_2| = |G_T|$. A bilinear map is a map $e : G_1 \times G_2 \to G_T$ with the following properties:

- Bilinear: for all $u \in G_1, v \in G_2$, and $a, b \in \mathbb{Z}$, $e(u^a, u^b) = e(u, v)^{ab}$.
- Non-degenerate: $e(g_2, g_2) \neq 1$.

$((\tau, t, \varepsilon))$-**bilinear group pair.** Two order-p groups (G_1, G_2) are a $((\tau, t, \varepsilon))$-bilinear group pair if satisfy the following properties:

- The group operation on both G_1 and G_2 and the isomorphism map ψ from G_2 to G_1 can be computed in time at most τ.
- A group G_T of order p and a bilinear map $e : G_1 \times G_2 \to G_T$ exist, and e is computable in time at most τ.
- No algorithm (t, ε) breaks co-CDH on (G_1, G_2).

[19] indicates that with e, the problem of co-DDH can be efficiently solved. This solution constructs the verification part of the BLS signature [7]. The threshold signature algorithm we used in our scheme is built by applying the method of [6] on the BLS signature.

2.2 Threshold Signature

Consider a scenario, a message M is regarded as authenticated by the group only when more than t members out of n members have signed for M. We use BLS threshold signature [7] to achieve this effect. To introduce the BLS threshold signature $(TKeyGen, TSign, Verify)$, the BLS signature $(KeyGen, Sign, Verify)$ should be introduced first.

Let G_1 and G_2 be bilinear group pair where $|G_1| = |G_2| = p$ and view the hash function $H : \{0, 1\}^* \to G_1$ as a random oracle.

- $(SK, PK) \leftarrow KeyGen(\lambda)$: As a PPT algorithm. On input a security parameter, generates a pair of secret and public keys.
- $\sigma \leftarrow Sign(M, SK)$: On input a secret key SK and a message M, generate the signature of M.
- $valid/invalid \leftarrow Verify(PK, M, \sigma)$: On input a public key PK, a message M, and a signature σ, return valid if the signature corresponds with the message given the public key, otherwise invalid.

Next, the t-out-of-n BLS threshold signature is introduced. The parameter n means how many users are there in the group having the right to sign, while t indicates at least how many shares of signatures are required to collect to reconstruct.

- $\{(SK_i, PK_i)\}^n \leftarrow TKeyGen(SK, PK, t, n)$: On input a secret key SK, a public key PK, two constant t and q where $t \leq q$, generates n shares of the secret key SK_i and public key PK_i.
- $\sigma_i \leftarrow TSign(M, SK_i)$: On input a share of secret key SK_i and a message M, generates a share of signature of M.

For clarity, two more functions are added for the BLS threshold signature.

- $valid/invalid \leftarrow TV(PK_i, SK_i, \sigma_i)$: On input of a share of PK_i, a share of secret key SK_i, a share of signature σ_i, return valid if the signature corresponds with the message given the public key, otherwise invalid.

- $\sigma \leftarrow TReconstruct(\{\sigma_i\}^t)$: On input t shares of signatures $\{\sigma_i\}^t$, a signature σ corresponds to the public key PK can be reconstructed.

However, we manage to limit the privilege of the consortium auditor. As a result of that, the process of threshold key generation $TKeyGen()$ is replaced by the method of [15]. The same outcome is acquired by running a protocol without trusted third parties. The protocol does not rely on the difficulty of DDH and thus can be used in our scheme [7].

3 System Model

In this section, the architecture of our system is initially introduced by describing different roles and their respective behaviors, and then follows the various attacks that our system may suffer, the design challenges we encountered, and the corresponding countermeasures against these obstacles.

3.1 System Architecture

The main objective of our system is to provide a mechanism through which any closed consortium can interface with the open network of end-users by the cross-chain architecture. In our vision, all the entities in our system need not worry about whom they should communicate with, and all the interactions are between the blockchain and themselves, through which an immutable history and possibility of auditing are provided, while a proper running of the system functions is ensured by implementing smart contracts. In particular, everyone can ask for a service or pieces of information from a consortium without joining it by posting their request in the public blockchain. Depending on the content of the request, the consortium members collaboratively generate and authenticate a response by posting their message in the consortium blockchain, respectively. According to [39], cross-chain communication requires trusted third party. Similar to the idea *Consensus on Consensus* of [16], it is reasonable that some consortium members are elected as trusted agents to bypass the requirement of trusted third parties. At last, to realize the auditability and preserve privacy, an auditor is needed in the consortium. However, the privileges of the auditor are limited. Malicious behaviors, such as forging a transaction that can be verified in the consortium blockchain, are hard to conduct for the auditor.

Accordingly, there are four types of entities in our scheme:

1. **End-users:** End-users are transaction initiators, requests from whom are mined by nodes running the consensus algorithm of the public blockchain. A transaction is initiated when a request is posted in the public blockchain. A transaction is completed when the corresponding response in the public blockchain is read and verified by the initiator.
2. **Consortium Members:** Consortium members are consortium blockchain nodes with their share of threshold signature secret key, running the consensus algorithm of the consortium blockchain. They generate responses or vote for the requests and respond by signing with their secret keys.

3. **Trusted Agents:** Trusted agents are public blockchain nodes as well as consortium blockchain nodes, running the consensus algorithms of both blockchains. They are responsible for transferring information between two blockchains. A trusted agent can be a consortium member at the same time.

4. **Auditor:** The auditor is a consortium blockchain node without a share of threshold signature secret key, running the consensus algorithm of the consortium blockchain. It is responsible for reconstructing the threshold signature and posting the reconstructed signature in the consortium blockchain. The reconstruction process can be revealed by it for auditing purposes when necessary.

3.2 Threats

Due to the data structure of the blockchain itself, systems based on blockchain may be vulnerable to several types of attacks. For a cross-chain architecture, an interface that safely transfers data between different blockchains should be developed. Meanwhile, the privacy of different entities from various perspectives should also be considered. The situations are discussed as follows, and our definitions of security and privacy are shown in Sect. 4.3.

Byzantine Behavior. It is assumed that at most t members out of all the n consortium members may exhibit some malicious actions [11]. Usually, the parameter t/n is less than 1/3. These t members may collaboratively manage to control the decision of the consortium. Besides, the parameters t and n are equal to the parameters of the same name in the threshold signature scheme in our scheme.

Sybil Attacks. *Sybil attacks* [13] denote attacks from those adversaries who can manipulate, imitate, or generate many identities to attack the system. In our system, before any request is processed by the consortium, it must have been mined by miners running the consensus algorithm of the public blockchain. For the fact that public blockchain can be joined without permission, consensus algorithms designed for public blockchains such as *PoW* and *Proof of Stake (PoS)* [20] have the feature of resisting *sybil attacks* natively. Therefore, whether our scheme can resist *sybil attacks* or not depends on the consensus algorithm of the chosen public blockchain.

Traceability. Traceability is one of the most important reasons we use blockchains. However, this characteristic should be further developed in cross-chain architectures. Our scheme focuses on the following requirements:

1. Consortium and public blockchain have their immutable transaction history separately, as they originally were.
2. Once a message is transferred from the public blockchain to the consortium blockchain; consortium members can find the corresponding history in the public blockchain.

3. Once a message is transferred from the consortium blockchain to the public blockchain; users can find the corresponding history in the consortium blockchain with the help of the auditor.

Interface Safety. Given the reality that a network in the real world cannot be completely synchronous, an upper bound is usually defined. A message with a transmission time more than that upper bound is considered missing and abandoned. However, the delay of unabandoned messages exists objectively and inevitably, which leads to the consequence that different users receive different sets of messages in different orders. Therefore, a safe cross-chain architecture requires consortium members to agree on which requests are transferred to the consortium and their specific order, without which confusion may be caused, and wrong responses may be returned to the customers. In particular, (1) Some consortium members may lose some mined blocks from the public blockchain. (2) Malicious members may reply to requests which have not been mined. (3) Conflicting requests from temporary forks [30] of the public blockchain. In our system, the elected consortium members compose the cross-chain interface, and the *First Signature*, which will be introduced in Sect. 4.1, ensures the consortium members have reached a consensus on the incoming requests.

We use the definition **Consortium Interface Safety** from [16] to define our safety as shown in Sect. 4.3.

Privacy. The privacy of the following entities is considered.

1. **End-users:** The request information may include sensitive information like invoices, credentials, etc. Given that the data on the public blockchain is available to everyone, information may be collected and used to identify the users. Moreover, in some scenarios, the request information contains no authentication information(like cloud federation providing cloud service to everyone), and the end customer is unwilling to let consortium members know which requests they have sent before. These problems can be addressed by public key encryption.
2. **Consortium Members:** Under the assumption that the manager is not corrupted, the identities of the consortium members should be concealed during the process of agreeing on an exact order of requests. This is achieved by threshold signature and public key encryption.

In our system, adversaries can read the information in the public and consortium blockchain, to corrupt consortium members or end-users. He may try to reveal a vote, forge a request or response with proper authentication, and reveal the advocators in a vote. Detailed security attributes we achieved are discussed in Sect. 4.3. Besides, our scheme does not consider network-level privacy issues, such as analyzing the data packets, network flows, or IP addresses.

4 Our Proposed Scheme

In this section, the workflow of a transaction is described first, which is the most used protocol in our scheme. Next, a comprehensive description of the whole scheme is given, and a security discussion follows.

4.1 Overview

A general transaction workflow includes the following three phases:

Initiate Transaction. This part describes the transaction initiation in the public blockchain.

1. An end-user seeks a service or some information. She sends her request with a user public key to the public blockchain miners.
2. Miners of the public blockchain collect the requests and public keys and pack them into a block, and then the block is committed in the public blockchain.
   - During this process, the *Blocknumber* of the block in the public blockchain and the *offset* of requests in this block are determined. *Blocknumber* and *offset* compose the unique order information of each request and determine the order in which requests are scheduled in the consortium.
3. Trusted agents (as a public blockchain node) are triggered upon a new block being committed. They verify it by methods like *Simplified Payment Verification (SPV)* and wrap the requests, user public keys, and their order information as consortium requests.

First Signature. This part describes the generation of the *First Signature*, which is not only for deciding the order of the consortium requests but also can vote on whether the consortium will schedule the request or not when necessary. After the *First Signature* is generated, requests can be scheduled and responded to.

1. Trusted agents (as a consortium blockchain node) post the consortium requests in the consortium blockchain by running the consensus algorithm.
2. The consortium members continuously read information from the consortium blockchain and sign the consortium requests. The consortium request, signature, and threshold public key are wrapped and encrypted by the auditor public key and posted in the consortium blockchain.
   - Here, the signature is a share of a threshold signature, which cannot prove that the consortium has admitted the consortium request. Only requests with a reconstructed signature, which can be verified by the consortium's unique threshold public key, are regarded as having achieved a consensus of the consortium and scheduled.

3. The auditor maintains a hash map to count the threshold signatures for each consortium request. Once the number of signatures for a request meets the threshold, the auditor reconstructs the signature and posts the reconstructed signature with the consortium request in the consortium blockchain. If the manager is given the right to assign tasks, she may designate a consortium member to respond.

It depends on the specific environment for whose response will be transferred to the public blockchain. Members can vote on the response content if the response is not encrypted. If the response is encrypted by the user's public key, members can vote on the identity of the responder. Maybe he is a certified expert in the field related to this request, the counterpart manufacturer, or the only one who knows the answer to the request, etc. Essentially, only the first response that completes the *Second signature* will be mined and committed in the consortium blockchain.

Second Signature. Up to here, there may be several [Consortium Request, First Signature] tuples in the consortium blockchain. To convince the end-users that the consortium has acknowledged the response, a signature representing the consortium must be attached to the response. This signature can be easily generated by off-chain multi-signature [6]. However, this approach is detrimental to the privacy and traceability of the system. We propose the *Second Signature* here, the process of which is very similar to steps 2,3 in *First Signature*.

1. Consortium members respond to the requests by posting their responses in the consortium blockchain, and the responses can be encrypted by the user public key when necessary.
2. Consortium members sign the response with their share of the threshold secret keys and encrypt their signature with the response by auditor public key, then post it in the consortium blockchain.
3. The auditor reconstructs the signature and posts the response with the signature in the consortium blockchain.
4. Trusted agents transfer the response with the corresponding signature to the public blockchain.

The proposed scheme is demonstrated in Fig. 1 and only the main parameters are shown. Notice that the *Second Signature* is omitted because its process is similar to the *First Signature*. A detailed description of the process can be found in Sect. 4.2.

Auditability. In the process described above, the auditor can reveal which consortium members have voted for which requests or responses. With the cooperation of the end-users, the auditor can reveal the encrypted response. In addition, the auditor can further corroborate his words by decrypting the corresponding record in the consortium blockchain.

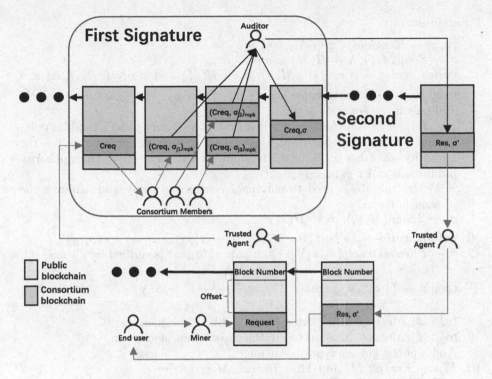

Fig. 1. The proposed scheme

4.2 Detailed Description

This section shows our detailed scheme, followed by the security and privacy theorem, with their proof sketch discussed.

Setup:

- Let G_1 and G_2 be a bilinear group pair conforms to Definition 2.1 with generators $g_1 \in G_1$ and $g_2 \in G_2$. $e : G_1 \times G_2 \to G_T$ be a bilinear map. The method to generate this type of group pair with proper parameters is introduced in [7,19].
- The auditor generates her keys for public key encryption (mpk, msk) and creates a hashmap $SignMap$ with $(Key, Values) = (Request, Signatures)$.
- End-users generate their keys for public key encryption (upk_i, usk_i).
- Consortium members run the none-trusted-party version $TKeyGen()$ with the other, achieve their share of secret key tsk_j and public key $tpk_j \leftarrow g_2^{tsk_j}$, publish their union public key tpk.
- Hash function $H : \{0,1\}^* \to G_1$ as a random oracle.

Functions:

1. $(v, x) \leftarrow KeyGen() : x \xleftarrow{R} \mathbb{Z}_p, v \leftarrow g_2^x$.
2. $\sigma \leftarrow Sign(M, x)$: $h \leftarrow H(M)$ and $\sigma \leftarrow h^x$.
3. $valid/invalid \leftarrow Verify(v, M, \sigma)$: $h \leftarrow H(M)$ and verify (g_2, v, h, σ) is a valid co-Diffie-Hellman tuple i.e. $e(h, v) \stackrel{?}{=} e(\sigma, g_2)$. The signature is valid if and only if the equation holds.
4. $\{(v_i, x_i)\}^n \leftarrow TKeyGen(x, v, t, n)$: A central authority picks a random polynomial $\omega \in \mathbb{Z}_p[X]$ of degree at most t-1 s.t. $\omega(0) = x$. For each user i, the authority gives her $x_i = \omega(i)$, its share of the secret key. The authority publishes v and n values $u_i = g_2^{x_i}$
   - Method of [15] is used to eliminate central authority and achieves the same outcome.
5. $\sigma_i \leftarrow TSign(M, x_i)$: $\sigma_i \leftarrow H(M)^{x_i}$.
6. $valid/invalid \leftarrow TVerify(v_i, M, \sigma_i)$: $h \leftarrow H(M)$, $e(h, v_i) \stackrel{?}{=} e(\sigma_i, g_2)$
7. $\sigma \leftarrow TReconstruct(\{\sigma_i, u_i\}^t)$: Each pair of (σ_i, u_i) is verified by $TVerify()$,

   then $\sigma \leftarrow \prod_{i=1}^{t} \sigma_i^{\lambda_i}$, $\quad where \quad \lambda_i = \dfrac{\prod_{j=1, j \neq i}^{t} -j}{\prod_{j=1, j \neq i}^{t} i-j} \quad (mod\ p)$.

8. $toP(M)$: Message M is posted in the public blockchain.
9. $toC(M)$: Message M is posted in the consortium blockchain.
   And a public key encryption scheme:
10. $M_{pk} \leftarrow Enc(pk, M)$ and $M \leftarrow Dec(sk, M_{pk})$
11. $SPV(B)$: Simplified Payment Verification to B.

Publish Consortium Announcements. Sometimes the consortium makes some announcement, and the announcement represents the group's will. Thus it should attach a signature verifiable by tpk and has a record in the consortium blockchain.

1. A member j draft an announcement ANC_j.
   - $\sigma_j \leftarrow Tsign(ANC_j, tsk_j)$
   - $[ANC_j, \sigma_j]_{mpk} \leftarrow Enc(mpk, [ANC_j, \sigma_j])$
   - $toC([ANC_j, \sigma_j]_{mpk})$
   - $toC(ANC_j)$
2. The other members such as j_2 read and advocate ANC_j.
   - $\sigma_{j2} \leftarrow Tsign(ANC_j, tsk_{j2})$
   - $[ANC_j, \sigma_{j2}]_{mpk} \leftarrow Enc(mpk, [ANC_j, \sigma_{j2}])$
   - $toC([ANC_j, \sigma_{j2}]_{mpk})$
3. As soon as the auditor has collected $[ANC_j, \sigma_{j2}]_{mpk}$.
   (Status: The auditor lacks 1 signature to generate the *First Signature* of ANC_j and has not collected $[ANC_j, \sigma_{j2}]_{mpk}$.)
   - $[ANC_j, \sigma_{j2}] \leftarrow Dec(msk, [ANC_j, \sigma_{j2}]_{mpk})$
   - $valid \leftarrow Tverify(tpk_{j2}, ANC, \sigma_{j2})$
   - $\sigma \leftarrow TReconstruct(\sigma_{1...t}, tpk_{1...t})$
   - $toC(ANC_j, \sigma)$
4. Trusted agents read (ANC_j, σ).
   - $toP((ANC_j, \sigma)$

Transactions. Three phases of a transaction are described separately as follows:

Initiate Transaction

1. An end-user i seeks services or information.
   - $toP([Request_i, upk_i])$
2. Trusted agents read the request.
   - Define $ID_i = [Blocknumber_i, Offset_i]$, where $Offset_i$ uniquely identify $Request_i$ in the block.
   - $SPV([Request_i, upk_i, ID_i])$
   - Define $Creq_i = [Request_i, upk_i, ID_i]$

First Signature are denoted as σs.

1. Trusted agents.
   - $toC(Creq_i)$
2. Consortium members j_2 reads $Creq_i$ and advocates it.
   - $\sigma_{j2} \leftarrow Tsign(Creq_i, tsk_{j2})$
   - $[Creq_i, \sigma_{j2}, tpk_{j2}]_{mpk} \leftarrow Enc(mpk, [Creq_i, \sigma_{j2}, tpk_{j2}])$
   - $toC([Creq_i, \sigma_{j2}, tpk_{j2}]_{mpk})$
3. The auditor, reads $[Creq_i, \sigma_{j2}, tpk_{j2}]_{mpk}$.
   (Status: The auditor lacks 1 signature to generate the *First Signature* of $Creq_i$ and has not collected $[Creq_i, \sigma_{j2}, tpk_{j2}]_{mpk}$.)
   - $[Creq_i, \sigma_{j2}, tpk_{j2}] \leftarrow Dec(msk, [Creq_i, \sigma_{j2}, tpk_{j2}]_{mpk})$
   - $valid \leftarrow TVerify(tpk_{j2}, Creq_i, \sigma_{j2})$
   - $\sigma \leftarrow TReconstruct(\sigma_{1...t}, tpk_{1...t})$
   - $ToC(Creq_i, \sigma)$

Second Signature are denoted as σ's.

1. Consortium member j_3 responds to $Creq_i$.
   - $Verify(tpk, Creq_i, \sigma)$
   - Generate the response Res_{j3}.
   - If required, $Res_{j3} \leftarrow Enc(upk_i, Res_{j3})$.
   - $toC(Res_{j3})$
   - $\sigma'_{j3} \leftarrow Tsign(Res_{j3}, tsk_{j3})$
   - $[Res_{j3}, \sigma'_{j3}, tpk_{j3}]_{mpk} \leftarrow Enc(mpk, [Res_{j3}, \sigma'_{j3}, tpk_{j3}])$
   - $toC([Res_{j3}, \sigma'_{j3}, tpk_{j3}]_{mpk})$
2. Consortium member j_4 reads Res_{j3} and advocates it.
   - $\sigma'_{j4} \leftarrow Tsign(Res_{j3}, tsk_{j4})$
   - $[Res_{j3}, \sigma'_{j4}, tpk_{j4}]_{mpk} \leftarrow Enc(mpk, [Res_{j3}, \sigma'_{j4}, tpk_{j4}])$
   - $toC([Res_{j3}, \sigma'_{j4}, tpk_{j4}]_{mpk})$
3. The auditor, reads $[Res_{j3}, \sigma'_{j4}, tpk_{j4}]_{mpk}$.
   (Status: The auditor lacks 1 signature to generate the *Second Signature* of Res_{j3} and has not collected $[Res_{j3}, \sigma'_{j4}, tpk_{j4}]_{mpk}$.)
   - $[Res_{j3}, \sigma'_{j4}, tpk_{j4}] \leftarrow [Res_{j3}, \sigma'_{j4}, tpk_{j4}]_{mpk}$
   - $valid \leftarrow TVerify(tpk_{j4}, Res_{j3}, \sigma'_{j4})$
   - $\sigma \leftarrow TReconstruct(\sigma_{1...t}, tpk_{1...t})$
   - $ToC(Res_{j3}, \sigma')$
4. Trusted agents reads Res_{j3}, σ'.
   - $ToP(Res_{j3}, \sigma')$

Audit. The manager may reveal a row in her *SignMap* and decrypt the corresponding history in the consortium blockchain when a request is considered suspicious. The response record in the consortium and public blockchain can be revealed if the user's secret key is provided.

4.3 Security Discussion

We discuss the security definitions as follows, and formal definitions and proofs will be shown in the full version of this paper.

Definition 1 (q-Consortium Soundness). *A cross-chain interaction scheme has q-Consortium Soundness if for all PPT adversary A, who is allowed to corrupt less than $(q \cdot |consortium|)$ consortium members, corrupt the manager, cannot produce a valid and verifiable response to a request without honest consortium member signing it.*

Theorem 1. *Our scheme has q-Consortium Soundness if the underlying t-out-of-n threshold signature algorithm is unforgeable, where $q = t/n$.*

Generally, a secure t-out-of-n threshold signature algorithm ensures that any PPT adversary, who is allowed to corrupt up to t users, cannot produce a valid signature(not one's share of signature). An adversary who can attack our scheme will generate a valid response, which contains a signature. This signature can be used to attack the unforgeability of the underlying threshold signature algorithm.

Definition 2 (Consortium Interface Safety). *The interface should ensure that all the correct consortium members agree on the same set of incoming consumer requests in the same order.*

Theorem 2. *Our scheme has Consortium Interface Safety if the underlying threshold signature is secure and the consensus algorithm of the chosen public blockchain provides a determined sequence of requests.*

Intuitively, the process of generating the *First Signature* is simultaneously deciding the order of requests.

Definition 3 (q-Consortium Member Privacy). *A cross-chain interaction scheme has q-Consortium Member Privacy if for all PPT adversary A, who is allowed to corrupt less than $(q \cdot |consortium|)$ consortium members, cannot give a correct list of consortium members advocating for a given request.*

Theorem 3. *Our scheme has q-Consortium Member Privacy if the underlying public key encryption algorithm is CPA secure and the underlying secret sharing scheme of the threshold signature scheme is secure.*

The definition of a secure *secret sharing* scheme and the proof of *Shamir's secret sharing scheme is secure* can be found in [8]. An adversary who can attack our scheme will generate a list of consortium members and a request, which can be used to attack the security of Shamir's secret sharing scheme.

5   Conclusion

By redesigning the protocols with various cryptographic tools, we enhanced the privacy of the consortium members by concealing their identities from the voting process. Also, we provided the auditability to the cross-chain architecture by revealing suspicious transactions. Our future work includes formal security proof as well as the evaluation of the scheme in a simulated scenario.

Acknowledgement. This work has been partly supported by the Fundamentral Research Funds for the Central Universities (No. 30106220482).

References

1. Abebe, E., et al.: Enabling enterprise blockchain interoperability with trusted data transfer (industry track). In: Proceedings of the 20th International Middleware Conference Industrial Track, pp. 29–35 (2019)
2. Al-Bassam, M., Sonnino, A., Bano, S., Hrycyszyn, D., Danezis, G.: Chainspace: a sharded smart contracts platform. arXiv preprint arXiv:1708.03778 (2017)
3. Au, M.H., Chow, S.S.M., Susilo, W., Tsang, P.P.: Short linkable ring signatures revisited. In: Atzeni, A.S., Lioy, A. (eds.) EuroPKI 2006. LNCS, vol. 4043, pp. 101–115. Springer, Heidelberg (2006). https://doi.org/10.1007/11774716_9
4. Azaria, A., Ekblaw, A., Vieira, T., Lippman, A.: MedRec: using blockchain for medical data access and permission management. In: 2016 2nd International Conference on Open and Big Data (OBD), pp. 25–30. IEEE (2016)
5. Bentov, I., Ji, Y., Zhang, F., Breidenbach, L., Daian, P., Juels, A.: Tesseract: real-time cryptocurrency exchange using trusted hardware. In: Proceedings of the 2019 ACM SIGSAC Conference on Computer and Communications Security, pp. 1521–1538 (2019)
6. Boldyreva, A.: Threshold signatures, multisignatures and blind signatures based on the gap-Diffie-Hellman-group signature scheme. In: Desmedt, Y.G. (ed.) PKC 2003. LNCS, vol. 2567, pp. 31–46. Springer, Heidelberg (2003). https://doi.org/10.1007/3-540-36288-6_3
7. Boneh, D., Lynn, B., Shacham, H.: Short signatures from the Weil pairing. J. Cryptol. **17**(4), 297–319 (2004)
8. Boneh, D., Shoup, V.: A graduate course in applied cryptography. Draft 0.5 (2020)
9. Bünz, B., Bootle, J., Boneh, D., Poelstra, A., Wuille, P., Maxwell, G.: Bulletproofs: short proofs for confidential transactions and more. In: 2018 IEEE Symposium on Security and Privacy (SP), pp. 315–334. IEEE (2018)
10. Cash, M., Bassiouni, M.: Two-tier permission-ed and permission-less blockchain for secure data sharing. In: 2018 IEEE International Conference on Smart Cloud (SmartCloud), pp. 138–144. IEEE (2018)
11. Castro, M., Liskov, B., et al.: Practical Byzantine fault tolerance. In: OsDI, vol. 99, pp. 173–186 (1999)
12. Chainalysis: The 2020 state of crypto crime. https://go.chainalysis.com/rs/503-FAP-074/images/2020-Crypto-Crime-Report.pdf. Accessed 24 Sept 2022
13. Douceur, J.R.: The Sybil attack. In: Druschel, P., Kaashoek, F., Rowstron, A. (eds.) IPTPS 2002. LNCS, vol. 2429, pp. 251–260. Springer, Heidelberg (2002). https://doi.org/10.1007/3-540-45748-8_24

14. Fuchsbauer, G., Orrù, M., Seurin, Y.: Aggregate cash systems: a cryptographic investigation of mimblewimble. In: Ishai, Y., Rijmen, V. (eds.) EUROCRYPT 2019. LNCS, vol. 11476, pp. 657–689. Springer, Cham (2019). https://doi.org/10.1007/978-3-030-17653-2_22

15. Gennaro, R., Jarecki, S., Krawczyk, H., Rabin, T.: Secure distributed key generation for discrete-log based cryptosystems. In: Stern, J. (ed.) EUROCRYPT 1999. LNCS, vol. 1592, pp. 295–310. Springer, Heidelberg (1999). https://doi.org/10.1007/3-540-48910-X_21

16. Ghosh, B.C., Bhartia, T., Addya, S.K., Chakraborty, S.: Leveraging public-private blockchain interoperability for closed consortium interfacing. In: IEEE Conference on Computer Communications, IEEE INFOCOM 2021, pp. 1–10. IEEE (2021)

17. Huang, H., et al.: Brokerchain: a cross-shard blockchain protocol for account/balance-based state sharding. In: IEEE INFOCOM (2022)

18. Jivanyan, A.: Lelantus: towards confidentiality and anonymity of blockchain transactions from standard assumptions. IACR Cryptology ePrint Archive **2019**, 373 (2019)

19. Joux, A., Nguyen, K.: Separating decision Diffie-Hellman from computational Diffie-Hellman in cryptographic groups. J. Cryptol. **16**(4), 239–247 (2003)

20. Kiayias, A., Russell, A., David, B., Oliynykov, R.: Ouroboros: a provably secure proof-of-stake blockchain protocol. In: Katz, J., Shacham, H. (eds.) CRYPTO 2017. LNCS, vol. 10401, pp. 357–388. Springer, Cham (2017). https://doi.org/10.1007/978-3-319-63688-7_12

21. Kokoris-Kogias, E., Jovanovic, P., Gasser, L., Gailly, N., Syta, E., Ford, B.: OmniLedger: a secure, scale-out, decentralized ledger via sharding. In: 2018 IEEE Symposium on Security and Privacy (SP), pp. 583–598. IEEE (2018)

22. Lai, R.W., Ronge, V., Ruffing, T., Schröder, D., Thyagarajan, S.A.K., Wang, J.: Omniring: scaling private payments without trusted setup. In: Proceedings of the 2019 ACM SIGSAC Conference on Computer and Communications Security, pp. 31–48 (2019)

23. Li, W., Sforzin, A., Fedorov, S., Karame, G.O.: Towards scalable and private industrial blockchains. In: Proceedings of the ACM Workshop on Blockchain, Cryptocurrencies and Contracts, pp. 9–14 (2017)

24. Liu, J.K., Wei, V.K., Wong, D.S.: Linkable spontaneous anonymous group signature for ad hoc groups. In: Wang, H., Pieprzyk, J., Varadharajan, V. (eds.) ACISP 2004. LNCS, vol. 3108, pp. 325–335. Springer, Heidelberg (2004). https://doi.org/10.1007/978-3-540-27800-9_28

25. Liu, J.K., Wong, D.S.: Linkable ring signatures: security models and new schemes. In: Gervasi, O., et al. (eds.) ICCSA 2005. LNCS, vol. 3481, pp. 614–623. Springer, Heidelberg (2005). https://doi.org/10.1007/11424826_65

26. Malavolta, G., Moreno-Sanchez, P., Schneidewind, C., Kate, A., Maffei, M.: Anonymous multi-hop locks for blockchain scalability and interoperability. Cryptology ePrint Archive (2018)

27. Morgan, J.: Virtuozzo. https://www.virtuozzo.com/. Accessed 24 Sept 2022

28. Nakamoto, S.: Bitcoin: a peer-to-peer electronic cash system. Decentralized Business Review, p. 21260 (2008)

29. Noether, S., Goodell, B.: Triptych: logarithmic-sized linkable ring signatures with applications. In: Garcia-Alfaro, J., Navarro-Arribas, G., Herrera-Joancomarti, J. (eds.) DPM/CBT -2020. LNCS, vol. 12484, pp. 337–354. Springer, Cham (2020). https://doi.org/10.1007/978-3-030-66172-4_22

30. Shahsavari, Y., Zhang, K., Talhi, C.: A theoretical model for fork analysis in the bitcoin network. In: 2019 IEEE International Conference on Blockchain (Blockchain), pp. 237–244. IEEE (2019)
31. Soliditylang.org: Solidity. https://soliditylang.org/. Accessed 24 Sept 2022
32. Sun, S.-F., Au, M.H., Liu, J.K., Yuen, T.H.: RingCT 2.0: a compact accumulator-based (linkable ring signature) protocol for blockchain cryptocurrency Monero. In: Foley, S.N., Gollmann, D., Snekkenes, E. (eds.) ESORICS 2017. LNCS, vol. 10493, pp. 456–474. Springer, Cham (2017). https://doi.org/10.1007/978-3-319-66399-9_25
33. Van Saberhagen, N.: Cryptonote v 2.0 (2013)
34. Wood, G., et al.: Ethereum: a secure decentralised generalised transaction ledger. Ethereum Project Yellow Paper 151(2014), 1–32 (2014)
35. Wüst, K., Kostiainen, K., Čapkun, V., Čapkun, S.: PRCash: fast, private and regulated transactions for digital currencies. In: Goldberg, I., Moore, T. (eds.) FC 2019. LNCS, vol. 11598, pp. 158–178. Springer, Cham (2019). https://doi.org/10.1007/978-3-030-32101-7_11
36. Xu, X., Rahman, F., Shakya, B., Vassilev, A., Forte, D., Tehranipoor, M.: Electronics supply chain integrity enabled by blockchain. ACM Trans. Des. Autom. Electron. Syst. (TODAES) 24(3), 1–25 (2019)
37. Yuen, T.H.: PAChain: private, authenticated & auditable consortium blockchain and its implementation. Futur. Gener. Comput. Syst. 112, 913–929 (2020)
38. Yuen, T.H., et al.: RingCT 3.0 for blockchain confidential transaction: shorter size and stronger security. In: Bonneau, J., Heninger, N. (eds.) FC 2020. LNCS, vol. 12059, pp. 464–483. Springer, Cham (2020). https://doi.org/10.1007/978-3-030-51280-4_25
39. Zamyatin, A., et al.: SoK: communication across distributed ledgers. In: Borisov, N., Diaz, C. (eds.) FC 2021. LNCS, vol. 12675, pp. 3–36. Springer, Heidelberg (2021). https://doi.org/10.1007/978-3-662-64331-0_1
40. Zhou, H., Ouyang, X., Ren, Z., Su, J., de Laat, C., Zhao, Z.: A blockchain based witness model for trustworthy cloud service level agreement enforcement. In: IEEE Conference on Computer Communications, IEEE INFOCOM 2019, pp. 1567–1575. IEEE (2019)

Data Cooperatives for Trusted News Sharing in Social Media

Abiola Salau$^{(\boxtimes)}$ ⓘ, Ram Dantu, Kritagya Upadhyay, and Syed Badruddoja

Department of Computer Science and Engineering, University of North Texas,
Denton, TX 76207, USA
{abiolasalau,kritagyaupadhyay,syedbadruddoja}@my.unt.edu,
ram.dantu@unt.edu

Abstract. The voluntary gathering and pooling of personal data by individuals via legal fiduciaries called data cooperatives is gaining a lot of attention as an approach to secure data management. Data cooperatives and blockchain are an excellent combination since they share fundamental features like decentralization and democratic design. In this paper, we leverage the power of blockchain to design a trusted news-sharing system for social media. We prove our concept by implementing a consumer news coop network on the Ethereum blockchain where members can voluntarily pool news information about their neighborhood for their benefit and also receive incentives in the form of an improved reputation for sharing credible news stories. We enforce honest behavior among the participants by implementing a trust and reputation scheme based on EigenTrust. Our results show that the blockchain approach to implementing a data cooperative is efficient with respect to memory consumption, scalability, and cost while also providing improved trust among participants. Furthermore, the reputation mechanism is effective in ensuring that malicious participants are severely penalized and removed from the system, while honest participants are rewarded. This approach can be used in a much bigger setup like Twitter so that the credibility of a shared post can be verified by a consensus before being shared on the network, thereby mitigating the spread of misinformation.

Keywords: Blockchain · Distributed Ledger Technology · Data cooperative · Reputation System · Social media · News sharing

1 Introduction and Problem Motivation

1.1 Data Cooperatives

Data cooperatives "refer to the voluntary collaborative pooling by individuals of their personal data for the benefit of the membership of a group or community" [1]. The data cooperative serves as a fiduciary for the data subjects, mediating between them and the data companies to help them negotiate the

© ICST Institute for Computer Sciences, Social Informatics and Telecommunications Engineering 2023
Published by Springer Nature Switzerland AG 2023. All Rights Reserved
W. Meng and W. Li (Eds.): BlockTEA 2022, LNICST 498, pp. 106–127, 2023.
https://doi.org/10.1007/978-3-031-31420-9_7

control and use of their personal data. The success of a data cooperative relies so much on the credibility of the kind of data that is pooled and how trustworthy the participants are in sharing credible data or information [1]. The kinds of resources that are pooled in a data co-op may be of varying types. For example, a community could come together to start a co-op where they pool personal health data, community news information, etc. [2]. Human beings are naturally inclined to attach some level of credibility to an individual based on how they perceive the reputation of that person, either through direct interactions or based on others' recommendations. In an online community such as a data co-op where members may not know each other enough to have some form of a trust relationship, a mechanism must be adopted to enable users to confidently interact or transact on the platform without fear of distrust [3]. *In a data cooperative platform, trust among the participants is necessary for the overall functioning of the co-op* [4,5]. *However, establishing and maintaining effective trust without a central control inherent in traditional systems where members may choose to be untrustworthy or malicious for their benefit is of concern—this is our focal point in this paper.* Specifically, but without loss of generality, our focus will be on news-sharing data co-ops where the members of the network can pool news about happenings in their community. This kind of system can help to create awareness about the events and security situations that exist in a community.

1.2 Fake News

The dissemination of news information used to be the sole responsibility of traditional media houses like TV, radio, and newspapers since they have the resources and are trained in fact-finding on a subject before broadcasting a news story [6]. However, since the advent of social media networks, every user now has the platform to share news posts and other information so that all their followers can read them in real-time. This real-time sharing and access to news information can be important for a thriving community. For instance, if people in a community come together to voluntarily share information about happenings in their respective neighborhoods. This gives them more knowledge about their community in a way that can help improve growth and innovation in the community, as shared data is the backbone of the knowledge economy [1]. The shared information or data can cover areas like health, weather forecasts, security, services, resources, and many more. Some benefits of this form of sharing may include: increased usage for an underutilized asset since a member can pool an asset currently underutilized and other members can benefit from it; a source of revenue for the data providers as the pooled data can be bought by service providers or researchers, and knowledge sharing among participating members.

Building on the concept of news information sharing on the social media networks and data cooperatives introduced in [1], we introduce our notion of a consumer news cooperative or co-op. A consumer news cooperative is a consumer-owned news-sharing platform where members of a community pool news information in their locality for the benefit of the members and the community at large. Members of this consumer news co-op can be professional news organizations, fact-checking organizations, or even individual citizens of a community. Media professionals coming together to share news information and resources have been existing for a long time with the Associated Press[1] as an example of media cooperatives formed by five newspapers. The Banyan project[2] is another such co-op that aims at providing daily coverage of events with trust, relevance, and respect in members' communities. To succeed in this form of cooperative, [7] pointed out some questions that need to be answered: what returns are the members going to get for their participation in the co-op, and how do we ensure trust in the system?

In this paper, we use blockchain technology as a bedrock for building a data co-op and leverage the inherent properties of the technology to establish trust among the participating members and also incentivize them through improved reputation, ensuring everyone in the co-op benefits either directly from the news information or resources shared or in the form of incentives from transactions on the blockchain.

1.3   Why Blockchain for Data Cooperatives?

A major challenge in any online community such as a data co-op is establishing and maintaining trust among participating members and thus, indirectly encouraging cooperation. The data co-op is modeled such that risk and reward are shared among its members [1]. They are also decentralized in the sense that there is no single member in a position of control or above the others. This is a key attribute of a democratic setting, and it is fundamental to the modeling of a co-op [8]. Coincidentally, this decentralized notion of power and democratic control is also a core attribute of the blockchain. The benefits of applying blockchain technology to this are multifold.

- It can provide a trusted mechanism for operational activities such as decision-making and record-keeping without the need for physical proximity in a secure and immutable manner, which is important in a news-sharing platform.
- The immutable property of the blockchain will provide a means to prove the provenance of a pooled data source and other transactions on the system if the need arises.
- Being inherently distributed, it aligns with the concept of a cooperative since the members may not necessarily be in proximity and each member will still have the same view of the distributed ledger.
- Blockchain, using smart contracts will help to enforce the laws and regulations binding the data cooperative and will also help to ensure that punishments and rewards mechanisms are automatically handled [9,10].

To implement a blockchain-based data cooperative, the design has to correlate to blockchain systems such that it will have a ledger that will hold the detail

---

[1] Associated Press, ap.org/en-us/.
[2] banyanproject.coop/.

of transactions, a consensus mechanism to agree on the pooled data (depending on the goal of the co-op), how new members can join and the requirements and a mechanism to build and maintain trust in the system and also a way of incentivizing participants to encourage them to keep being on the network [11]. We have addressed these fundamental elements in this work.

1.4 Our Contributions

The main contributions of this paper are summarized as follows:

- We prove our concept by implementing a consumer news sharing prototype using blockchain as the underlying technology for a news pooling data co-op and our results show that the system is effective, scalable, and secure.
- Then, we integrate a reputation scheme to track malicious members and dishonest consensus nodes as well as incentivize honest behavior on the system which is a gap in related papers that we studied.
- We propose the use of a modified Eigentrust model which takes the transaction history of a user into account in the reputation computation for the reputation computation.
- Lastly, we evaluate our system experimentally, discuss its performance in terms of efficiency, scalability, and security and present defense mechanisms against potential attack.

1.5 Outline

The rest of the paper is organized as follows: Sect. 2 describes the existing literature and works relating to ours while also mentioning the differences between our work and these existing works. Section 3 describes the proposed system architecture and framework in detail. Section 4 talks about the experimental setup for the project and the implementation. In Sect. 5, results and discussion are provided, as also the security analysis. We conclude the paper in Sect. 6 by discussing future works and summarizing the key concepts and ideas of this paper.

2 Background and Related Work

The idea of data providers getting better control over their data is gradually developing due to the declining level of trust between users and service providers [12]. With the volume of data generated daily by users of the internet and especially the social media networks, individuals are increasingly concerned about the privacy of their data and how the social network platforms handle their data [12,13]. [7] describes a data cooperative as a community where individuals come together to pool their personal data for the benefit of its members. The authors further discussed the advantages communities can get from such a collaboration, among which is the economic growth a community can derive from having access to its data and being able to analyze it.

There are existing forms of data cooperatives [8] with the goal of individuals collaborating for the common good of the group while ensuring the members have control of their personal data. One such platform is MIDATA[3] where account holders can actively contribute to medical research by granting controlled access to their personal data. HAT[4] is a micro-server platform that gives the right of personal data to individuals through ownership of their personal data. Enigma [14] which is a peer-to-peer platform where different parties can jointly run computations on their data while keeping the data private. A common concept behind these platforms is to ensure that the data owners have absolute control over their data and can grant control-based access to whomever they want to.

In the world of news information broadcast, the Associated Press and the Banyan Project are examples of media cooperatives where news media organizations can come together to pool their resources for better news coverage or facility sharing. The media cooperatives report news based on the interests of their members and their geographical location[5] The application of blockchain as a technology for "sharing" has gained much attention with copious research work in literature. For a comprehensive review on the blockchain and trust in a sharing economy, we refer readers to paper [15]. However, we highlight some of these existing works that are similar to ours. Worthy of mention are the works of [6,16–19] where the authors propose the use of blockchain in sharing and analyzing news, while some others propose a hybrid of blockchain and ML or DL to tackle fake news [20–23] but our paper has a fundamental difference from these papers in the implementation of a reputation scheme based on Eigentrust [24] and a penalty system, which are missing from these previous works. Although our work leverages the concept introduced in [16], we have addressed some of the gaps identified in the paper.

In this paper, we present a data cooperative blockchain framework that can help to address the challenge of declining trust among members of an online community. It proposes a novel implementation of a consumer news data co-op using blockchain as the underlying technology, with comparable results (see Sect. 5) It also develops a novel reputation tracking system for participants to encourage and ensure honesty in the community and a punishment system to penalize dishonest players, effectively removing malicious members from the community after a limited number of rounds.

3   System Architecture

A high-level overview of the framework architecture is depicted in Fig. 1. Community members can interact with the blockchain using a news-sharing distributed application (DApp) on their client device. The news shared by a user is sent as a transaction to the blockchain through a smart contract implemented to manipulate the blockchain. This interaction is achieved through the Python web3 API.

---

[3] midata.coop/en/home/.

[4] Hubofallthings.com/main/what-is-the-hat.

[5] Cooperatives of the Americas - http://www.aciamericas.coop/Who-we-are.

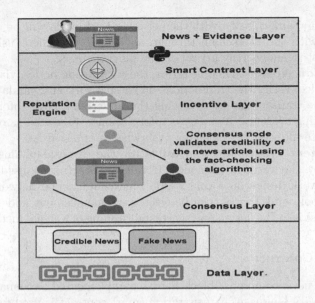

Fig. 1. Overview of the Blockchain-based Consumer News Co-op Framework. We have a client-accessible news-sharing DApp at the topmost application layer, which interacts with the blockchain through a smart contract on the second layer. The incentive layer includes a reputation engine that computes the reputation values of each validator that participates in the consensus process. The transaction data is stored on the blockchain ledger in the data layer.

In the smart contracts layer, the smart contracts have different functionalities based on the option selected by the user. An Eigentrust-based reputation engine in the incentive layer computes the trust level and reputation of the participants taking into account their historical behavior on the network.

The consensus algorithm layer can be any of several consensus algorithms like Proof of Stake [25], Proof of Reputation [26,27], Proof of Review (PoR) [28], etc., depending on implementation requirements. Note that if the consensus algorithm is reputation-based as in [26], the reputation engine may be omitted or embedded into the consensus layer if required.

3.1   Participants and Their Roles on the Blockchain

There are three types of nodes: news sharing nodes, verification nodes, and management nodes.

– *News Sharing Nodes* are registered members of the cooperative that post news content. Examples may include TV channels, radio, newspapers, or any citizen of the community, etc., as shown in Fig. 2. A news-sharing node shares "newsworthy" information with the network. Each node will be able to communicate with the blockchain through an HTTP web client using a REST API to post a newsworthy article on the blockchain.

- **Verification Nodes.** In simple terms, the verification nodes, via an external oracle service, verify the transactions on the network and validate the credibility of the transactions by reviewing the underlying news information and its supporting evidence. If the news information is validated as credible, it is broadcast to all users of the co-op; otherwise, it is discarded.
- **Management Nodes** are responsible for the disposal of misinformation detected by the verification nodes. If this architecture is used in a social media network design on a consortium blockchain, social network providers like Facebook, and Twitter can be elected as management nodes since their only interest is in the design and successful running of a social media platform.

3.2   Smart Contract

To design the news co-op on a blockchain, we implemented two smart contracts using the Solidity language. A registration smart contract is used for user registration when joining the co-op, creating a digital identity profile with a UserID and digital signature for the new user, while another smart contract, called the Function smart contract, implements the logic for news sharing and management. The reputation value update is also done in this smart contract. In the Function smart contract, three key functions are implemented: a news sharing function, which creates the logic for the user to post news; a verification and management function, which is run by the verification nodes and management nodes; and a reputation function, which is the implementation of our modified Eigentrust algorithm [24,31] that computes the reputation of each of the nodes based on their transaction history and the credibility of the news posted by a news sharing node.

As depicted in Fig. 1, a sharing node can post news information along with IPFS[6] links to supporting evidence (such as verifiable media files) by running the news sharing function from its DApp. On receipt of this transaction, nodes interested and available online to verify the transaction, and run the verification and management algorithm on their DApp. This algorithm collates a set of userIDs comprising all the interested nodes, $u_i \in U$ and orders them according to their reputation, t_i on the system. It then randomly selects the userIDs with the top 20% reputation into a set of verification and management committees. From this set, one is randomly chosen as the management node while the others are verification nodes. The other users that were not selected for the committee will play no further part at this time until another news item has been posted.

The verification nodes review the transaction and, based on the evidence given, assign a flag of 0 for False or 1 for True to the transaction, sign it with their respective signature, and send it to the management node. The management node gathers all the signed transactions and checks for the majority flag. If a

---

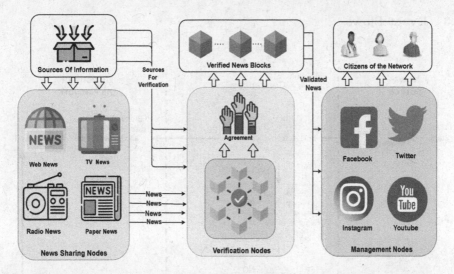

Fig. 2. Participants in the Blockchain. This figure shows a high-level overview of the news sharing ecosystem, with the news sharing nodes sharing a piece of newsworthy information along with supporting evidence, which is verified by the verification nodes via oracle services and broadcast to the citizens of the network or disposed of by the management nodes based on its credibility.

majority of the verification nodes assign a flag of 1, then the news is broadcast to the community and the transaction hash is added to the blockchain, but if the majority assigns a flag of 0, then the news information is tagged as false and not broadcast to the community. Lastly, if there is no majority, then the transaction is tagged as "undecided" and not added to the chain until the sharing node can re-share with more supporting evidence.

After the management node has completed its task, the reputation algorithm collects the userIDs of all the users that played a role in the last transaction, which includes the sharing node and the members of the verification and management committee, into a reputation set R, then computes and updates their respective reputations, as described in the reputation system subsection of this paper.

3.3   Event Flows

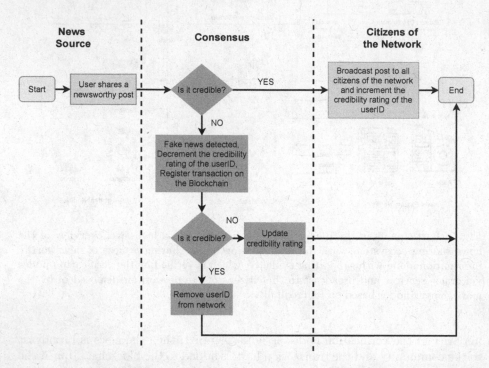

Fig. 3. Flow chart of Events. A user, through its client DApp shares a news transaction on the blockchain. The blockchain environment activates validators who validate the news credibility through an oracle that feeds the implemented smart contract. Depending on the credibility of the transaction based on the validator's outcome, the news is either broadcast and meta-data added to the ledger or discarded by the management nodes. The reputation values of validators are updated accordingly using Eq. 4.

Figure 3 shows the flow of events in the consumer news co-op. For example, if Bob shares a news post, it is sent as a transaction to the blockchain where the verification nodes will review the news information based on the supporting evidence and, if adjudged credible, the news information is broadcast to all users of the co-op and Bob's credit rating is incremented. However, if the news is not credible, the information is discarded and not broadcast to all users, and their reputation is updated with a decreased. We defer further discussion on the reputation computation to Sect. 3.4. Transactions meta-data will be stored on the blockchain ledger with details including the userID, timestamp, news source, etc. while the news article itself is stored off-chain for memory management. This would consume less space on the blockchain and also give the opportunity to delete news content that is illegal (e.g., a death threat). Note that in such a case, the meta-data remains on the blockchain as it is immutable. This feature also helps to track any misinformation that may have been wrongly reported as credible. Real-time APIs will be able to query the reputation of a userID which can be used to notify users whenever a news post is shared from that userID. The reputation feature incentivizes the users to avoid posting false information.

3.4 Reputation System

To begin, we assume that the reader is familiar with the standard equations for trust computation in EigenTrust (see [24]). We modify the equations to address its limitations and the inherent vulnerabilities identified by Fan et al. in their work, Eigentrust++ [29] to make it more attack resilient. The Eigentrust approach has been well established in the literature [24,30–32], as an effective trust model in P2P systems due to its algorithmic approach to enhancing the overall system security by detecting malicious peers, making it easy to punish such behavior, and encouraging honest peers, thereby encouraging cooperative behavior and enforcing trust in the system.

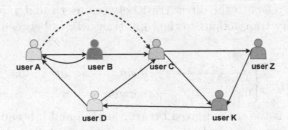

Fig. 4. Trust transitivity principle showing the relationship between users

Equation 4 shows the formulation of the global trust value (or reputation) by combining a direct trust value between a user and other users it had direct transactions with and a recommended trust value, which is a type of trust that is based on transitive trust [33]. As described [3,33] and illustrated in Fig. 4, a direct trust is what exists between user A and user B and it is derived using Eq. 1. If user A trusts user B, user B trusts user C, and user B recommends user C to user A, then user A can derive a measure of trust in user C based on the recommendation, and due to its direct trust in user B, this type of trust is derived trust. The derived trust is computed as shown in Eq. 3.

$$c_{i,j} = \begin{cases} \frac{max(s_{i,j},0)}{\sum_k max(s_{i,k},0)} & \text{if } \sum_k max(s_{i,k},0) \neq 0; \\ p_i, & \text{otherwise} \end{cases} \quad (1)$$

where p_i represents a case where peer i may be new and does not trust any other peer, it will have to choose the pre-trusted peers and its value is given as:

$$p_i = 1/|P|, \quad (2)$$

where P is the set of pre-trusted peers.

$$c_{i,k} = \sum_j c_{i,j} c_{j,k} \tag{3}$$

To address the possibility of malicious users colluding to assign arbitrary high trust values to each other and arbitrary low trust values to good peers in a distributed setting, a proliferation parameter a is used, thereby recalculating the current reputation of each peer as in Eq. 4, where a represents the probability of a peer having an interaction with any other, therefore relying on the pre-trusted peers. We also incorporate an Additive Increase and Multiplicative Decrease penalty component to it such that the reputation value of a malicious node is drastically reduced by half, resulting in its quick removal from the system when its reputation is below an acceptable threshold.

$$t_i = (1 - a)(c_{1,i}t_1 + c_{2,i}t_2 + ... + c_{n,i}t_n) + ap_i \tag{4}$$

where a is a constant ≤ 1.

In Eq. 1, $c_{i,j}$ refers to the direct trust between user i and j, $s_{i,j}$ is the ratio of the satisfactory transactions to the total transactions between users i and j, computed as

$$s_{i,j} = \begin{cases} \frac{sat_{i,j}}{sat_{i,j}+unsat_{i,j}} & \text{if } sat_{i,j} + unsat_{i,j} > 0; \\ 0, & \text{otherwise} \end{cases} \tag{5}$$

In Eq. 3, $c_{i,k}$ is the trust derived between users i and k because of the transitive trust between user i and other users that have direct trust with user k.

In Eq. 4, t_i is the global trust, also known as reputation of user i as perceived by the network, and $c_{n,i}$ is the local trust between users n and i computed from Eqs. 1 and 2.

At the completion of a news sharing, verification, and management round, the reputation engine recomputes and updates the global trust of all the participants in that round. If the news information is flagged as false, then the news-sharing user is penalized with a reduction in its reputation. But if found credible by a minimum 51% majority, then its reputation rises. Likewise, for the verification nodes, the erring minority will have their reputation reduced to serve as a punishment for not adequately verifying the news for its authenticity before making a decision, while the majority will have their reputation raised for the honest work they performed. This will help to ensure that the nodes carefully verify the news and the supporting evidence before assigning a tag and thus discourage malicious behaviors from the nodes while also encouraging cooperation and trust-building for the success of the data co-op.

3.5   Incentive Structure

This work relies on a simple incentive structure in the form of improved reputation scores for well-behaved nodes in the system. This is based on the assumption that humans do not require any monetary incentive to report the news happening in their locality. However, some approaches may be explored to enforce the incentives, such as the game-theoretic approaches studied in papers like [34–36] where the nodes can self-police themselves with a reward and penalty system such that if any participating node can verifiably report another malicious node, it gets a reward greater than the normal increment in its reputation for a round, while the dishonest node has its reputation either decreased by half or set to 0, depending on the game strategies. Another good approach is to have the reputation of the nodes tied to a monetary stake invested in the system so that they get to lose their money when they behave dishonestly, while honest nodes get to earn monetary rewards as well.

4   Experimental Setup and Implementation

Technologies software/tools that were used for this project include: i) Remix Web IDE ii) Truffle.js iii) Web3.js and Web3.py iv) Node.js v) Ganache vi) Ropsten test net vii) Solidity

The application will be developed on an Ethereum-based blockchain network; a smart contract will be written using Solidity, and a graphical user interface will be developed for interaction with users. The API services will be designed using a web3.js client in Node.js. Through this, the user can connect to the blockchain to post news transactions or request the reputations of users. Ganache was used as a local blockchain during the development stage of the smart contract. Performance results were measured on the Ropsten test net. The Metamask plug-in was used to interact with the blockchain for user accounts.

Data-set for the blockchain implementation was collected from Twitter through its developer API[7]. The dataset is described as a trending topic, e.g. #Covid19, #USElections2020, #RusyaUkrayna, etc., which involves several newsworthy tweets from various information sources. Possible news sources include newspapers, magazines, TV channels, radio stations, blogs, etc. A total of 5000 tweets were collected on the trending topic "#US Elections" between October 28, 2020, and November 4, 2020. Tweets that were not in English were removed, and duplicates were also removed. This reduced the total number of tweets in our test data set to 4153. For the initial set of users, we created multiple accounts on the Ropsten test net, starting with 50 accounts, and assigned random initial reputation scores with a minimum of the average reputation value to the nodes. This is based on the assumption that, as obtainable in reality, the developers of the system are less likely to want to destroy the system. We also started with 10 news-sharing users, each sharing a news message from the available dataset to the network, and in further iterations, we allowed new users to join and continue to increase and observe the system as we add new users and reputations being computed. In the next section, we present and discuss the results of our experiments.

---

[7] Twitter API - developer.twitter.com/en/docs/twitter-api/enterprise/search-api/ove rview.

5   Results and Discussion

The system testing was done on the Ropsten test net and performance data was generated on metrics that measure the relevance of blockchain as a platform for the pooling of news information on consumer news co-ops. Results from [37], show that evaluating the system on the Ropsten test net gives similar performance results when compared to the Ethereum main net only with increased transaction receipt times on the main net, which may be attributed to the volume of transactions in the pool at the time of making the transaction.

The transaction times on the Ropsten Test Net show that, on average, the time taken for a user to share a news post on the blockchain network is 14.24 s, with times ranging between 3.61 s and 43.25 s. This variation may be attributed to the size of the news information being shared and the time it takes to mine each transaction on the blockchain. This mining time is also dependent on the amount of gas offered by the sender of the transaction. This variation can also be attributed to traffic on the blockchain network [2]. However, the read time is close to real-time, which is important in a quick assessment of how credible the news source is.

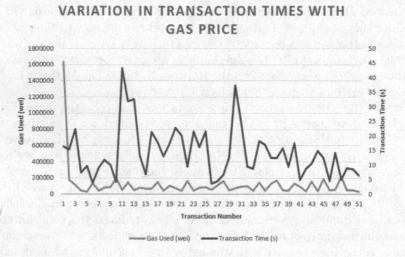

Fig. 5. Variation Between the Gas Used and Transaction Receipt Times for News Sharing Transactions. Transaction 1 with a gas used of 1630773 Wei is the gas consumed for the deployment of the smart contract. Observe that the gas used for the transactions with the exception of the deployment transaction is almost constant. This is because of the limitation on the number of characters acceptable per tweet on Twitter.

Figure 5 shows the variation between the gas used and transaction receipt times for each news-sharing transaction on the blockchain. A total of 50 tweets were used for the experiment and each of the tweets representing a piece of news information to be shared is depicted on the horizontal axis as the transaction number while the left vertical axis represents the gas used in Wei and the right vertical axis shows the latency in sharing the news post on the blockchain. We notice that the time taken per transaction differs. The variation may be attributed to the time taken to validate and add the transaction to the blockchain.

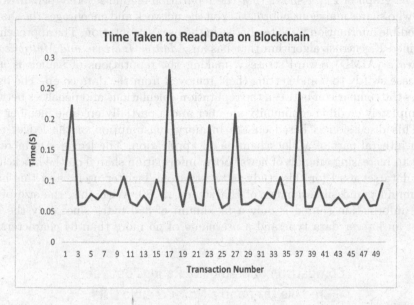

Fig. 6. Time Taken To Retrieve Reputations of Users On The Blockchain. An average of 0.09 s was used for reading the reputation of a user, with a minimum of 0.06 s and a maximum of 0.28 s.

A total of 1630773 Wei of gas was consumed for smart contract deployment. The news sharing function, which is one of the two write functions in the smart contract, consumed an average of 90707 Wei of gas, with consumption volume varying between a minimum of 33271 Wei and a maximum of 212781 Wei. The other write function, which is the user registration function, consumed an average of 20724 Wei of gas, with consumption volume varying between a minimum of 10844 Wei and a maximum of 47125 Wei. The amount of gas used for the deployment of the smart contract on the blockchain is dependent on the logic in the functions of the smart contract, i.e., the more complex the function logic, the higher the gas consumed. Another function in the smart contract is the one that reads the reputation of a user. This function only reads from the blockchain, and reading from the blockchain does not consume gas.

Figure 6 shows a plot of the time taken to read the reputations of users on the blockchain. For every piece of news shared by a user, its reputation is computed based on the outcome of the validation of the news information by the verification nodes. A user can query the system for its reputation score. We simulate this by querying the reputation scores of different users and the time taken to get the ratings was plotted as depicted in Fig. 6. We may observe from the points on the plot that the credit ratings were retrieved in close to real-time, unlike the time taken in the news sharing plot of Fig. 5. This difference is because the function that generated the plot of Fig. 6 is a read function, and it does not require any transaction cost, so it can read from the blockchain in about real-time.

The graph of Fig. 7 shows that the reputation engine severely penalizes any user who shares malicious information on the network and encourages the sharing of credible information by a steady rise in the user's reputation. The approach is a modified Eigentrust algorithm that has an *Additive Increase and Multiplicative Decrease* (AIMD) reward strategy, making the reputations of malicious users decrease swiftly to 0 and getting them removed from the data co-op. The figure shows the comparison between the reputation calculations and penalties between a completely credible community member and a partially credible member.

This discussion is based on the memory consumption of the ledger as it is an integral part of a blockchain-based application. The ledger size increases with an increasing amount of newsworthy information shared on the blockchain. The data set used for this study is tweets from Twitter users, and this has a maximum permissible number of characters of 280. With this, the size of the news information shared is only a maximum of 350 bytes since only the user ID of an integer data type and a username of no more than 64 characters are

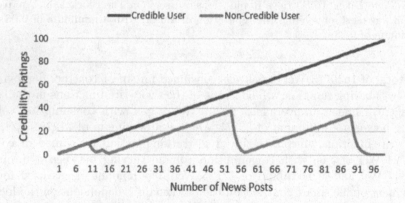

Comparison of Credibility Ratings Between Credible User and a Non-Credible User

Fig. 7. Comparison Between The Reputation Calculations And Penalties Between A Fully Honest Member And A Partially Malicious Member. We can observe that the reputation of the honest user steadily increases while that of the malicious user drastically reduces after being severely punished by the 11th, 55th, and 91st rounds. Notice also that the reputation value of malicious users decreased to zero after the 93rd round and would be effectively removed from the system.

stored in addition to the news text. The blockchain also maintains data about the reputation of users.

Storing a user profile and its credit rating on the blockchain only consumes about 97 bytes per user considering the data types of the variables used. After the addition of 10,000 used, the ledger size will be 0.97 Mb, which is very small. [38] reports that, as of May 2020, there is an average of 6000 tweets per second on the Twitter social media platform. It is also reported that this has been the average number of tweets since the year 2014. According to Ethereum Transaction growth chart[8] the highest number of the 1,406,016 transactions occurred on Thursday, September 17, 2020, achieving a transaction rate of 16.27 Tx/s. This is very small compared to the number of average tweets per second on the Twitter social media platform.

5.1 Security Analysis

In this section, we will describe the defense of our model against potential threats and attacks relating to similar systems. We argue that, provided the reputation computation engine is accurate, it reflects the probabilities that the selected consensus nodes (the verification and management nodes) are not corrupted [27]. Thus, the verification and management node selection processes will always select an honest majority committee, and the outcome of the consensus will be added to the blockchain, proving the blockchain's safety.

To show the guarantee of an honest majority-of-reputation in the committee, we follow the approach presented in [39,40]. In similarity to [39] we employ Hoeffding inequality [41] rather than Chernoff bound in this context since the set of reputation values for the nodes is not equally distributed. In essence, given a set of reputation vectors randomly selected, it allows us to provide an upper bound on the probability that the sum of reputation vectors deviates from its expected value by more than a certain constant ϵ. Concretely, given a family $Rep = \{r^{n(\kappa)}\}_{\kappa \in N}$ and a set of stakeholders $n = n(\kappa)$ participating in a certain round of consensus, for all sufficiently large k's, using Hoeffding inequality, the average of the reputations is expected to be greater than $\frac{1}{2} + \omega(\sqrt{\frac{\log n}{n}})$, or that the expected number of honest parties should be greater than $\frac{n}{2} + \omega(\sqrt{n \log n})$. κ is a system security parameter that determines the difficulty level of selection.

Lemma 1 *(The Hoeffding Inequality)* [41]. *Let $X_1, \cdots, X_m$ be m independent random variables, each ranging over the (real) interval [0, 1], and let $\mu = \frac{1}{Q} \cdot E[\sum_{i=1}^{Q} X_i]$ denote the expected value of the mean of these variables. Then, for every $\epsilon > 0$, $Pr\left[\left|\frac{\sum_{i=1}^{Q} X_i}{Q} - \mu\right| \geq \epsilon\right] \leq 2e^{-2\epsilon^2 m}$.*

Theorem 1 *(Honest Majority)* [39]. *With overwhelming probability in the security parameter κ for some constant $\Delta > 0$, adversary $\mathcal{A}$ controls at most an $1/2 - \Delta$ fraction of the reputation of stakeholders in P_{sel}. Where P_{sel} is the set of nodes selected into the formed committee.*

---

[8] Etherscan - https://etherscan.io/chart/tx.

Assumptions:

1. $Rep = \{\mathbf{r}^{n(\kappa)}\}_{\kappa \in N}$ and a polynomial $n = n(\kappa)$, for all sufficiently large κ, the average of the reputations is greater than: $\frac{1}{2} + \omega(\sqrt{\frac{\log n}{n}})$, or equivalently, that the expected number of honest parties is greater than: $\frac{n}{2} + \omega(\sqrt{n \log n})$
2. Reputation vector $\mathbf{r} = (r_1, \cdots, r_n)$. Let $\mathbf{I} \leftarrow r$ be subset of $\mathbf{I} \subseteq [n]$ with $i \in \mathbf{I}$ chosen with probability $1 - r_i$ and the probabilistic choice of $\mathbf{I}$ is given to a distinguisher.

Claim:

With the assumptions stated above, if it holds that $\sum_{i=1}^{n} r_i > \lfloor \frac{n}{2} \rfloor + \omega(\sqrt{n \log n})$ then there exists a negligible function $\mu(\kappa)$ such that for every κ, $Pr\left[|\mathbf{I}| \geq \lfloor \frac{n}{2} \rfloor \right] \leq \mu(\kappa)$.

Proof:

Fix n and let $n = n(\kappa)$

For every $i \in [n]$, let X_i be a random variable that is 1 if P_i is honest and 0 otherwise.

$$Pr[X_i = 1] = r_i$$

Let $\bar{X} = \frac{\sum_{i=1}^{n} X_i}{n}$,

by linearity of expectations,

$$E[\bar{X}] = \frac{1}{n} \sum_{i=1}^{n} r_i$$

Intuitively, we will have an honest majority when $|\mathbf{I} < n/2|$ (or when $\sum_{i=1}^{n} X_i \geq \lfloor \frac{n}{2} \rfloor + 1$).

Let $\Delta = (\sum_{i=1}^{n} r_i) - \lfloor \frac{n}{2} \rfloor = nE[\bar{X}] - \lfloor \frac{n}{2} \rfloor$.

Following Lemma 1,

$$Pr\left[\sum_{i=1}^{n} X_i \leq \lfloor \frac{n}{2} \rfloor \right] = Pr\left[\sum_{i=1}^{n} X_i - nE[\bar{X}] \leq \lfloor \frac{n}{2} \rfloor - nE[\bar{X}] \right]$$

$$= Pr\left[\sum_{i=1}^{n} X_i - nE[\bar{X}] \leq -\Delta \right] = Pr\left[\sum_{i=1}^{n} X_i - nE[\bar{X}] \leq -n\frac{\Delta}{n} \right]$$

$$= Pr\left[\frac{\sum_{i=1}^{n} X_i}{n} - E[\bar{X}] \leq -\frac{\Delta}{n} \right] \leq 2e^{-\frac{2\Delta^2}{n}}$$

By the assumption in the claim, $\Delta = \omega(\sqrt{n \log n})$, we have $\frac{\Delta^2}{n} = \omega(\log n)$ Hence,

$$Pr\left[|I| \geq \lfloor\frac{n}{2}\rfloor\right] = Pr\left[\sum_{i=1}^{n} X_i \leq \lfloor\frac{n}{2}\rfloor\right] \leq 2e^{-\frac{2\Delta^2}{n}} < 2e^{-\omega(\log n)} \qquad (6)$$

which is negligible in n. Thus, it holds that $e^{-\omega(\log n(k))}$ is a function that is negligible in κ as required. □

Figure 8 visualizes Eq. 6. It shows the probability of an attacker controlling the majority of reputation with changing committee size. It is worthy of note that as the committee size increases, the attacker's chances drastically reduce.

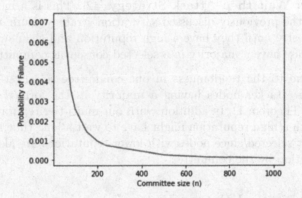

Fig. 8. Probability of an adversary having a majority in a sampling committee of size n

Next, we address the possibility of a Sybil attack on our system. In our proposed blockchain-based solution, the reputation of an individual plays a vital role in the successful operation of the data cooperative since it is a major criterion in the selection of nodes for system-specific tasks such as validating transactions, adding a new block to the chain, and so on. Thus, the reputation computation system is a major target for an attack.

Assumptions on the Reputation System

1. A reputation must be earned. It cannot be purchased, traded, or spent.
2. The reputation of a node is the aggregation of all reputation adjustments for the current round for that node.
3. Peers should not be responsible for directly computing their respective reputation values, and neither should they be able to modify these values.
4. Reputation values must be stored on the blockchain and be verifiable by all peers.

Sybil Attack: Saturation. In a Sybil attack with a saturation strategy, the attacker registers a large number of new users on the system with the aim of using its control over them to subvert the system [42]. The goal of the attacker is to either bring down the reputation of honest nodes or increase the reputation of a certain node that it controls, which has to improve its chances of getting selected for system tasks and then subvert the system.

Mitigation: This type of attack is designed to fail on our proposed system since the newly-joined nodes will have a reputation of zero and will require time and good behavior on the system to build their reputation before being chosen for system tasks. In addition, if a lot of nodes are joining the network at the same time, this would make it easily detectable and it could be a trigger for a transition to more stringent selection conditions.

Sybil Attack: Wait then Attack Strategy [42]. This is a more dangerous strategy than the previously discussed saturation strategy. Here, the attacker's nodes act honestly until they have a high reputation and then switch to a bad action when they have a majority in a selected consensus committee.

Mitigation: Due to the randomness in our committee selection protocol, the chances of the attacker nodes having a majority in the formed committee is negligible (see Theorem 1). In addition, with our multi-tier reputation protocol, even nodes with a high reputation might have to wait a long time before getting a chance to get selected since nodes with lower reputations are also given a fair chance of selection by the committee.

6   Conclusion and Future Work

In this work, we showed the development of a novel blockchain-based approach to the data cooperative concept using a consumer-owned news cooperative use case. Applying blockchain to data co-ops solves the challenge of incentivizing the news providers, as this was a major setback in the traditional system. Also, the addition of a reputation system ensures that the participants are honest since they are penalized when they post any misinformation. This will provide a platform for a transparent, multi-party system where all participating nodes can post newsworthy information and get rewarded with an improved credit rating.

For the blockchain to serve as the preferred platform for peer-to-peer news sharing platforms, it will have to support the number of news posts reported by [38] per second. Theoretically, with a block gas limit of $12{,}472{,}493^9$ with the gas cost of around 21,000 for each transaction, we achieve approximately 594 transactions per block. With the current block time of $13.08\,\mathrm{s}^{10}$, Ethereum can theoretically support 45.69 TXN/s. This number is obviously below the requirement for real-time support for news sharing. We will explore other blockchain platforms and consensus algorithms like proof-of-stake, where validators can be

---

[9]   etherscan.io/chart/gaslimit.

[10]   ethstats.net/.

selected based on stakes or permission from blockchain platforms depending on production requirements. This will enable us to examine how well the blockchain platform will scale with an increasing number of participants.

In future work, we aim to explore the application of game theory in the design of the consensus mechanism as well as the reward and penalty system. Some of the existing work in this area include [34–36]. We also plan to implement access controls in the system since it is an integral aspect of any data cooperative. A user should be able to control who gets access to their data, for what duration, and also be able to revoke this granted access. We will also further evaluate the system against threats and attacks that could result in the possibility of forking the blockchain. The work of Kleinrock et al. [27], showed how a consensus committee can be selected using a fair lottery tier-based approach such that new nodes whose reputation is naturally low would have a fair chance of being selected into the consensus committee while simultaneously ensuring that older yet highly reputable nodes have a higher probability of being chosen than the new nodes. This approach can be useful in our work since we only consider the top 20% reputable nodes and have no chance of newly joined nodes.

References

1. Pentland, A., Hardjono, T.: 2. Data Cooperatives in Building the New Economy (2020)
2. Salau, A., Dantu, R., Upadhyay, A.: Data cooperatives for neighborhood watch. In: 2021 IEEE International Conference on Blockchain and Cryptocurrency (ICBC), pp. 1–9 (2021). https://doi.org/10.1109/ICBC51069.2021.9461056
3. Jøsang, A., Ismail, R., Boyd, C.: A survey of trust and reputation systems for online service provision. Decis. Support Syst. **43**(2), 618–644 (2007)
4. Data Co-Ops Workshop: Executive Summary of a December 22, 2019 Workshop Hosted at the Hebrew University of Jerusalem, The Federmann Cyber Security Research Center (2019). https://csrcl.huji.ac.il/sites/default/files/csrcl/files/data_co-ops_summary.pdf
5. Salau, A., Dantu, R., Morozov, K., Upadhyay, K., Badruddoja, S.: Multi-tier reputation for data cooperatives. In: Pardalos, P., Kotsireas, I., Guo, Y., Knottenbelt, W. (eds.) MARBLE 2022. LNOR, pp. 253–273. Springer, Cham (2022). https://doi.org/10.1007/978-3-031-18679-0_14
6. Kim, B., Yoon, Y.: Journalism model based on blockchain with sharing space. Symmetry **11**(1), 19 (2019). https://doi.org/10.3390/sym11010019
7. Kaiser, J.E.G.: Media Cooperatives: Challenges and Opportunities (2019). https://medium.com/@jgksfconsulting/media-cooperatives-challenges-and-opportunities-e6803c0716ae. Accessed 30 Jan 2021
8. Pentland, A., Hardjono, T., Penn, J., Colclough, C., Ducharmee, B., Mandel, L.: Data cooperatives: digital empowerment of citizens and workers (2019)
9. Upadhyay, K., Dantu, R., He, Y., Salau, A., Badruddoja, S.: Paradigm shift from paper contracts to smart contracts. In: 2021 Third IEEE International Conference on Trust, Privacy and Security in Intelligent Systems and Applications (TPS-ISA), pp. 261–268. IEEE (2021)

10. Upadhyay, K., Dantu, R., He, Y., Badruddoja, S., Salau, A.: Can't understand SLAs? Use the smart contract. In: 2021 Third IEEE International Conference on Trust, Privacy and Security in Intelligent Systems and Applications (TPS-ISA), pp. 129–136. IEEE (2021)

11. Salau, A., Dantu, R., Morozov, K., Badruddoja, S., Upadhyay, K.: Making blockchain validators honest. In: The Fourth International Conference on Blockchain Computing and Applications (BCCA). IEEE (2022)

12. Madden, M.: Public perceptions of privacy and security in the post-snowden era (2014)

13. World Economic Forum: Rethinking Personal Data: A New Lens for Strengthening Trust (2014). http://reports.weforum.org/rethinkingpersonal-data

14. Zyskind, G., Nathan, O., Pentland, A.: Enigma: decentralized computation platform with guaranteed privacy. ArXiv abs/1506.03471 (2015)

15. Hawlitschek, F., Notheisen, B., Teubner, T.: The limits of trust-free systems: a literature review on blockchain technology and trust in the sharing economy. Electron. Commer. Res. Appl. **29**, 50–63 (2018)

16. Balouchestani, A. Mahdavi, M., Hallaj, Y., Javdani, D.: SANUB: a new method for sharing and analyzing news using blockchain. In: 2019 16th International ISC (Iranian Society of Cryptology) Conference on Information Security and Cryptology (ISCISC), pp. 139–143 (2019). https://doi.org/10.1109/ISCISC48546.2019.8985152

17. Saad, M., Ahmad, A., Mohaisen, A.: Fighting fake news propagation with blockchains. In: 2019 IEEE Conference on Communications and Network Security (CNS), pp. 1–4 (2019). https://doi.org/10.1109/CNS.2019.8802670

18. Islam, A., Kader, M.F., Islam, M.M., Shin, S.Y.: NEWSTRADCOIN: a blockchain based privacy preserving secure NEWS trading network. In: Patel, D., et al. (eds.) IC-BCT 2019. BT, pp. 21–32. Springer, Singapore (2020). https://doi.org/10.1007/978-981-15-4542-9_3

19. Paul, S., Joy, J.I., Sarker, S., Ahmed, S., Das, A.K.: Fake news detection in social media using blockchain. In: 2019 7th International Conference on Smart Computing & Communications (ICSCC) pp. 1–5. IEEE (2019)

20. Katal, A., Singh, J., Kundnani, Y.: Mitigating the effects of fake news using blockchain and machine learning. In: 2021 2nd International Conference for Emerging Technology (INCET), pp. 1–7 (2021)

21. Jaroucheh, Z., Alissa, M., Buchanan, W.: TRUSTD: combat fake content using blockchain and collective signature technologies. ArXiv, abs/2008.13632 (2020)

22. Agrawal, P., Anjana, P.S., Peri, S.: DeHiDe: deep learning-based hybrid model to detect fake news using blockchain. In: International Conference on Distributed Computing and Networking 2021 (ICDCN 2021), pp. 245–246. Association for Computing Machinery, New York (2021)

23. Torky, M., Nabil, E., Said, W.: Proof of credibility: a blockchain approach for detecting and blocking fake news in social networks. Int. J. Adv. Comput. Sci. Appl. **10**(12), 321–327 (2019)

24. Kamvar, S.D., Schlosser, M.T., Garcia-Molina, H.: The eigentrust algorithm for reputation management in P2P networks. In: Proceedings of the 12th International Conference on World Wide Web (2003)

25. Nguyen, C.T., Hoang, D.T., Nguyen, D.N., Niyato, D., Nguyen, H.T., Dutkiewicz, E.: Proof-of-stake consensus mechanisms for future blockchain networks: fundamentals, applications and opportunities. IEEE Access **7**, 85727–85745 (2019)

26. Gai, F., Wang, B., Deng, W., Peng, W.: Proof of reputation: a reputation-based consensus protocol for peer-to-peer network. In: Pei, J., Manolopoulos, Y., Sadiq, S., Li, J. (eds.) DASFAA 2018. LNCS, vol. 10828, pp. 666–681. Springer, Cham (2018). https://doi.org/10.1007/978-3-319-91458-9_41

27. Kleinrock, L., Ostrovsky, R., Zikas, V.: Proof-of-reputation blockchain with Nakamoto fallback. In: Bhargavan, K., Oswald, E., Prabhakaran, M. (eds.) INDOCRYPT 2020. LNCS, vol. 12578, pp. 16–38. Springer, Cham (2020). https://doi.org/10.1007/978-3-030-65277-7_2

28. Zaccagni, Z., Dantu, R.: Proof of review (PoR): a new consensus protocol for deriving trustworthiness of reputation through reviews. Cryptology ePrint Archive, Report 2020/475 (2020)

29. Fan, X., Liu, L., Li, M., Su, Z.: EigenTrustp++: attack resilient trust management. In: 8th International Conference on Collaborative Computing: Networking, Applications and Worksharing (CollaborateCom), pp. 416–425 (2012)

30. Gao, S., Yu, T., Zhu, J., Cai, W.: T-PBFT: an EigenTrust-based practical Byzantine fault tolerance consensus algorithm. China Commun. **16**, 111–123 (2019)

31. Abrams, Z., McGrew, R., Plotkin, S.: A non-manipulable trust system based on EigenTrust. SIGecom Exch. **5**(4), 21–30 (2005)

32. Kurdi, H.A.: HonestPeer. J. King Saud Univ. Comput. Inf. Sci. **27**(3), 315–322 (2015)

33. Jøsang, A., Gray, E., Kinateder, M.: Simplification and analysis of transitive trust networks. Web Intelli. and Agent Sys. **4**, 139–161 (2006)

34. Nojoumian, M., Golchubian, A., Njilla, L., Kwiat, K., Kamhoua, C.: Incentivizing blockchain miners to avoid dishonest mining strategies by a reputation-based paradigm. In: Arai, K., Kapoor, S., Bhatia, R. (eds.) SAI 2018. AISC, vol. 857, pp. 1118–1134. Springer, Cham (2019). https://doi.org/10.1007/978-3-030-01177-2_81

35. Samanta, A.K., Sarkar, B.B., Chaki, N.: Quantified analysis of security issues and its mitigation in blockchain using game theory. In: Dutta, P., Mandal, J.K., Mukhopadhyay, S. (eds.) CICBA 2021. CCIS, vol. 1406, pp. 3–19. Springer, Cham (2021). https://doi.org/10.1007/978-3-030-75529-4_1

36. Liu, Z., et al.: A survey on blockchain: a game theoretical perspective. IEEE Access **7**, 47615–47643 (2019). https://doi.org/10.1109/ACCESS.2019.2909924

37. Muttavarapu, A.S., Dantu, R., Thompson, M.: Distributed ledger for spammers' resume. In: 2019 IEEE Conference on Communications and Network (2019)

38. Sayce, D.: The number of tweets per day in 2020. Accessed 26 Nov 2020

39. Asharov, G., Lindell, Y., Zarosim, H.: Fair and efficient secure multiparty computation with reputation systems. In: Sako, K., Sarkar, P. (eds.) ASIACRYPT 2013. LNCS, vol. 8270, pp. 201–220. Springer, Heidelberg (2013). https://doi.org/10.1007/978-3-642-42045-0_11

40. Larangeira, M.: Reputation at stake! A trust layer over decentralized ledger for multiparty computation and reputation-fair lottery. Cryptology ePrint Archive (2021)

41. Hoeffding, W.: Probability inequalities for sums of bounded random variables. In: Fisher, N.I., Sen, P.K. (eds.) The collected works of Wassily Hoeffding. Springer Series in Statistics, pp. 409–426. Springer, New York (1994). https://doi.org/10.1007/978-1-4612-0865-5_26

42. Biryukov, A., Feher, D., Khovratovich, D.: Guru: universal reputation module for distributed consensus protocols. Cryptology ePrint Archive (2017)

NFT and Machine Learning

A Novel Fast Recovery Method for HT Tamper in Embedded Processor

Wanting Zhou[1]([✉])[iD], Shiwei Yuan[1], Lei Li[1], and Kuo-Hui Yeh[2][iD]

[1] Research Institute of Electronic Science and Technology, University of Electronic Science and Technology of China, Chengdu, SC 611731, China
zhouwt@uestc.edu.cn
[2] Department of Information Management, National Dong Hwa University, Hualien 97001, Taiwan

Abstract. Nowadays, embedded processors face various hardware security issues such as hardware trojans (HT) and code tamper attacks. In this paper, a novel cycle-level recovery method for HT tamper in embedded processor is proposed, which consists two units, a General-Purpose Register (GPRs) backup unit and a PC rollback unit. The former one is designed to replace original register files with backup function extra. And the latter one is composed for rollback operations based on the exact PC address corresponding to the wrong instruction. If a HT tamper is detected, the backup unit works in conjunction with PC rollback unit allowing the processor to resume the instruction execution. The proposed method has been implanted into a RISC-V core of PULPino, and the experimental results show that the processor can restore from fault state caused by inserted HT in real time with the latency of 7 clock cycles, including 2 clock cycles for detection.

Keywords: hardware security · GPRs · fault recovery · embedded processor

1 Introduction

In recent years, processors are facing potential security risks due to hardware Trojan (HT) malicious attack [1–13] and code tamper attacks [14–16]. Facing the security issues abovementioned, a fast and effective recovery mechanism is important to protect processor working normal after a fault is detected.

Existing methods for processor fault recovery mechanism mainly include: 1) checkpoint backup and rolling back [17–26], 2) method on combing attack detection and fault repairing [27–30]. The former one is the most common method for recovery, which is based on building a checkpoint file of recording the state of executing program. If a fault occurs, the checkpoint file would be loaded to cover

Supported by University of Electronic Science and Technology of China.

W. Meng and W. Li (Eds.): BlockTEA 2022, LNICST 498, pp. 131–139, 2023.
https://doi.org/10.1007/978-3-031-31420-9_8

the state. There are some shortcomings of this method, including low real-time performance and higher requirements of memory resources. The latter one needs to build a basic block (BB) depended on monitoring and recovery architecture. However, this method leads to a large number of signatures for extraction of all executing program in advance. Besides, the BB dividing according special instruction may ignore the attack on other instructions.

To overcome these inadequacies mentioned above, a real-time recovery approach is proposed herein, which is an extension of our previous work [31] with performance improvement and hardware implantation. If an attack is detected, recovery mechanism is triggered, a GPRs backup unit with dynamic selection is responsible for restoring the right value which should write to GPRs. Meanwhile, the pipeline of processor is suspended, and the PC of the processor is replaced by the corresponding PC value at the exact moment of an attack occurs. Then, the proposed method has been verified into RI5CY, which is a 4-stage in-order RISC-V core of PULpino [32,33]. And the experimental results show that the processor can restore from fault state caused by HT attack only with a latency of 7 clock cycles, including 2 clocks for detection.

2   The Proposed Recovery Method

The fundamental idea of the proposed method is that the instructions are dispatched sequentially and executed sequentially for in-order processors. Instruction sequences in the program often have data dependencies. For example, consider the following two register instructions to a pipeline processor as shown in Fig. 1. The instruction 1 deposits the data into R1 as its execute stage at time t3. Instruction 2 would be decoded at time t3 by using R1 data, and its execution would be complete at t4. In this scenario, the result of current executed instruction is relied on the instruction itself and the GPRs data, which is updated from execution or write-back stage result of the previous instruction.

When a HT attack is detected, fast recovery scheme can be realized through re-executing the wrong instruction. If PC of wrong instruction, PC pointed at the exact time when the attack occurs, and backup GPRs data are provided simultaneously, cycle-level recovery mechanism can be built by PC rollback. Based on this idea, recovery scheme has been proposed which consists two units, a GPRs backup unit and a PC rollback unit. Besides, a GPR-State Real-Time Detection Module (GSRTM) unit, presented in our previous work [34], are adopted to monitor the state of GPRs, the indication signal will be generated to start the recovery operation once an attack detected. Meanwhile, the corresponding wrong instruction and its PC value are provided for rollback unit to perform recovery scheme. The hardware implementation has been implanted into RI5CY, which is shown in Fig. 2.

2.1   The Design and Implement of GPRs Backup Unit

According to analysis above, the GPRs backup unit should have two functions. It needs to bypass the EX or WB stage information which writes to GPRs

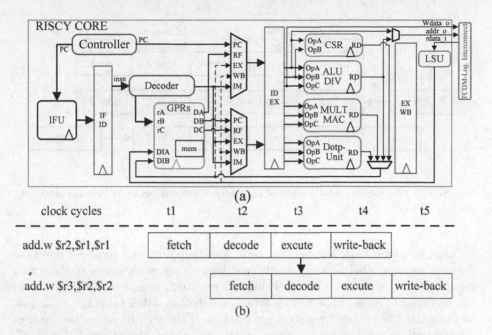

Fig. 1. The function of GPRs information in processor pipeline.

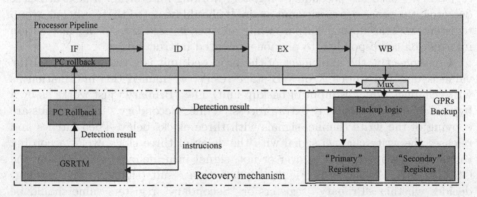

Fig. 2. System diagram based on backup and PC rollback techniques.

registers in normal execution of the program. In addition, it also stores the GPRs information corresponding to the previous executed instruction. Herein, two register groups are needed, "Primary" registers are used in normal work while "Secondary" registers are worked as backup information corresponding the previous executed instruction, which used for restoring. The registers information relationship of instruction life time (an instruction between ID stage to EX or WB stage) between "Primary" and "Secondary" is shown in Fig. 3.

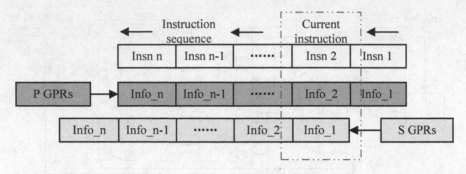

Fig. 3. The information relationship of instruction stream between Primary and Secondary GPRs.

In order to minimize the recovery time, a backup unit with dynamic selection through register label is built, which used to indicate work states of these two groups. If tag = 1, it works as "Primary" registers, else if tag = 0, it works as "Secondary" registers. When an attack is detected, label value is exchanged, and original "Secondary" registers are used as "Primary" registers, the backup information are output for restoring. In the meantime, the original "Primary" registers are used as "Secondary" registers working for storing. If next attack is detected, the process is carried out again. It should be noted that, only one group registers work as normal output, while another is used for storing instruction information corresponding to previous executed instruction.

Consequently, the implement of the proposed unit is given in Fig. 4. GPRs' value is updated from EX or WB stage result, we named this information as write channel, which is input of backup unit. The "Primary" just works as by a bypass channel without any extra process. While "Secondary's input signals are copying of the write channel signals with three clocks delay. Then latches and releases the write channel signal with the delay of three clock cycles according to the current instruction is over or not, signal insn_life_over generated by the GSRTM unit. As shown in Fig. 4, the detection result (signal_strong_warning) decides whether "Primary" registers or "Secondary" registers value should be chosen for output. It should be noted that, the "Primary" or "Secondary" group is decided by a tag, which can guarantee the backup unit would either affect the normal execution of the program or reduce the performance of the embedded processor.

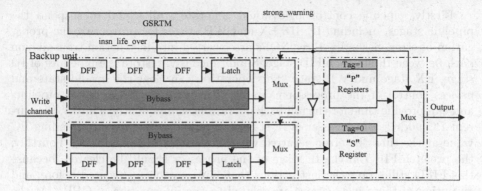

Fig. 4. The implementation of GPRs backup unit.

2.2   The Design and Implement of PC Rollback Unit

The PC rollback unit is similar to program rollback, which is responsible for rolling-back of the exact PC address corresponding to the wrong instruction rather than program checkpoint. Then, utilize the PC address and GPRs information storage in "Secondary" registers to realize fast recovery.

There is an instruction should be processed specially, the STORE instruction stores data from GPRs into a specified location in memory. Thus, if the wrong instruction is STORE, it is necessary to block this instruction from storing memory immediately to ensure that the memory information is corresponding to the previous instruction.

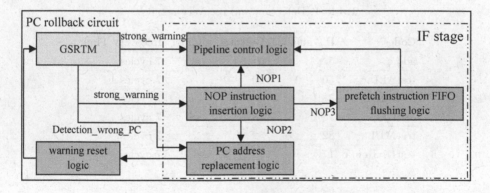

Fig. 5. The implementation of PC rollback unit.

The strong_warning signal is a key signal, which is used to indicate an attack occurs. In order to perform recovery, there are five steps: suspend pipeline, insert NOPs, PC replacement, flushing prefetch FIFO and resetting warning signal. The implementation of PC rollback unit is shown in Fig. 5 which has five logic parts corresponding to the steps mentioned above.

Firstly, pipeline control logic would generate stall signal to suspend the pipeline stages, including IF, ID, EX and WB stages for preventing the propagation of error. Secondly, three NOPs are inserted into instruction transmission path between IF stage and ID stage. Simultaneously, restore the pipelines of ID stage, EX stage and WB stage. This operation can clear the invalid state and useless control of the processor caused by suspending the processor pipeline, and can provide time for the roll back operations subsequently. Thirdly, the current PC address of processor in IF stage is replaced with the corresponding PC value at the time the error occurred when inserting the second NOP. Fourthly, the prefetch FIFO in the IF stage of the processor should be cleared, because this FIFO still stores the instructions that have not been executed before, and execution of these instructions are related to the information of GPRs. At the same time, restoring the pipeline of the IF stage. Lastly, when the instruction prefetched after the PC rollback is detected in the ID stage, it means that the PC rollback recovery has been completed, at the same time reset the warning signal generated by the GSRTM unit.

3   Experimental Results

In order to demonstrate the fast and effectiveness of the proposed method, six programs with different functions were implanted for test, and the test results were shown in Table 1, including number of HT implanted, detection number and recovery time. The experimental results showed that all six programs with 207 HTs had been detected and recovered with the latency of 7 clocks.

Table 1. Detection and recovery results.

Codes	HT number	Detected number	Recovery Time
add.c	5	6	7 cycles
testALU.c	50	50	7 cycles
testClip.c	38	38	7 cycles
testCnt.c	18	18	7 cycles
testMUL.c	82	82	7 cycles
testDivRem.c	17	17	7 cycles

Further, an example, a HT maliciously tampered with x15 of the GPRs, is used to explain the tamper flow which is shown in in Fig. 6. Moreover, the the recovery process which is shown in Fig. 7.

When GPRs are subject to malicious tampering attacks (x15 is changed from 4 to 5, the PC address corresponding to the abnormal moment is 0x0000_041C, and the instruction is 0x0010_0537), the inserted HT attacks can be recovered in real time with the latency of 7 clock cycles, including 2 clock cycles for detection.

The proposed method can realize fast recovery with cycle-level recovery conjunction with detection technology, which has performance improvement compared with the part work in [6],which has at least 100 us sample length for HT detection and more time for analysis and recovery.

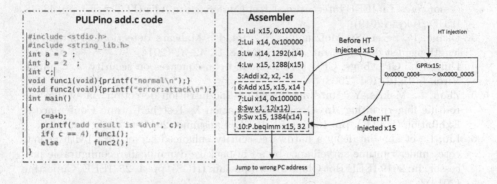

Fig. 6. An example of tamper attack on x15 of GPRs.

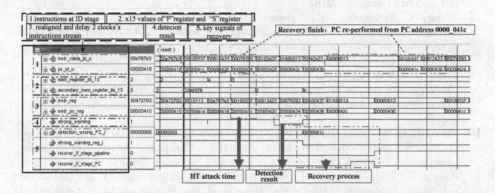

Fig. 7. Simulation wave of HT activated, detection and recovery mechanism.

4   Conclusion

This paper proposes a real-time recovery method after real-time detection, and its implemented way is also given, which has been verified in the RISC-V core of PULpion. The experimental results show that the proposed method can effectively guarantee that processor restored from abnormal state with the latency of 7 clock cycles.

Acknowledgments. This work is partly supported by Sichuan Science and Technology Program under Grant 2021YJ0082. And the authors would like to thank IC Team for providing advice and discussion.

References

1. Bhunia, S., Hsiao, M.-S., Banga, M., Narasimhan, S.: Hardware trojan attacks: threat analysis and countermeasures. In: Proceedings of the IEEE, pp. 1229–1247. IEEE (2014)
2. Kuo, M.-H., Hu, C.-M., Lee, K.-J.: Time-related hardware trojan attacks on processor cores. In: IEEE International Test Conference in Asia (ITC-Asia), pp. 43–48. IEEE, Tokyo (2019)
3. Okane, P., Sezer, S., McLaughlin, K., Im, E.: Malware detection: program run length against detection rate. IET Softw. **8**(1), 42–51 (2014)
4. Duflot, L.: CPU bugs, CPU backdoors and consequences on security. J. Comput. Virol. **5**(2), 91–104 (2008)
5. Zhou, L., Makris, Y.: Hardware-based on-line intrusion detection via system call routine fingerprinting. In: Design, Automation & Test in Europe Conference & Exhibition (DATE), pp. 1546–1551. IEEE, Lausanne (2017)
6. Liu, L., et al.: Jintide®: a hardware security enhanced server CPU with xeon® cores under runtime surveillance by an in-package dynamicall reconfigurable processor. In: 2019 IEEE Hot Chips 31 Symposium (HCS), pp. 1–25. IEEE, Cupertino (2019)
7. Hoque, T., Wang, X., Basak, A., Karam, R., Bhunia, S.: Hardware Trojan attacks in embedded memory. In: 2018 IEEE 36th VLSI Test Symposium (VTS), pp. 1–6. IEEE, San Francisco (2018)
8. Wang, X., Mal-Sarkar, T., Krishna, A., Narasimhan, S., Bhunia, S.: Software exploitable hardware Trojans in embedded processor. In: 2012 IEEE International Symposium on Defect and Fault Tolerance in VLSI and Nanotechnology Systems (DFT), pp. 55–58. IEEE, Austin (2012)
9. Zhao, Y., Wang, X., Jiang, Y., Mei, Y., Singh, A.-K., Mak, T.: On a new hardware Trojan attack on power budgeting of many core systems. In: 31st IEEE International System-on-Chip Conference (SOCC), pp. 1–6. IEEE, Arlington, VA, USA (2018)
10. Zhou, J., Li, M., Guo, P., Liu, W.: Mitigation of tampering attacks for MR-based thermal sensing in optical NoCs. In: 2020 IEEE Computer Society Annual Symposium on VLSI (ISVLSI), pp. 554–559. IEEE, Limassol, Cyprus (2020)
11. Zaraee, N., Zhou, B., Vigil, K., Shahjamali, M., Joshi, A., Selim, Ü.M.: Gate-level validation of integrated circuits with structured-illumination read-out of embedded optical signatures. IEEE Access **8**, 70900–70912 (2020)
12. Chhabra, S., Lata, K.: Key-based Obfuscation using HT-like Trigger Circuit for 128-bit AES Hardware IP Core. In: 34th International System-on-Chip Conference (SOCC), pp. 164–169. IEEE, Las Vegas, NV, USA (2021)
13. Ma, H., et al.: On-chip trust evaluation utilizing TDC-based parameter-adjustable security primitive. IEEE Trans. TCAD **40**(10), 1985–1994 (2021)
14. Lin D, Wu C.: Real-time active tampering detection of surveillance camera and implementation on digital signal processor. In: 2012 Eighth International Conference on Intelligent Information Hiding and Multimedia Signal Processing, pp. 383–386. IEEE, Piraeus-Athens, Greece (2012)
15. Baba Y, Homma N, Miyamoto A, Aoki T.: Design of tamper-resistant registers for multiple-valued cryptographic processors. In: 40th IEEE International Symposium on Multiple-Valued Logic, pp. 67–72. IEEE, Barcelona, Spain (2010)
16. Yang, J., Zhang, Y., Gao, L.: Fast secure processor for inhibiting software piracy and tampering. In: 36th Annual IEEE/ACM International Symposium on Microarchitecture, pp. 351–360. IEEE, San Diego, CA, USA (2003)

17. Bashiri, M., Miremadi, S.-G., Fazeli, M.: A Checkpointing technique for rollback error recovery in embedded systems. In: 2006 International Conference on Microelectronics, pp. 174–177. IEEE, Dhahran, Saudi Arabia (2006)
18. Xu, M., Zhao, H., Li, J., Zhang, H.: Steady rollback and recovery policy based on integrity measurement. In: 2010 IEEE International Conference on Intelligent Computing and Intelligent Systems, pp. 834–836. IEEE, Xiamen (2010)
19. Chen, C.-H., Ting, Y, Heh, J.-S.: Low overhead incremental checkpointing and rollback recovery scheme on windows operating system. In: Third International Conference on Knowledge Discovery and Data Mining, pp. 268–271. IEEE, Phuket, Thailand (2010)
20. Tamir, Y., Tremblay, M.: High-performance fault-tolerant VLSI systems using micro rollback. IEEE Trans. Comput. **39**(4), 548–554 (1990)
21. Slegel, T.-J., et al.: IBM's S/390 G5 microprocessor design. IEEE Micro **19**(2), 12–23 (1999)
22. Sorin, D., Martin, M., Hill, M., Wood, D.: SafetyNet: improving the availability of shared memory multiprocessors with global checkpoint/recovery. In: 29th Annual International Symposium on Computer Architecture, pp. 123–134. IEEE, Anchorage, AK, USA (2002)
23. Salehi, M., Khavari, T.-M., Rehman, S., Shafique, M., Ejlali, A., Henkel, J.: Two-state checkpointing for energy-efficient fault tolerance in hard real-time systems. IEEE Trans. VLSI **24**(7), 2426–2437 (2016)
24. Li, T., Ambrose, J., Parameswaran, S..: RECORD: reducing register traffic for checkpointing in embedded processors. In: 2016 Design, Automation & Test in Europe Conference & Exhibition (DATE), pp. 582–587. IEEE, Dresden, Germany (2016)
25. Do, X., Ha, V., Tran, V., Renault, É.: The technique of locking memory on Linux operating system - application in checkpointing. In: 6th NAFOSTED Conference on Information and Computer Science (NICS), pp. 178–183. IEEE, Hanoi, Vietnam (2019)
26. Wang, X., Zhao, Z., Xu, D., Zhang, Z., Hao, Q., Liu, M.: An M-cache-based security monitoring and fault recovery architecture for embedded processor. IEEE Trans. VLSI **28**(11), 2314–2327 (2020)
27. Chaudhari, A., Park, J., Abraham, J.: A framework for low overhead hardware based runtime control flow error detection and recovery. In: 31st VLSI Test Symposium (VTS), pp. 1–6. IEEE, Berkeley, CA, USA (2013)
28. Huu, N., Robisson, B., Agoyan, M., Drach, N.: Low-cost recovery for the code integrity protection in secure embedded processors. In: 2011 IEEE International Symposium on Hardware-Oriented Security and Trust, pp. 99–104. IEEE, San Diego, CA, USA (2011)
29. Gizopoulos, D., et al.: Architectures for online error detection and recovery in multicore processors. In: 2011 Design, Automation & Test in Europe, pp. 1–6. IEEE, Grenoble, France (2011)
30. Kundu, K., Khan, O.: Efficient error-detection and recovery mechanisms for reliability and resiliency of multicores. In: 29th International Conference on VLSI Design and 2016 15th International Conference on Embedded Systems (VLSID), pp. 12–13. IEEE, Kolkata, India (2016)
31. Zhou, W.-T., Li, L., Yuan, S.-W.: China Patent, vol. 202210262087, pp. 4 (2022)
32. PULpino Datasheet. https://pulp-platform.org/docs/pulpino_datasheet.pdf
33. PULpino Project. https://github.com/pulpplatform/pulpino
34. Yuan, S.-W., Li, L., He, Y.-H., Zhou, W.-T., Li, J.: Real-time detection of hardware trojan attacks on general-Purpose Registers in a RISC-V processor. IEICE Electron. Express **18**(10), 1–3 (2021)

MIA-Leak: Exploring Membership Inference Attacks in Federated Learning Systems

Chengcheng Zhu, Jiale Zhang[✉][iD], Xiang Cheng, Weitong Chen,
and Xiaobing Sun

School of Information Engineering, Yangzhou University, Yangzhou 225009, China
mx120220554@stu.yzu.edu.cn, {jialezhang,wtchen,xbsun}@yzu.edu.cn

Abstract. Federated learning has achieved significant success in both academia and industry scenarios since it can train a joint model among unbalanced datasets while protecting the training data privacy. Recent research has shown that, by inferring whether a given data record belongs to the model's training dataset, the membership information could be leaked by malicious participants. However, when deploying member inference attacks in federated learning, the core problem is how to obtain the membership inference attack data with the same distribution as the training data. In this paper, to tackle this problem, we mainly focus on exploring membership inference attacks in federated learning based on the data augmentation method. Specifically, we present two types of membership inference attacks based on the generative adversarial nets, in which a class-level attack aims to infer the global model and a user-level attack tries to focus on a specific victim. We conduct extensive experiments to evaluate the effectiveness of our proposed two types of membership inference attacks on two benchmark datasets. The experimental results have shown that both class-level and user-level attacks can achieve extraordinary attack accuracy on federated learning.

Keywords: Federated learning · Membership inference · Generative adversarial nets · Privacy leakage

1 Introduction

To prevent privacy leakage, federated learning has been introduced into distributed computing systems due to its specific privacy-preserving structure,

This work is partially supported by the National Natural Science Foundation of China (62206238), Natural Science Foundation of Jiangsu Province (Grant No. BK20220562), Natural Science Foundation of Jiangsu Higher Education Institutions of China (Grant No. 22KJB520010), Future Network Scientific Research Fund Project (FNSRFP-2021-YB-47), Yangzhou City-Yangzhou University Science and Technology Cooperation Fund Project (YZ2021158).

W. Meng and W. Li (Eds.): BlockTEA 2022, LNICST 498, pp. 140–154, 2023.
https://doi.org/10.1007/978-3-031-31420-9_9

where the central server trains a joint global model via uploaded gradients from participants instead of the raw data [1–3]. Unlike the traditional centralized distributed computing system which aggregates raw data from participants, federated learning distributes the training models to local devices, and only transmits the parameters between the central server and participants to update the global model [4]. Hence, data privacy can be large extend preserved, while participants keep their local datasets on their own end.

However, recent researches reveal that the federated learning framework is vulnerable to various inference attacks, such as membership inference [5], representatives inference [6], properties inference [7], and gradients inference [8]. Among these inference attacks, membership inference is one of the most powerful active attacks against private training datasets. Shokri et al. [9] first proposed the membership inference attack against machine learning models through a black-box API, which reveals the fact that membership information can be leaked by distinguishing the difference between model predictions from training and non-training inputs. Notably, the purpose of membership inference attacks is to determine whether a certain data sample is used to train the model (Fig. 1).

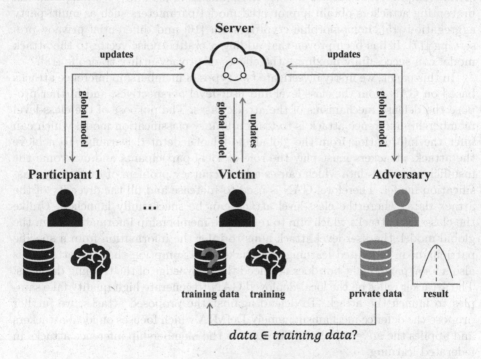

Fig. 1. Membership inference attack in federated learning.

Membership inference attacks are ongoing threats to the data of participants in federated learning, which lead to user privacy leakage issues [10]. For example, a membership inference attack can be initialized by an attacker who aims to reveal the medical records of specific patients [11]. To initial certain attacks, the attacker train a binary model and take the confidence score vector of the Victims as input [9]. In federated learning, the attacker may play the role of a benign participant or central server to perform the attacks. The attackers can either join the federated learning as a participant to observe the latest model parameters from the server and perform the membership inference attacks or play the server role to collect the parameters uploaded from participants to modify the model [12]. The user data is exposed to attackers in either scenario, where existing defense mechanisms have little effect on membership inference attacks.

Therefore, the defense mechanism on membership inference attacks attracts more attention in the research area. It is worth noticing that Generative adversarial networks (GAN) could be the reason for the recent success of membership inference attacks [13]. GAN is designed and widely applied in the computer vision area due to its excellent data augmentation features. By using the discriminator and generator in GAN, attackers may leverage the parameters from the training models to generate the fake samples or obtain the data from other participants which has the same distribution in the training dataset [14]. State-of-the-art membership inference attack defense mechanisms in federated learning focus on preventing attackers obtain unprotected model parameters such as multi-party aggregation [15], homomorphic cryptosystem [16] and differential privacy preserving [17]. It has been proven that adding a crafted noise vector to the attack model can successfully maximize the effects of privacy-utility tradeoffs [18].

In this paper, we firstly investigate two types of membership inference attacks based on GAN from the class-level and user-level perspectives, and further propose the defense mechanisms of the attack cases. The purpose of the class-level membership inference attack is to train a binary classification model which can infer the information from the global model of federated learning. To achieve the attack, attackers must play the role of local participants and overcome the insufficient attack data which causes a low accuracy problem of the binary classification model. Therefore, GAN is used to increase and fill the diversity of the attack data, where the class-level attack can be successfully launched. Unlike the class-level attacks which aim to reveal the membership information from the global model, the user-level attack aims to infer the information from a specific participant in federated learning. We make an assumption that the attacker is also a local participant but does not need the knowledge of the training datasets. The attacker relies on the local-deployed GAN to generate high-quality fake samples to launch the attack. To defend against the proposed attacks, we further propose the defence mechanism namely DefMIA which focuses on local attackers and applies the adversarial samples against the membership inference attacks in federated learning.

The main contributions of this paper are as follows.

- We first demonstrate that constructing membership inference attacks in federated learning faced the problem of lacking attack training data. Then, we point out that GAN is a promising technology to generate fake samples with the same distributions as participants' training data.

- We present two types of membership inference attacks, in which class-level attack aims to attack the global model and user-level aims to attack the specific victim. We explore the weakness point of the current federated learning and initialize the attacks which are enhanced by GAN. We prove that both of the attacks are efficient and can achieve excellent accuracy when attacking federated learning.
- Exhaustive experimental evaluations on two benchmark datasets show that both class-level and user-level attacks achieve extraordinary attack accuracy on federated learning. However, the attack accuracy reduced dramatically after we explore the DefMIA method in the federated learning system.

The rest of this paper is organized as follows. Section 2 reviews the related works. The membership inference attacks in federated learning are analyzed in Sect. 3. Follow by the experiment and evaluation in Sect. 4. Finally, Sect. 5 summaries the whole paper and gives future directions.

2 Related Work

2.1 Attacks in Federated Learning

Compared to traditional machine learning approaches, federated learning does not require participants to upload their local raw data to the central server. Therefore, federated learning has its native advantage of privacy-preserving, where participants only need to upload the parameters of their local trained model to the central server [19]. Although federated learning can efficiently handle unbalanced data while protecting training data privacy, security issues still exist. Firstly, the central server does not know the local training data, hence, the server cannot verify the uploaded parameters are correct or not. Furthermore, parameters can be easily leaked by the malicious server or external adversaries, which leads to privacy leaking problems.

Attackers target the aforementioned drawbacks in federated learning, and launch the different types of attacks such as model inversion attack [20], poisoning attack [21,22], and adversarial attack [23]. The types attack can be classified by different purposes, which are confidentiality, integrity, and availability [24]. The purpose of confidentiality is to protect the sensitive data from users. Confidentiality attacks are not only trying to steal the local training data, but also trying to expose the privacy data or infer the training models [3]. Attackers in confidentiality attacks will not interfere the training progress and the training models, they just act like participants to initialize the attacks. Integrity attacks aims to destroy the model outputs by poisoning the model. Typical integrity attacks such as label-flipping [25] and backdoor attack [26], which mislead the target model to a specific direction which given by the attackers [27]. Availability attack aims to attack the availability in classification including errors, false positives and false negatives [28]. The main purpose of availability attack is to make the target model in federated learning unusable.

2.2   Membership Inference

Membership inference refers to attacks on machine learning models to determine the certain data is from the training set or not [11]. Membership inference attacks can target both traditional machine learning and federated learning which is a severe security threat to user information [29]. For traditional machine learning membership inference attacks, Shokri et al. [9] designed a shadow model which can simulate the target model to give results. Additionally, attackers also set up a testing dataset that has the same distribution as the training dataset to train the inference model.

Membership inference against federated learning systems has been introduced by Nasr et al. [12]. The attackers can either play the role of server who collects the uploaded parameters from participants or play the role of participants to obtain the aggregated models. Attackers also can launch the attacks actively, where the malicious server and participants can generate adversary data to realize the attacks [2].

2.3   Defense Proposals

Previous researches on attacks show that federated learning is vulnerable to membership inference attacks, where the adversarial example can mislead the prediction results of the attack models [30]. To defend the adversarial attacks, MemGuard [18] is proposed, which applies formal utility-loss guarantees to defend membership inference attacks under the black-box setting. The carefully designed noise has been added into the confidence score vector of the model, where the attack models can be misleading to a random result. In summary, Federated learning is vulnerable to membership inference attacks since the parameters can be easily observed by malicious participants. To tackle this problem, the proposed DefMIA adds the crafted noises to the model, where the main challenge is to restrict the loss of the target model in multiple training iterations.

3   Membership Inference Attacks in Federated Learning

3.1   Threat Models

Adversary's Objectives. The objective of the threat model is to obtain indirect information about the target models. Therefore, the classification task of the threat model will be measured by the following metrics: 1) membership inference accuracy: which is the performance of the classification on the target dataset; 2) main task accuracy: which represents the performance of the global model of the federated learning. The threat model expects to achieve the high performance of the membership inference accuracy and keep the high performance of the main task accuracy.

Adversary's Observations. The threat model will be set under a white-box setting, where the adversary observes can initialize the inference attack. The attacker can observe the latest model which the server distributed to every participant each iteration in federated learning. Therefore, the attack obtains every detail of the distributed global model, including structure, learning algorithm L, and the parameter θ of the model. This information can be used to train a GAN to generate the samples and initialize the membership inference attack.

Adversary's Capabilities. The capabilities of the adversary will be listed in this part. The adversary can: 1) obtaining details of the global model for each training iteration, 2) controlling the local training and local data as a participant, 3) modifying the hyper-parameters of the model, 4) updating the select parameters randomly. But cannot: 1) observing the parameters from other participants because the global model averaging all the uploaded gradients on the server, 2) accessing the data from other participants.

3.2   Case1: Class-Level Attack

Overview of Attack. The goal of the class-level attack is to wreak the confidentiality of the models and obtain the membership information, where the attacker plays the role of a participant in federated learning and passively trains the attack model. The attack model will be considered as a white-box setting to the attacker since it can observe all the model structures and gradients of each layer of the model. Based on the aforementioned white-box setting, the attacker joins the federated learning as a participant in the proposed class-level attack method, where the attacker train a binary classification model with GAN-generated data to distinguish members from non-members in the training data. To achieve this target, We propose a two-phase GAN enhanced membership inference attack, which includes data augmentation and attack model training phases.

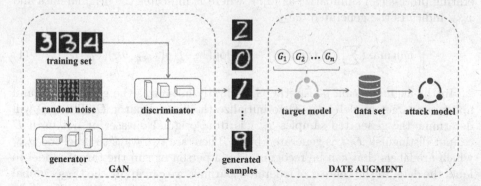

Fig. 2. Class-level membership inference attack in federated learning.

Figure 2 illustrates the architecture of the class-level membership inference attack in federated learning. We leverage the true labels and prediction results from the target model to train the attack model, where the attack model can learn the distribution of prediction to distinguish members from non-members of the target model. We define $f_{target}()$ as the target model, and D_{target}^{train} as the training set of the target model, where the labeled data $(x\{i\}, y\{i\})_{target}$ belongs to D_{target}^{train}. ($x\{i\}$ represents the target model input, and $(y\{i\}$ represents the true label of $(x\{i\}$ which is from the label classes c_{target}. The prediction of target model $Y = f_{target}(x)$ is computed and applied to train the attack model, due to Y is highly dependent on the true label. Therefore, the attack model can distinguish that if the data is from the training dataset of the target model or not.

However, the lack of diversity in D_{target}^{train} is challenging. The attacker only has limited data as a participant, and a data augmentation model is designed to overcome the challenge which uses GAN to generate new data. In the data augmentation phase, the GAN sets the target model as the discriminator and generates new data which follows the same distribution as the original training set. The enhanced dataset will be used to train the attack model which will have the capacity to launch the membership inference attack with high inference accuracy.

Augment Training Data with GAN. We apply GAN to overcome the problem of low training data diversity in class-level attacks, which can generate the extra data x_{gen} with the same distribution of original data. We will detail the GAN in this part with model structure and augmentation progress. As shown in Fig. 2, the generator G is initialized by a random noise $g(z; \theta_G)$, in the meantime, the discriminator D is initialized by the target federated learning model $f(x; \theta_D)$. The goal of the GAN is to generate the data to increase the training set which shares the same distribution of the original data. Hence, the discriminator will lead the generator to generate the training data. After certain training iterations, the quality generated data x_{gen} is close to the original data. The generating process can summarize as Eq. 1, where x_i indicates the original data and x_{gen} indicates the generated data.

$$\min_{\theta_G} \max_{\theta_D} (\sum_{i=1}^{n_+} \log f(x_i; \theta_D) + \sum_{j=1}^{n_-} \log(1 - f(g(x_{gen}; \theta_G); \theta_D))) \tag{1}$$

In the augmentation phase, the GAN firstly initializes the generator G and apply the target model $f_{target}()$ to initialize the discriminator D. Then, D will determine the generated samples x_{gen} is from original dataset or not until D cannot distinguish x_{gen} is generated by G. There are two ways to label the x_{gen} which are labels that can be recognized by a person or run the target model to label the data. In the context of federated learning, we can apply the target global model to label the generated samples x_{gen} easily. In the classification phase, the original data and generated data are combined as one training dataset to train the attack model.

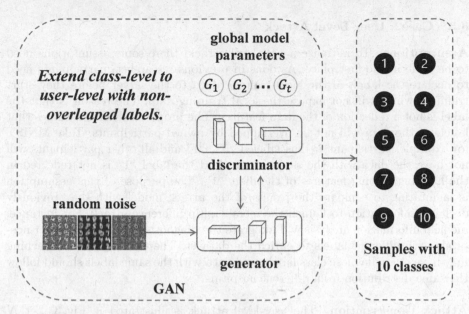

Fig. 3. User-level membership inference attack in federated learning.

Train Attack Model. The object of the attack model is leveraging the GAN to reveal the data distribution of the target model and apply the generated data to train the attack model. As shown in Fig. 2, the training data is integrated by original and generated data after the data augmentation phase. The integrated data includes predictions, true labels, and member states, which will be learnt by the attack model. The final training data of the attack model $x\{i\}_{attack}$ consists of prediction, true label and two attributes "in" or "out" which indicates a member or non-member of the target model.

According to GAN, we query the predictions Y from D_{target}^{train}. Then, the dataset D_{target}^{gen} with $(record, label)$ will be generated. Therefore, the enriched training set D_{target}^{train} is the combination of D_{target}^{ori} and D_{target}^{gen}.

The object of the classification model is the classify the member state through the distribution of prediction around the true label. Therefore, the GAN enhanced membership inference attack model is trained based on the labels. We further divide training dataset D_{attack}^{train} into n categories, where $f_{attack}()$ represents the attack mode and the input of the model x_{attack} is $(y, Y, in/out)$. Each category will be used to train one attack model, where the attack model can classify the membership state for giving a certain data record. The reasons for launching a successful membership inference attack are generalizability and training data diversity, where GAN is a good way to increase the diversity due to the outstanding performance on data augmentation.

3.3 Case2: User-Level Attack

Assumptions. To initialize a user-level attack, there some assumptions need to be done in the first place. As done in previous researches, participants need to declare the labels of the local training data to the server before they start training, which will not expose the local training data. The reason is that the label is not a reflection of the data features. The proposed scheme assumes that labels of the data will not be overlapped by owned participants. Take MNIST for example, participant P_1 has labeled "0", "1" and all other participants will not have the data with the same labels. And the label "1" is not reflected in the handing writing features of the digit "1". The purpose of this assumption is facilitating to compare the results of the attack model with the previously declared information to launch the membership inference attack. For instance, medical information analysis will integrate the diagnosis data from different hospitals with different labels to enrich the dataset. Therefore, federated learning may have more diagnose class labels, and data with the same labels should follow the same distribution from different hospitals.

Attack Construction. The user-level attack is illustrated in Fig. 3. Let N participants join the federate learning, and V represents the victim. A represents the attacker who also join the federated learning as a participant. After k training iterations, A and V have the same global model with parameter θ_d downloaded from the central server. Normally, A and V will use the global model and local data to training a new local model, and upload the updated parameters θ_u to the server. The federated learning central server will firstly average all the parameter updates from all participants, then update the global model. Therefore, it is hard for A to launch the membership inference on the V directly. We take the same structure of GAN in Sect. 3.2, where the θ_d is used to train the discriminator D, and generator G can generate the fake data which similar to real data. We use the generated data to train a binary classifier, once we obtained the target dataset, the classifier can predict the result as "in" which means the results are consistent with the declaration information, otherwise mark as "out". As shown in Fig. 3, we train the classifier with the generated data with all labels. As we described in Sect. 3.2, we can choose inference algorithm after analyzing the generated data. In our experiment, we choose MNIST as dataset and CNN as the classifier.

4   Experimental Evaluation

This section firstly introduce the dataset and experimental setup, then we evaluate the performance of class-level attacks, user-level attack and defense methods.

4.1   Datasets and Experimental Setup

Dataset. We apply two famous datasets MNIST and Fashion MNIST to evaluate our experiment.

MNIST is a handwritten digits dataset that consists of 60000 training data and 10000 testing data from digits "0" to "9". Each image is a 28 × 28 image with white text on black background [31].

Fashion MNIST (F-MNIST) is a Zalando's article images dataset which consists of 60,000 training data and 10000 testing data with 10 classes of clothes, pants, and shoes, etc. Each example is also a 28 × 28 grayscale image [32].

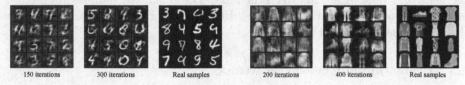

(a) Reconstructed samples of MNIST dataset   (b) Reconstructed samples of F-MNIST dataset

Fig. 4. Data reconstruction results on MNIST and F-MNIST datasets based on GAN.

Experimental Setup. All the experiments are conducted on an Ubuntu 16.04 Linux server with 32 GB RAM and NVidia Quadro P4000 GPU. All the codes are written under Python 3.6 with Pytorch and Tensorflow with Keras framework.

Class-Level Attack Configuration: We set 100 participants in federated learning, and each of them has 60 MNIST samples. The participants will train 10 epochs and the learning rate is set to 0.001.

User-Level Attack Configuration: We apply a basic CNN model for the membership inference model on both datasets. The model of MNIST includes two convolutional layers and two dense layers. The kernel size is set to 5 × 5. The model for F-MNIST has four convolutional layers and the kernel size is set to 3 × 3. Each participant will train MNIST for 30 epochs and the learning rate is 0.01. For F-MNIST, each participant will train 60 epochs with a learning rate of 0.0001. All the experiments are run for 400 communication rounds of federated learning.

Defense Configuration: The number of participants of the target federated learning model is set to five, one of the participants is considered as an attacker. Each of the participants has 12000 training samples and train the model for 10 epochs with a learning rate of 0.01. The class-level and user-level attack models will be implemented in the experiment. The settings of the defense model are based on the white-box scenario, and we assume that the defense model does not share the same network structure as the attack models.

4.2   Effectiveness of Data Augmentation

To evaluate the effectiveness of the data augmentation by using GAN in federated learning. The reconstruction process is being monitored, where the number of participants and samples remains unchanged. The generator G will generate the samples with 100 lengths and reshape them to 28×28. The generator will start to generate samples when the accuracy of the global model reaches 0.93.

Figure 4 shows that sample visualization during different iterations. The comparison of the reconstruction results between 150 iterations, 300 iterations, and original samples of the MNIST dataset are shown on the left, and the reconstruction results between 200 iterations, 400 iterations, and original samples of the F-MNIST dataset are shown on the right. The generated samples are getting more clear once the iteration increases. Hence, GAN can successfully simulate the original samples of all participants.

4.3 Evaluation of Class-Level Attack

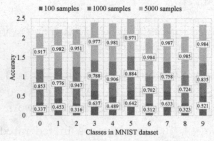

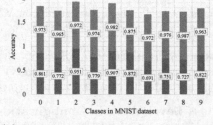

(a) Performance under different generated data size

(b) Performance under different learning epochs

Fig. 5. Evaluation results of class-level inference attack under different variables.

The performance of the class-level attack is measured by prediction accuracy and recall metrics. The prediction accuracy represents the attack accuracy directly, and the coverage of the attack method is measured by the recall. To evaluate the prediction accuracy, the training set and testing set have been reshuffled to train and test the attack model. We also set the random conjecture accuracy as 0.5 for comparison purposes. Table 1 shows the performance of the proposed membership inference attack model. By increasing the training set from 100 samples to 5000 samples, the proposed membership inference attack achieves 97.63% test accuracy on the MNIST dataset, and the recall is 88.36% We also use the F1 score to measure the ability of classification. The result shows that the F1 score reaches 0.94, which means the proposed attack method has good generalization and membership inference capability.

Figure 5(a) shows how the different size of training data affects the prediction of membership inference attack method on each class of MNIST dataset. Results show that the overall accuracy is 52.9% when the attacker only has 100 data samples. However, the accuracy has increased dramatically to 97.9% after the training set is reached 1000s samples. To explore how the impact of the

Table 1. Performance of class-level inference attack

Attack Accuracy	Recall Ratio	F1 Score
97.63%	88.36%	0.94

settings of the target model affects the accuracy of the proposed attach model, we implement experiments on different learning epochs. Figure 5b show that the attack accuracy of 100 epochs is much higher than 10 epochs, and the attack precision is close to 1, which means overfitting could lead to the model being more vulnerable to membership inference attacks.

4.4 Evaluation of User-Level Attack

According to Fig. 6(a), the accuracy of models achieves 99.45% and 93.71% on MNIST and F-MNIST, respectively, which is high enough to complete all the classification tasks on the testing dataset. In the meantime, the attacker also generates enough samples via a local deployed GAN to train the attack model. After the membership inference attack, we further measure the attack effectiveness from the label point of view. Figure 6(b) shows the attack effectiveness on the two datasets, where TP represents the true positive and FN represents the false negative. We compare the number of classes held by each participant, and we assume that the victim has more than one class of the dataset, which may affect the membership inference. We compare the effectiveness of membership inference between different numbers of classes held by the victim, where the effectiveness of the attack model getting worse the more classes held by the victim.

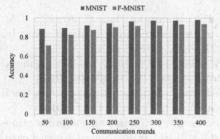

(a) Performance of benchmark federated learning

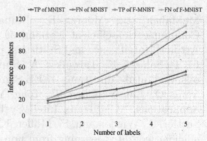

(b) Performance of user-level inference attack

Fig. 6. Evaluation results of benchmark federated learning and user-level inference attack.

To elaborate on the advantage of the proposed user-level attack, we compare our user-level attack with the active inference attacks using the SGA algorithm proposed by Nasr et al. [12]. The attack accuracy of SGA can reach about 76% on the F-MNIST dataset, which is close to our experiment settings while the victim holds just one class of the data of F-MNIST. However, the novelty of our user-level attack is the attack objective. Nasr et al. [12] claim that their attack methods against all the participants in federated learning, which means their attack only aim the whole training set. However, the proposed user-level attack method can launch an inference attack on a specific victim who joins the federated learning.

5   Summary and Future Work

In this paper, we give a comprehensive study on exploring membership inference attacks and mitigation methods in federated learning systems. We firstly proposed two types of membership inference attacks based on GAN, which are class-level attack and user-level attack. For class-level attack, GAN is used to increase and fill the diversity of the attack data, so as to increase the accuracy of the binary classification attack model. For user-level attack, it aims to infer the membership information from a specific participant, which is a more deep-level attack method. The experimental results have shown that both class-level and user-level attacks can achieve extraordinary attack accuracy on federated learning. In future work, we plan to explore the membership inference attacks in an untrusted federated learning environment, where a part of participants tries to jeopardize the global model through poisoned local model updates. In this situation, how to guarantee the attack accuracy of inferring the membership information of certain data records is becoming a big challenge.

References

1. McMahan, B., Moore, E., Ramage, D., Hampson, S., y Arcas, B.A.: Communication-efficient learning of deep networks from decentralized data. In: Artificial Intelligence and Statistics, pp. 1273–1282. PMLR (2017)
2. Li, T., Sahu, A.K., Talwalkar, A., Smith, V.: Federated learning: challenges, methods, and future directions. IEEE Signal Process. Mag. 37(3), 50–60 (2020)
3. Yang, Q., Liu, Y., Chen, T., Tong, Y.: Federated machine learning: concept and applications. ACM Trans. Intell. Syst. Technol. (TIST) 10(2), 1–19 (2019)
4. Sattler, F., Wiedemann, S., Müller, K.R., Samek, W.: Robust and communication-efficient federated learning from non-IID data. IEEE Trans. Neural Netw. Learn. Syst. 31(9), 3400–3413 (2019)
5. Truex, S., Liu, L., Gursoy, M.E., Yu, L., Wei, W.: Demystifying membership inference attacks in machine learning as a service. IEEE Trans. Serv. Comput. 14, 2073–2089 (2019)
6. Wang, Z., Song, M., Zhang, Z., Song, Y., Wang, Q., Qi, H.: Beyond inferring class representatives: user-level privacy leakage from federated learning. In: IEEE INFOCOM 2019-IEEE Conference on Computer Communications, pp. 2512–2520. IEEE (2019)

7. Melis, L., Song, C., De Cristofaro, E., Shmatikov, V.: Exploiting unintended feature leakage in collaborative learning. In: 2019 IEEE Symposium on Security and Privacy (SP), pp. 691–706. IEEE (2019)
8. Zhu, L., Liu, Z., Han, S.: Deep leakage from gradients. Adv. Neural. Inf. Process. Syst. **32**, 14774–14784 (2019)
9. Shokri, R., Stronati, M., Song, C., Shmatikov, V.: Membership inference attacks against machine learning models. In: 2017 IEEE Symposium on Security and Privacy (SP), pp. 3–18. IEEE (2017)
10. Chen, J., Zhang, J., Zhao, Y., Han, H., Zhu, K., Chen, B.: Beyond model-level membership privacy leakage: an adversarial approach in federated learning. In: 2020 29th International Conference on Computer Communications and Networks (ICCCN), pp. 1–9. IEEE (2020)
11. Hayes, J., Melis, L., Danezis, G., De Cristofaro, E.: LOGAN: membership inference attacks against generative models. arXiv preprint arXiv:1705.07663 (2017)
12. Nasr, M., Shokri, R., Houmansadr, A.: Comprehensive privacy analysis of deep learning: passive and active white-box inference attacks against centralized and federated learning. In: 2019 IEEE Symposium on Security and Privacy (SP), pp. 739–753. IEEE (2019)
13. Goodfellow, I., et al.: Generative adversarial nets. Adv. Neural Inf. Process. Syst. **27** (2014)
14. Qu, Y., Yu, S., Zhang, J., Binh, H.T.T., Gao, L., Zhou, W.: GAN-DP: generative adversarial net driven differentially privacy-preserving big data publishing. In: ICC 2019–2019 IEEE International Conference on Communications (ICC), pp. 1–6. IEEE (2019)
15. Jónsson, K.V., Kreitz, G., Uddin, M.: Secure multi-party sorting and applications. IACR Cryptol. ePrint Arch. **2011**, 122 (2011)
16. Aono, Y., Hayashi, T., Wang, L., Moriai, S., et al.: Privacy-preserving deep learning via additively homomorphic encryption. IEEE Trans. Inf. Forensics Secur. **13**(5), 1333–1345 (2017)
17. Abadi, M., et al.: Deep learning with differential privacy. In: Proceedings of the 2016 ACM SIGSAC Conference on Computer and Communications Security, pp. 308–318 (2016)
18. Jia, J., Salem, A., Backes, M., Zhang, Y., Gong, N.Z.: MemGuard: defending against black-box membership inference attacks via adversarial examples. In: Proceedings of the 2019 ACM SIGSAC Conference on Computer and Communications Security, pp. 259–274 (2019)
19. Zhou, Y., Ye, Q., Lv, J.C.: Communication-efficient federated learning with compensated overlap-FedAvg. IEEE Trans. Parallel Distrib. Syst. **33**, 192–205 (2021)
20. Fredrikson, M., Jha, S., Ristenpart, T.: Model inversion attacks that exploit confidence information and basic countermeasures. In: Proceedings of the 22nd ACM SIGSAC Conference on Computer and Communications Security, pp. 1322–1333 (2015)
21. Yang, C., Wu, Q., Li, H., Chen, Y.: Generative poisoning attack method against neural networks. arXiv preprint arXiv:1703.01340 (2017)
22. Zhang, J., Chen, J., Wu, D., Chen, B., Yu, S.: Poisoning attack in federated learning using generative adversarial nets. In: 2019 18th IEEE International Conference On Trust, Security And Privacy In Computing And Communications/13th IEEE International Conference On Big Data Science And Engineering (TrustCom/BigDataSE), pp. 374–380. IEEE (2019)
23. Lyu, L., Yu, H., Yang, Q.: Threats to federated learning: a survey. arXiv preprint arXiv:2003.02133 (2020)

24. Proudfoot, D.: Anthropomorphism and AI: turing's much misunderstood imitation game. Artif. Intell. **175**(5-6), 950957 (2011)
25. Zhang, J., Chen, B., Cheng, X., Binh, H.T.T., Yu, S.: PoisonGAN: generative poisoning attacks against federated learning in edge computing systems. IEEE Internet Things J. **8**(5), 3310–3322 (2020)
26. Bagdasaryan, E., Veit, A., Hua, Y., Estrin, D., Shmatikov, V.: How to backdoor federated learning. In: International Conference on Artificial Intelligence and Statistics, pp. 2938–2948. PMLR (2020)
27. Xu, G., Li, H., Liu, S., Yang, K., Lin, X.: VerifyNet: secure and verifiable federated learning. IEEE Trans. Inf. Forensics Secur. **15**, 911–926 (2019)
28. Lu, Y., Huang, X., Dai, Y., Maharjan, S., Zhang, Y.: Blockchain and federated learning for privacy-preserved data sharing in industrial IoT. IEEE Trans. Industr. Inf. **16**(6), 4177–4186 (2019)
29. Salem, A., Zhang, Y., Humbert, M., Berrang, P., Fritz, M., Backes, M.: ML-leaks: model and data independent membership inference attacks and defenses on machine learning models. arXiv preprint arXiv:1806.01246 (2018)
30. Nguyen, A., Yosinski, J., Clune, J.: Deep neural networks are easily fooled: high confidence predictions for unrecognizable images. In: Proceedings of the IEEE Conference on Computer Vision and Pattern Recognition, pp. 427–436 (2015)
31. Deng, L.: The MNIST database of handwritten digit images for machine learning research [best of the web]. IEEE Signal Process. Mag. **29**(6), 141–142 (2012)
32. Xiao, H., Rasul, K., Vollgraf, R.: Fashion-MNIST: a novel image dataset for benchmarking machine learning algorithms. arXiv preprint arXiv:1708.07747 (2017)

SoK: Can NFTs Solve the Economic Problems of Countries with Ancient Heritage? Egypt as a Case Study

Shymaa Arafat[✉]

Computer Science and Engineering, Cairo, Egypt
shymaa.arafat@gmail.com, shar.academic@gmail.com

Abstract. A lot of research has been done on the debatable role cryptocurrencies can play in developing countries; in this paper we look from a different angle at NFTs. We believe that NFTs, especially with MetaVerses, came as a bless to nations with ancient heritage that attract tourists. Online tourism existed from the year 2000, and nowadays with COVID-19 travelling restrictions along with the advance of VR/AR/XR museum tours many projects are there and gained satisfaction. In this paper we propose and analyze the merit of adding the NFT component to this recipe; NFTs of museum pieces can be sold for money, and NFT games can be made based on historical stories or famous characters. There is also the use of NFTs inside Metaverses whether by selling country original NFTs on existing ones like brands do, or by building special Metaverses of ancient civilizations and places like the Red Sea with its rare coral reefs; we trace similar starting projects around the world. Then we discuss the challenges and design decisions involved in the development cycle of such projects, including Blockchain choice, auction & pricing mechanisms, economical analysis; also NFT copyrights problems and Metaverses security risks along with the newest available and under research solutions. We end the journey with the conclusion that NFTs & Metaverses can monetize the country's heritage without selling the physical assets, and will promote research and education of human resources as a bonus advantage.

Keywords: NFT · Metaverse · Blockchains · tourism economics · cryptocurrency · security & privacy · developing countries

1 Countries and Cryptocurrencies

With the emergence of cryptocurrencies, especially at the prices rise up time of Bitcoin and Ethereum, a lot of developing countries thought that mining crypto can provide them with an economic boost like it enriched some people [1]; many voices inside developing countries see crypto as a gate to escape poverty and connect equally with the

W. Meng and W. Li (Eds.): BlockTEA 2022, LNICST 498, pp. 155–175, 2023.
https://doi.org/10.1007/978-3-031-31420-9_10

developed world [2] and thus encourage governments to do so [3–5][1]. As for developed countries the USA, which was the origin of Bitcoin & Ethereum, there are more than 8000 Bitcoin ATM by the end of 2020 [6]; the government of Fort Worth in Texas did started mining recently [7]. Other countries created their own digital currency [8]; from the middle east Tunisia created eDinar[2], according to [9], Egypt, UAE, and Israel had some thoughts. Then with the popularity of individuals usage of cryptocurrencies, where there are no law regulations along with the anonymity nature of blockchains could hide a lot of money laundering, criminal, or against-government activities, a lot of governments became repulsive and took an offensive position against cryptocurrencies [10^3 –12]. Other countries took a conceptual risk by adopting Bitcoin as their main currency which led to dramatic losses [13, 14]. In fact, most of the described experiment failure reasons contradicts with the *Financial Inclusion* incentives described in[2]; dealing with digital wallets is not easier than holding bank accounts, and doesn't necessarily measured by possessing smart phones. All those economic factors on developing countries have been studied extensively in the literature [2, 6, 15, 16]; a side note in [17] about *"currency inconvertibility problems"* between African countries that plagued trading for long times and could be solved by using a cryptocurrency, is worth mentioning. We here clarify that all the above is not the scope of this paper, we avoid those controversy risk vs return crypto usages, and concentrate on different cultural and entertainment uses of *NFTs* [18] that will be detailed in what follows.

2   Countries and NFTs

In November 2021, a European Parliament report about NFTs [19] stated that *"NFTs might act as a boost to support the creator economy. NFTs are highly innovative technologies, with a clear market value proposition, which might nurture a new techno-cultural movement. It is recommended that the EU supports NFTs through European projects aimed to promote culture, arts, and youth creativity. Generally, a clear European policy regarding NFTs will support entrepreneurs to choose EU member states as their base, while supporting the creation of new jobs in the EU"*. In this section we will explore different countries and institutional uses of NFTs.

---

[1] We even believe the electricity needed for crypto mining in Ethiopia may have changed the valuation of different cards in the Game Theory model of the Nile Basin conflict of interests towards GERD at some moments; agriculture water was the most important in the introduction of (https://www.academia.edu/15471274/A_Game_Theory_Approach_to_Understanding_the_Nile_River_Basin_Conflict), while electricity is the dominant factor in recent statements (https://twitter.com/FdreService/status/1557674864454078464).

[2] We found conflicting news about Tunisia: a negating fact checking site (https://misbar.com/en/factcheck/2022/05/25/tunisia-did-not-pioneer-the-use-of-cryptocurrency-and-blockchain), the early launching of eDinar (https://cointelegraph.com/news/tunisia-to-launch-e-dinar-national-currency-using-blockchain), the Finance minister statement: (https://www.coindesk.com/policy/2021/06/14/tunisian-finance-minister-says-bitcoin-ownership-should-be-decriminalized/). However, this is beyond the scope of this paper focusing on Egypt.

[3] Malaysia didn't prevent trading, only mining & what they described as illicit activities (https://www.malaymail.com/news/malaysia/2022/02/21/malaysias-illegal-crypto-mining-reaches-an-all-time-high-in-2021/2042862.)

Existing governmental and institutional uses of NFTs include holding health or educational records. Ethiopia 5 million child educational NFT records on the Cardano Blockchain is an example [17, 20, 21] list different universities and professors in USA, China, and South Korea that use NFTs to hold students results; the first DeFi MOOC course offered by Berkeley University in Aug 2021 has just offered students success NFT badges [22].

The use of NFTs to collect donations money has been widely adopted by NGOs and universities [23–25], and even countries recently [26]. There were some rejecting voices from environmental activists earlier [27] due to the carbon inflation environmental harm from the very high energy consumption in *Proof of Work (POW)* blockchains, however this has not become a problem anymore. Lately, a Crypto Climate Accord has been signed which seeks to decarbonizing the cryptocurrency and blockchain industry and achieve net-zero greenhouse gas emissions by 2040 through different solutions [28]. *Proof of Stake (POS)* blockchains with their low energy consumption is the current dominant solution; in 2021 [29] conducted a comperative study of energy consumption between POW blockchains, different POS systems and more. As for now in 3rd quarter of 2022, Cardano [30] and Solana [31] are well known of their low energy consumption, also Ethereum, the first Blockchain to deploy NFTs, will soon (6th Sep) perform Ethereum L2, POS, merge phase that is said to consume 99% less energy [32]; a longer list of the 10 most Eco-Friendly blockchains can be found in [33]. So we go forward on our proposed variety of applications, with a clear conscious towards environment and climate change.

3   NFTs Profitable Uses

Now let us span the NFT well known commercial uses, as the main purpose of this paper is to propose money rewarding solutions especially for Egypt. The *PWC global entertainment and media outlook* 2022–2026 [34] reports a 10.4% increase in 2021 revenue, and expects it to reach US$3tn in 2026; a section was dedicated to NFTs $55bn[4] exchange in 2021 featuring it to put more power in creators hands (what most youth love about the crypto world in general). From Blockchain specific analytical sites, glassnode [35] reported a $100m NFT trading in *OpenSea* in just the early days of Aug2021, also the *Axie Infinity* NFT game market cap have risen in July 2021 from $200m to $2bn. Examples for celebrity NFTs the Johnny Depp NFT collection *"Never Fear Truth"* selling has made about $300–400K (an average price of 0.8 ETH each) after his famous trial [36], and Nelson Mandela *"My Robben Island"*.

Musicians, and similarly football celebrities [37], use NFTs as a form of trading digital copies, posters, or what could be similar to baseball cards; where people, specially youth, naturally buy excessive amounts from those things in cheap to moderate prices.

---

[4] [18] says that NFTs trading volume in 2021 is only $17 bn, but maybe this because PWC number may include repeated selling as they stated in in their report, also "Non Fungible" recorded a potential decrease in the 2022 NFT quarterly report (https://nonfungible.com/rep orts/2022/en/q2-quarterly-nft-market-report) mainly due to the noticable fall of crypto prices, we believe this will not destroy our case since we are targeting tourists and Egyptology fans not for FOMO (https://www.spiceworks.com/tech/innovation/guest-article/the-future-of-nfts-is-fomo-the-best-business-model/); will be explained in more detail later in the paper.

The business nourished at first by those who looks for everything new, for those who are nostalgic about rare old records [38]; and finally as cases mentioned in the same reference because public figures are used to internet copyrights concept to prevent impersonating them or stealing their material. In addition, NFTs have evolved to add more features to attract target customers like adding some bonuses or special rights to their buyers, to benefit their issuers like *royalty* that gives the the celebrity a ratio of each resell value,......etc. The tactics of sometimes selling and sometimes giving free air drops of such NFTs, the feel of fairness, the proof of identity techniques (*proof of personhood*) to prevent monopoly possession of free drops, and more issues are summarized in Vitalik Buterin blog [39].

The popularity and profits from such uses encouraged educational (Yale University in June 2021 [40]) and cultural (Russian museum in July 2021 [41])[5] institutions to gain money through NFTs as a mean of digital copyrights. An NFT of a rare first-edition printed copy of the US Constitution was sold in November 2021 at $43.2m [42]; recently the *White House Historical Association* is also minting NFTs through *Iconic Moments* [43]. [44–46] consolidate and discuss around the globe museums NFT selling experience, while [47] is a webinar debating the subject; [48] is an interview discussion by Los Angeles museum with a computer scientist from *UNCOPIED;* the article is interestingly featuring an NFT of an Egyptian piece in the museum. Although halted at the moment[6], in 2018 some Italian museums and galleries signed a 5 year deal with *Cinello.com* company to create *DAWs* (*Digital Art Work*) which are much more expensive 3D encrypted digital objects, and usually accompanied with a minted NFT on the Blockchain [49] that could be viewed as a new piece of art itself; in 2019 DAWs were used instead of real pieces in Leonardo da Vinci's exhibition in Saudi Arabia [50]. To our knowledge, UAE is the pioneer Arab country in the field of NFTs; since the beginning of 2022 museum NFTs have been launched tioned [51], and governmental[7] NFTs had been minted by Dubai police department twice; their enthusiasm to Metaverse is no less with $54m investment aiming to $4bn gains by 2030[52]. The producers of *the Squid Game,* South Korea, has dedicated $200m for Metaverses projects [53] including culture and tourism. In fact, several projects have already started to build museums

---

[5] The Russian Central Bank consultation paper Aug2022 is described as a *blanket ban* (https://www.cbr.ru/Content/Document/File/132241/Consultation_Paper_20012022.pdf) and this doesn't prevent or contradict with the NFTs selling, the same stands for China banning mining & trading while supporting crypto research, Blockchain conferences, and Museum NFTs. In addition Russia has another problem with most of the crypto community taking the Ukrainian side (https://cointelegraph.com/news/crypto-community-reacts-to-russia-s-war-in-ukraine), collecting donations for them [26], and calling to ban Russian TXs (https://blog.chainalysis.com/reports/cryptocurrency-liquidity-russia-sanctions/), this naturally is expected to affect the Russian government strategy towards crypto.

[6] The Italian government found out that Uffizi Gallery got only 70,000€, about 30% of the selling price, because the DAW creation costed 100,000€, see (https://www.museumnext.com/article/italian-government-halts-museum-nft-sales/). However, we don't know about the 2019 Saudi Arabia and 2022 exhibitions profits.

[7] In fact UAE government has a stated policy about it in their official website https://u.ae/en/about-the-uae/strategies-initiatives-and-awards/local-governments-strategies-and-plans/dubai-metaverse-strategy.

Metaverse that combine NFTs, and games in *learn & earn* schemes to serve educational and commercial purposes. The *Morpheus* project [54] is one of the earliest (starting 2019) and the largest with the collaboration of many international entities, Vastari Labs is running another [55]; [56, 57] covers those and more different projects that follow the same approach.

4 The Egyptian Case

In light of the above, we propose in this paper different NFT lines of use for Egypt, mainly in heritage-based projects, that we believe may have a considerable impact on its economy. In fact, if the government didn't do it someone else will; there exists already Egyptian heritage inspired NFT games [58] done by non-Egyptians, even the egyptian women in debt donation NFTs was originally created by Horizon FCB Dubai [25].

In fact Egypt was one of the countries poineering online tourism; an international golden medal in 2000 prove it [59] as documented by a remote tourism USA located *EgyptTours* company founded 1996; a joint project was launched in 2007–2013 to archive the Mediterranean Heritage [60], and gained a lot of satisfaction. As for the NFT market taste, a PhD study named *crypto connections* project let users freely mint an NFT from whatever they felt spiritual connection with in Liverpool museum [61]; the fact that one of the users chose the Egyptian *Book of the dead* from all existing pieces, reveals that there is a market for Egyptian NFTs. So, we believe it is time due for Egypt to step in this full of magic varieties empowering creators NFT world and start its own large scale projects; there are eneromus number of ancient pieces, sights, rare coral reefs that can be sold as NFTs with different prices according to value. There are also scientifically valuable Egyptology digital images (like mummies CAT scans, and Pyramids inside angles,..) which can be made as *DAWs* and rented to scientific gatherings or sent in abroad exhibitions. Historical legends and stories from different eras can be used to create tons of games; joining NFTs with Metaverse can reach even more higher domains. If recent research-based virtual museum tours has gained such satisfaction [62, 63], especially with recent pandemics and other factors that promote remote tourism activities, then different ancient eras and temple Metaverses, red sea navigation between colored fishes and rare coral reefs are expected to gain more for having more user interactivity and role varieties. Hence, such Metaverses can be designed on commercial basis, not just for educational purposes as mentioned in the first few lines in [64]. In addition, based on the popularity of Egyptology fans real life activities [65], virtual historical clothes and jewelries from different eras can be traded as NFTs inside different existing Metaverses in a similar way to fashion brands NFTs [66–68]. A team of 42 authors surveyed the Metaverse possible research areas in [69], while the Current economy volume and Future estimates were discussed thoroughly in the World Economic Forum 2022 [70, 71], along the debatable need[8] [64, 72] and different uses of NFTs and Blockchain technology inside

---

[8] In [64] Stanford University professor Jeremy Bailenson explains why he thinks Metaverses can exit without Blockchains using a 2003 project called "Second Life" with 70m registered accounts till now; this 2016(before NFTs) paper (https://www.sciencedirect.com/science/art icle/abs/pii/S026840121630175X) supports his point proposing a Metaverse deployment plan with no Blockchains.

160   S. Arafat

it [72, 73]. On 28 June, the *European Parliament research service (EPRS)* organized a round table discussing "The Metaverse: a unique opportunity for innovation and growth – or a dangerous 'parallel reality'?", a note was released followed by a more recent paper [74].

5   Issues, Challenges, and Design Decisions

Naturally, these fancy financially promising projects comes with some design and implementation issues and problematic areas that remains a subject of research; things that must be studied and design decesions, the network and infrastructure needed to implement them should also be studied. Figure 1 is an example roadmap from the Morpheus project [54].

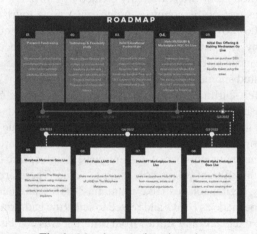

Fig. 1. Morpheus project time phases

- *Network Readiness:*

For a start let us agree that any investment in enhancing the network and internet infrastructure in Egypt, or any country, will be beneficial for many sectors in the country not just what we propose in this paper; ie, it's always worth it. Articles in [13, 14] concludes that network readiness problems was the main failure element for El Salvador Bitcoin adaption, going back to table3 in [15] network readiness in Egypt was scaled to be **38.58%**, while El Salvador's was 37.27%. However, network facilities required in cryptocurrency adoption is not necessarily the same as for minting NFTs or implementing games and Metaverses; the target customer here is abroad tourists and thus what we care most about is to cope with the most advanced network speeds and capacities of people with high tech capabilities to spend hours in Metaverse worlds without being bored of low download or having fears of trojan horses attached to the software. Finally like El Salvador minister said in [14], adding a crypto payment option increased their USA tourists by 30% from youth generations who only use crypto money, thus we expect that adding NFTs and Blockchain technology to whatever remote tourism activity the government plans to do, will add a ratio from people who pay online only through crypto wallets.

- *Developers and team qualifications:*

There are many sites that facilitate minting NFTs without much coding experience, still Egyptology experts and tourism economics experts need to be there to decide what to mint and in what floor price. However, designing NFT games or Metaverses that use NFTs and Blockchain technology does need programming experience; see [75] for an example of developing an NFT game, while [76] is a post graduate students experience in learning the technicalities of minting an NFT. We believe this is not much of a problem, Egyptian universities graduate no less than 4000 qualified students every year[9]; regarding virtual tours, the samples in [60, 63, 77] are done by Egyptians, with the first project starting as early as 2007 and keeping an open source framework available for interested developers [78]. In any case, training generations to code smart contracts and design games or Metaverses increases the country human resources. Artistic and creativity drawing will be needed to inspire from the history, and Egypt do not lack cartoon designers or applied arts faculties. Also, lawyers with enough information technology skills, and DeFi knowledge will be needed at some stage to review the terms in the contract deals (recall the Italian case), and formulate the necessary usage regulations. The study in [15], as a peer reviewed study, has scaled *Egypt Human Development Index (HDI)* as **0.707** and *Education* to be **0.618**, both in a 0 to1 scale.

- *Blockchain Choice & Design decisions*

There are a lot of existing Blockchains each with certain features and characteristics; countries do thorough studies and examine different aspects and deal proposals before choosing to mint their NFTs on a certain Blockchain. Examples from the above are El Salvador choice of Bitcoin, Ethiopia choice of Cardano, and Dubai choice of Ethereum; Appendix A is a table consolidating different choices of museums and cultural entities. Factors that affect such choice include transaction fees [76], popularity of the network, being *un-forkable*[10], energy consumption and eco-friendly (Tezos were chosen by WitWorth art Gallery for that [79], Palm, and Algorand by others). Other design decisions include off-chain NFT data storage [80], available auction mechanisms and whether it would be possible to divide the NFT ownership into stakes that could be

---

[9] In2011 Computer&Information Sciences graduated 2643 + 1383 Computer Engineering (https://censusinfo.capmas.gov.eg/Metadata-ar-v4.2/index.php/catalog/447/download/2411), more faculties opened since then; there's also governmental training (https://www.iti.gov.eg/iti/home) & presedential initiative (http://www.epmp.gov.eg/Default.aspx).

[10] Blockchains fork (the append-only ledger splits into separe two ledgers with one parent block, the last one before the fork) when the decentralized community majorly disagrees, like Bitcoin cash and Ethereum classic. After forks the data state on-chain and off-chain would may be inconsistent (https://dl.acm.org/doi/10.1007/978-3-030-95391-1_1).

traded separately[11] to sell the NFTs, security guarantees; *interoperability* between different Metaverses, liabilities and defining responsibilities in an interactive user empowering environment as Metaverse, were some of the issues pointed out by the EPRS paper [74].

- **NFT Copyrights and IP rights**

As the NFT community which was initiated mainly by enthusiased youth gradually matures, it started to recognize and define different copyrights for different NFT types; there are edit rights, intellectual rights, resell rights, royalty rights for original owner resell profit ratio, buyers group membership rights, and IP copyrights [81]. Buyers also sometimes are confused and sometimes get, or feel, decieved about they actually bought [82, 83]. [84] is a starting project offering *'Can't Be Evil'*[12] alpha version NFT licences smart contract (*CantBeEvil.sol*)[13]; the team contains legal consultants too. In general, governmental scale projects should make carefully thought choices about each NFT kind they sell and be clear to their customers. For example, one may expect rare heritage NFT photos should have the same rights as physical pieces sold in international auctions with additional country's royalty ratio from any resell, while memorial moderate to cheap NFTs may be user editable, maybe royalty rights from using the NFT in media clips or shows, and maybe buyers benefits like bonuses or discounts on tours, also Metaverse NFTs could be rentable (not just sellable) to be worn in a certain Metaverse world gathering.

- **Security & Privacy, Data Protection**

It's expected that any virtual or augmented reality application will get some information about its users that will increase with like the dimensions of the room they're in, their figure shape, arm length or strength,...etc. all these information are used by the application [85]; naturally a complete Metaverse world with clothes and accessories to be worn will know more about its users [86, 87]. For those threats and more many voices claim blockchains are essential to Metaverses; blockchains provide cryptographically secure transactions and authentication. *Meta Guard* is a recently proposed solution [88], where techniques we could relate to differential privacy that protects people privacy when gathering statistics, or to obfuscation that is sometimes used in web browsers [89] or blockchains to hide transactions details or smart contract codes [90], by mangling different users data so none is revealed, or injecting random data is in each user data; see

---

[11] See (https://youtu.be/8WpIGsmyF2A) for a securitization and repurchase scheme for shared NFTs based on Stakelberg game model, (https://timroughgarden.github.io/fob21/reports/r2.pdf)for constraints/goals and impossibility results in designing an optimal NFT auction, and (https://a16zcrypto.com/nft-sales-market-clearing-gas-wars-auction-mechanism-design-for-builders/) for a very recent follow up on [39].

[12] As cited in [84], the name is a guiding principle in web3 (https://twitter.com/OnChainBuilders/status/1554591962182946816) as a follow up on the 'don't be Evil' Google popularized slogan (we are not asking you not to be Evil, we will prevent you, https://twitter.com/milesjennings/status/1564991866340184065?s=20&t=40UgFzrjtdJ5D9K6KkW_LA).

[13] The smart contract is written in Solidity; ie, for Ethereum NFTs but they will extend the project later to include other blockchains.

the original paper [91] for the details and the trade offs. We have to know also that NFT different attacks are still there and have to be dealt with [92]. In general, users should feel more confident to buy or get into authorities backed NFTs and Metaverses, and thus states are expected to design more robust and cryptographically secure applications. A merit or advantage which could be promoted is that parents should feel more safe for their children to spend time playing and learning history at the same time (*learn & earn* concept) in governmental backed games and metaverses, with the all going talks about a massive number of risky games and expectedly future metaverses around.

● *Regulations & Liabilities*

In any case, countries ought to decide on larger scope regulations for NFTs and cryptocurrency trading. In addition the EPRS paper [74] pointed out in its paper to the necessity of defining responsibilities in data sharing between different Metaverses and the challenge of allocating liabilities in an often overlapping roles environment as Metaverses; what the PWC [34] described as *"empowering users"* feature. Meaning that this users attracting feature that gives them the power to be creative and make their own rules, will make it harder for regulators to separate such overlapping roles and define responsibilities when something wrong happens. So, if governments will design their state backed Metaverses, they have to be more cautious in defining user capabilities and constrains inside the Metaverse without being so repulsively constraining them. Also governments will have to make their own regulations that NFT buyers should obey, because users are expected to be from different countries and there's no unique international law till now.

● *Economical Decisions & Analysis*

Many studies and discussions are there in the literature about NFTs risk & return analysis [93, 94], and more is expected to evolve about Metaverses. However, we believe this can't be considered enough to judge the proposed tourism applications; the analysis should be done in a case by case basis, where the people passion about the NFT or Metaverse subject is a correlated variable. The target customers willing to pay amount should be studied with the project cost to determine fees and prices. We have virtual museum tours prices as a starting guide [95], then [96] is an example of a recent (April 2022) marketing study on metaverse's potential audience focusing on the specific case of museums Metaverses. Decisions may include what to sell and what to use as an advertising promo or free NFT drops, the geo distribution of free drops in correlation to tourists ratios, how to assess customers satisfaction (performance metrics) and use it as a feedback to enhance the Metaverse or game. DAWs as being more expensive to create should be done according to prior selling or renting demands, along with a comparative study of using them in abroad exhibitions instead of real pieces (less transformation cost, needed guards,…etc.). Existing literature examples for analyzing the economic potential of virtual tours and other factors during COVID-19 are [97, 98], with [97] focusing on Egypt although done in Oman; while [99] is a forecasting study using neural networks. Note that NFT royalties profit can help in measuring Market preferences as will be explained shortly.

6   NFTs.. The Concept, and Technical Details

This section gives the necessary scientific background to understand NFTs from the developers view.

6.1   The Conceptual Meaning of an NFT

The term NFT stands for *Non Fungible Token*, and was first introduced then standardized by the Ethereum foundation in Jan 2018, to represent, and hence trade, uniquely identified items through transactions in the Blockchain [18, 100]. The term *Token* is adopted from Systems Programming where it refers to the item currently processed by the parser of a programming language compiler; tokenizing an item in Blockchain terminology means allocating a storage type to it and define the necessary interface functions to be processed in smart contracts code and thus transactions. In Ethereum, NFTs are represented by the ERC-721 token type as opposed to the original ERC-20 token type representing fungible tradable money[14]. ERC-721 evolved in the year 2017 through Cryptopunks then the famous Cryptokitties game [18] till it was standardized by EIP-721, because those items needed more data attributes to be attached to them, like Metadata, and different interface functions to handle them [101].

The *fungiblility* of currency in general, whether fiat or crypto, means money is only identified by its value; even in fiat currency, people normally do not care about its serial number unless there's an authority tracing investigation. On the other hand, your ticket seat for example is unique and have a unique time date & seat position, even though there could be many tickets with the same price. See [102] for a law suit example illustrating fiat currency fungiblility, and to understand that even UTXO-based blockchains treats cryptocurrency as fungible.

6.2   Implementing NFTs in Different Smart Contract Blockchains

Ethereum was the poineer Blockchain in introducing and massive usage of NFTs through two standard token types ERC-721 and ERC-1155, however most current blockchains like Solana, Flow, Cardano, Algorand,... Offer standard handling of NFTs. In fact they had a chance to be explored and nourish when Ethereum transaction gas fees became too high[15] for gamers and artists at the early days of EIP-1559. It's merely like handling different abstract data structures, Fig. 2 [81, 103], in different programming languages, where each blockchain has a different smart contracts coding language; examples are

---

[14] Another token type is ERC-1155, which is used to represent a collection of mixed tokens to simplify batch processing in one smart contract (https://eips.ethereum.org/EIPS/eip-1155). There are more improvement proposals to be discussed in (https://eips.ethereum.org/EIPS/); examples in pp.30–31 of [19].

[15] Reached a max of 196$ in May 2022, but back to 1.57$ average (https://cointelegraph.com/news/ethereum-average-gas-fee-falls-down-to-1-57-the-lowest-since-2020), and still (https://news.bitcoin.com/ethereums-post-merge-transfer-fees-remain-low-since-mid-may-high-priority-eth-fees-are-93-cheaper/), although an extreme was reported for an NFT recording the merge (https://www.theblock.co/post/170278/an-nft-minted-after-the-merge-cost-60000-in-transaction-fees).

Solidity in Ethereum, Rust in Solana, Cadence in Flow. [76] is post graduate students report describing Ethereum's Solidity to be as abstract as Python, while developing on Solana's Rust to be similar to programming in C. A detailed thorough comparison of different NFTs standards may extend to a complete technical report, graduation project, or thesis, and we believe it is recommended to be done if Egypt is to go forward in implementing the proposed ideas; see sec.2.2 in [19] for a condensed survey. Other than coding methodology, implementations differ on how Metadata is handled and stored, what do they contain [104], where the original NFT image itself is stored [80], how batch minting is handled in one transaction to save gas fees, what cryptographic functions and techniques are used, how royalties are handled to trace original owner with a certain ratio with each resell. We will suffice here with a brief few remarks and terminologies to make things clear; we also selected an NFT learning example diagram from *OpenSea.com* in Fig. 3, more with different implementations are included in the Mandiant report [80].

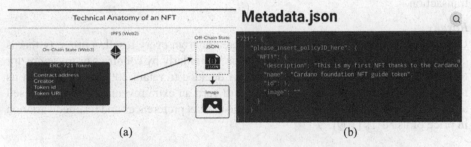

(a)   (b)

Fig. 2. (a) abstract anatomy of NFT [81], (b) example NFT JSON [103].

Fig. 3. An NFT with it's ERC-721 and metadata (OpenSea)

Metadata
The term means in general *data about data*; ie, data needed to identify or classify the stored data. This is an optional extension in Ethereum ERC-721, and a must in Cardano; usually contains name, symbol, URL, description of the NFT, could contain thumbnail image,…. Blockchains may differ in the way Metadata is stored, because it would be expensive to store all the metadata about every NFT on the Blockchain. Such details should be part of the Blockchain choice decision depending on the usage purpose; for example the cryptographic hash in Cardano metadata make it more suitable for identity and traceability management [103, 105], the flexibility and continuous evolve of Ethereum make it more popular in Game NFTs.

Where's the NFT Physically Stored? In addition to the Blockchain token, and the metadata, the digital image representing the NFT has to be stored somewhere. NFTs could be stored in a centralized server like the *Amazon **CloudFront***, or in a distributed peer-to-peer networks like the *InterPlanetary File System (**IPFS**)* and more recently *arweave.org* which is a permissioned Blockchain[16]; [80] goes through all such methods and the data availability risks and loss incidents in each, while [106] proposes a similar side Blockchain solution named ***StateSnap***, [104] also suggests data blockchains proliferation. We in this paper think this decision should be carefully studied, since the incidents in [80] include a penetration to a US state government server.

The ***Enumeration Extension*** in Ethereum allows an NFT issuer contract to publish its full list of NFTs and make them discoverable. Solana [76, 107] has the ***candy machine*** to mint multiple NFTs, and the ***Gumdrop*** to give NFTs to a large number of users through the use of Merkle trees [108]. Cardano also allows the mint of multiple NFTs in one transaction.

Royalty

Used to retain a profit ratio to the original creator from every resell, a property that is considered useful for art creators; could be used similarly by countries or museums for their NFTs. The Whitworth for example has decided to retain 20% royalties from its minted NFTs; this means that the gallery will earn an extra revenue from every resell along with the statistical benefit of reading the market preferences and resulted variation in price of its NFTs [109].

6.3   Implementing NFTs in Bitcoin

Although NFTs got their popularity through Ethereum, historical surveys relate NFTs to as early as 2012 ***colored coins*** in Bitcoin [19]. The problem with implementing NFTs in Bitcoin does not support smart contracts; however more functionality is possible through lightning networks and side chains. Typically a transaction with minimum possible BTC value, dust UTXO, moves the action to another side chain (Bitcoin pegged blockchain) where the NFT is minted or processed in any way [110]. A lot of Bitcoin NFTs providers are given in [111]; in fact this could be one of the reasons behind the increase of dust UTXOs in Bitcoin lately[17]. It's also worth mentioning that Cardano too as a UTXO-based blockchain, and in spite of providing coding capabilities, needs a 1.4 ADA minimum value UTXO in each transaction minting one or possibly multiple NFTs [103]. Supporters of Bitcoin NFTs say that it is more robust and safe for users to mint their NFTs on a Bitcoin empowered Blockchain than on a newer one that may disappear or fork after sometime; however, we point out that Bitcoin remains a *POW* Blockchain for massive

---

[16] Named *Block-weave* as stated in their light-paper, arweave is said to be deployed by Solana, and *Valuables* which is a market place for NFTs of tweets screenshots.

[17] Observing the most richest Bitcoin addresses daily (https://bitinfocharts.com/top-100-richest-bitcoin-addresses.html), one can always find more than 10m addresses holding less than 2$. Tracing UTXOs in the dustiest addresses (https://bitinfocharts.com/top-100-dustiest-bitcoin-addresses.html) reveals another 10 m; ie., ~ 20 m dust UTXOs probably attaching side projects to Bitcoin Blockchain.

NFT minting plans. It's also worth mentioning that buying other blockchains NFTs with Bitcoin money is possible through tokenizing BTC into Wrapped token WBTC offered by most DEXs which can be then traded or used as a collateral [110].

7   Conclusions and Prospectives

We aimed at this paper to study the potential of all NFTs uses as collectables, in games, and in Metaverses uses to monetize heritage, ancient civilizations, and all tourism resources for a country like Egypt. We wrote a Systemization of knowledge paper trying to consolidate all what is there in the literature and in the internet as well. The hardest part was sifting through a tremendous amount of information, deciding what was more important to document in the big picture, and also doing it in a way that the deeper details are accessible to the reader through the provided links and references. We conclude our paper with recommending that Egypt, which started thinking of virtual online tourism as early as 1996, should catch-up with the developed world and launch its NFT collections, a number of learn, play, and earn history games and Metaverses as well; we proposed a number of choices in this paper. We also touched on the security problems and different design decisions involved in the development cycle of such series of projects. At the end, we don't say it is an easy task, we showed example similar project that planned a 3 years roadmap, however we believe it is worth it. In addition to the impact of direct revenue for a country in debt, there's the advantage of digitaly archiving all the existing heritage and whatever is under the threat of destruction or elimination; in fact the government usually pay for that while here it will be a source of income. Also, we emphasize on the beneficial impact of increasing the number of qualified Human resources; in 2022 Egypt Central Bank statistics Egyptians working abroad remittances added \$31.9bn to the country's foreign currency balance which is much more than tourism revenue [112]. We believe such up-to-date Blockchain and Metaverse projects will promote research and experience in all Blockchain, web3, and multimedia related fields; in a way it will be a learn & earn process like that in existing museums projects. Every participant will have to learn about Blockchains, DeFi systems, smart contracts coding; each implementation problem or debatable design decision can start a scientific research thread, maybe a thesis or a graduation projecy. At the end, this will provide them with distinguished work chances in a variety of applications, and will raise Egypt HDI & Education in studies like [15].

Acknowledgements. I'm grateful to everyone participated in making me acquire this level of knowledge & research skills: from my graduation faculty Alexandria Computer Engineering department (the encouragement of Prof. Nagwa Elmekky, and the guiding soul of Prof. Ahmed Belal), to everyone who has put their work free online (MIT, Prof. Roughgarden, Berkeley MOOC, arXiv). I also thank EAI for the given discount to an independent researcher from a developing country.

Appendix A

We tried to consolidate all musuems NFT experiments around the world with their Blockchain choices and any necessary remarks.

Museum/Gallery	Country	Blockchain	Remarks
Liverpool	England		Crypto Connections, free, PhD study, "Book of the Dead" NFT https://jingculturecomm erce.com/national-mus eums-liverpool-crypto-con nections/
British Museum	England	planning to switch to Ethereum 2.0 POS	have been fiercely criticized for corporate and private philanthropy linked to fossil fuels, planning to switch to the Ethereum 2.0 blockchain https://rga.com/futurevis ion/articles/new-nft-ser vice-industry-courts-cul ture-amid-controversy
State Hermitage	Russia	Binance	https://cointelegraph.com/ news/russian-state-hermit age-raises-440k-via-bin ance-nft-auction
Uffizi Galleries & 8 more	Italy	Ethereum	DAWs, Cinello https://news.artnet.com/ art-world/unit-london-dig ital-artwork-2074552
the Belvedere	Vienna, Austria	planning to switch to Ethereum 2.0	did receive some negative comments around sustainability issues https://rga.com/futurevis ion/articles/new-nft-ser vice-industry-courts-cul ture-amid-controversy
WitWorth & Manchester Srt Galleries	England	Tezos https://tezos.com/	Vastari Labs https://blooloop.com/sus tainability/news/green- nfts-sustainable-museum- technology-greenloop/
Aspen Museum	USA	Palm https://palm.io/	https://www.ft.com/con tent/76cacb9e-ba20-44e7- 9ced-f570553af5e1
Data History Artifacts Museum	NY-USA	Algorand	https://www.binance.com/ en/news/top/7038222 https://museum.datahi story.org/about

(*continued*)

(*continued*)

Museum/Gallery	Country	Blockchain	Remarks
Moco Museum	USA	Algorand	https://mocomuseum.com/mocoverse/
Himalayas Museum	India	Re-NFT Shards Protocol	https://renft-shards-protocol.medium.com/himalayas-museum-created-the-first-global-nft-artverse-by-cooperating-with-renft-shard-protocol-c3d04c4b5430
Museum of The Future	Dubai, UAE	Ethereum	https://jingculturecommerce.com/museum-of-the-future-dubai-immersive-superflux-marshmallow-laser-feast/
Universal Hip Hop Museum	Bronx-NY-USA	Near Protocol	https://afrotech.com/universal-hip-hop-museum-nft-series
National Art Museum of Ukraine	Ukraine		In partnership with Estonia-based startup, STAMPSDAQ https://www.ukrinform.net/rubric-society/3339822-works-of-ukrainian-artists-could-be-purchased-in-nft-version.html
St. Petersburg institution	Russia	Binance	https://news.artnet.com/art-world/guernica-tapestry-un-returned-2069976
Shanghai Museum	China	Shangbo Chain	Made their own special purpose Blockchain https://jingculturecommerce.com/shanghai-museum-museum-of-the-sea-shangbo-nfts-blockchain/
	England	DEN tokens (a special purpose Blockchain)	The Morpheus A joint learn to earn project Metaverse + HOLO-NFTs https://www.morpheus.art/ https://whitepaper.morpheus.art/

(*continued*)

(*continued*)

Museum/Gallery	Country	Blockchain	Remarks
IWM Imperial War Museums	England		
EPIC The Irish Imigration Museum	Ireland		
The Hunt Museum	Ireland		
MM The Museum of Menerology	Romania		
Anglo-Boer War Museum	South Africa		
UNHCR The UN Refugee Agency	UN		

References

1. Toronto Universit. https://citizenlab.ca/2018/03/bad-traffic-sandvines-packetlogic-devices-deploy-government-spyware-turkey-syria/. Cited by Bitcoin News and market watch. Accessed 10 Aug 2022
2. https://guardian.ng/opinion/outlook/bitcoin-adoption-and-its-impacts-on-the-developing-world. Accessed 7 Aug 2022
3. Written (2017). https://allaboutethio.com/blockchain-cryptocurrency-bitcoin-in-ethiopia.html. Accessed 7 Aug 2022
4. How Ethiopia Could Monetize Bitcoin & Escape The Industrial Phase. https://projectmano.com/plan. Accessed 7 Aug 2022
5. https://twitter.com/betelhem_dessie/status/1369390186115833857. Accessed 8 Aug 2022
6. https://www.pelicoin.com/blog/what-is-the-economic-impact-cryptocurrency. Accessed 7 Aug 2022
7. https://www.cnbc.com/2022/04/26/fort-worth-tx-the-first-city-in-the-us-to-mine-bitcoin.html. Accessed 10 Aug 2022
8. Smith, I.: https://www.euronews.com/next/2022/03/09/cbdcs-these-are-the-countries-are-using-launching-or-piloting-their-own-digital-currencies. Accessed 11 Aug 2022
9. https://nilefm.com/geekdom/article/4750/betting-on-bitvoin-egypt-to-release-a-digital-currency-framework-soon. Accessed 10 Aug 2022
10. Sigalos, M.: https://www.cnbc.com/2021/07/19/malaysian-police-steamroll-1point25-million-worth-of-bitcoin-mining-rigs.html. Accessed 12 Aug 2022
11. Orji, C.: https://www.euronews.com/next/2022/04/27/bitcoin-ban-these-are-the-countries-where-crypto-is-restricted-or-illegal2. Accessed 12 Aug 2022
12. Thomas, D.: https://beincrypto.com/national-bank-of-ethiopia-warns-of-illegal-crypto-use/. Accessed 7 Aug 2022

13. Bloomberg, "El Salvador.s Big Bitcoin Gamble Backfires to Deepen Debt Woes". https://www.bloomberg.com/. Accessed 7 Aug 2022
14. Sigalos, M.: https://www.cnbc.com/2022/06/25/el-salvador-bitcoin-experiment-not-saving-countrys-finances.html. Accessed 7 Aug 2022
15. Bhimani, A., Arif, S.: Do national development factors affect cryptocurrency adaption. Sci. dir. Technol. Forcast. Soc. Chang. **181**, 121739 (2022). https://doi.org/10.1016/j.techfore.2022.121739
16. Nabben, K.: RMIT University. https://theconversation.com/cryptocurrency-has-an-impact-on-economies-thats-why-some-are-afraid-of-it-and-some-welcome-it-175911. Accessed 7 Aug 2022
17. Salami, I.: University of East London. https://theconversation.com/amp/ethiopias-blockchain-deal-is-a-watershed-moment-for-the-technology-and-for-africa-160719. Accessed 26 July 2022
18. Ethereum use cases, "Non-fungible Tokens (NFT)". https://ethereum.org/en/nft/. Accessed 28 Aug 2022
19. Demystifying Non-Fungible Tokens. A Thematic Report Prepared ByThe European Union Blockchain Observatory & Forum. https://www.eublockchainforum.eu/files/reports/DemystifyingNFTs_November%202021_2.pdf
20. https://www.terminalfour.com/blog/posts/fad-or-future-can-nfts-transform-higher-education.html. Accessed 11 Aug 2022
21. Knack. https://nonfungible.com/news/opinions/nfts-and-higher-education-part-1. Accessed 11 Aug 2022
22. DeFi MOOC. https://medium.com/%40defi.mooc/announcing-the-defi-mooc-2021-nft-and-badge-collection-c8a42fbdc998. Accessed 23 July 2022. The mintcd NFTs https://gallery.metamirror.space/collection/?name=defimooc2021nft. Accessed 15 Aug 2022
23. https://news.bitcoin.com/ngo-announces-plan-to-use-nfts-for-famine-victims-of-ethiopia-tigray-war/. Accessed 2/2022
24. https://www.insidehighered.com/news/2022/01/20/colleges-cash-nfts-new-fundraising-mechanism. Accessed 11 Aug 2022
25. Corr, A.: https://musebycl.io/digital-data/nft-sales-free-egyptian-women-jailed-defaulting-loans. Accessed 10 Aug 2022
26. https://www.outlookindia.com/business/ukraine-raises-600-000-through-nfts-to-rebuild-museums-destroyed-in-russian-invasion-news-189742. Accessed 18 Aug 2022
27. Abdou, M.: https://egyptianstreets.com/2021/08/21/why-charity-nfts-wont-save-palestine/. Accessed 16 Feb 2022
28. Crypto Climate Accord, "Powering Crypto with 100% Renewable". https://cryptoclimate.org/solutions/. Accessed 16 Aug 2022
29. Platt, M., et al.: The energy footprint of blockchain consensus mechanisms beyond proof-of-work. In: IEEE 1st International Conference on Software Quality, Reliability and Security Companion (QRS-C) (2021). https://ieeexplore.ieee.org/document/9741872
30. Bignell, F.: https://thefintechtimes.com/traders-of-crypto-finds-cardano-to-be-the-least-energy-intensive-crypto-coin-in-2021/. Accessed 16 Aug 2022
31. https://solana.com/news/solanas-energy-use-report-march-2022. Accessed 10 Aug 2022
32. Frost, L.: https://decrypt.co/71353/ethereum-foundation-eth-2-0-will-use-99-95-less-energy. Accessed 16 Aug 2022
33. https://www.thetimes.co.uk/money-mentor/article/eco-friendly-cryptocurrencies/. Accessed 10 Aug 2022
34. PWC, "Perspectives from the Global Entertainment & Media Outlook 2022–2026". https://www.pwc.com/gx/en/industries/tmt/media/outlook/outlook-perspectives.html. Accessed 14 Aug 2022

35. https://insights.glassnode.com/nfts-and-gaming-lead-the-eth-rally/amp/#click=https://t.co/2Hx3hOJdkk. Accessed 12/2021

36. Nelson, J.: https://decrypt.co/101922/johnny-depp-ethereum-nfts-surge-after-actor-wins-suit-against-amber-heard. Accessed 12 Aug 2022

37. Priyadarshi, A.: https://thesportsrush.com/nfl-news-patrick-mahomes-joined-rob-gronko wski-after-selling-3-4-million-worth-nft-art-pieces-in-just-20-minutes/. Accessed 11 Aug 2022

38. Rice,   J.:   https://cointelegraph.com/news/thanks-to-bauhaus-i-totally-get-nfts-now. Accessed 4 Aug 2021

39. Buterin, V.: Alternatives to selling at below-market-clearing prices for achieving fairness (or community sentiment, or fun). https://vitalik.ca/general/2021/08/22/prices.html. Accessed 23 Jan 2022

40. https://statistics.yale.edu/news/yale-statistics-and-data-science-auctions-nft.   The   NFT: https://foundation.app/%40YaleDataScience/foundation/41810. Accessed 11 Aug 2022

41. Helen Partz, https://cointelegraph.com/news/russian-state-hermitage-raises-440k-via-bin ance-nft-auction. Accessed 12 Aug 2022

42. Megan, C.: Hills, CNN, "First-edition copy of US Constitution sells for record $43.2 million".   http://edition.cnn.com/style/article/us-constitution-sothebys-sale/index.html. Accessed 18 Aug 2022

43. https://www.iconicmoments.co/proof-collective-partners-with-iconic-moments-for-gra ils-ii. Accessed 31 Aug 2022

44. Valoneti, F., et al: Crypto collectibles, museum funding and OpenGLAM: challenges, oppor-tunities and the potential of non-fungible tokens (NFTs). Appl. Sci. **11**(21), 9931 (2021) A Special Issue on Advanced Technologies in Digitizing Cultural Heritage. https://doi.org/10.3390/app11219931

45. https://cuseum.com/blog/2021/11/16/how-21-museums-amp-cultural-organizations-eng aged-with-nfts-in-2021. Accessed 31 Aug 2022

46. Reyburn,   S.:   https://www.nytimes.com/2022/03/25/arts/design/museums-nfts.html. Accessed 7 Aug 2022

47. https://cuseum.com/webinars/discussing-and-debating-the-potentials-of-nfts-in-the-mus eum-sector-overview. Accessed 19 Aug 2022

48. Carsenat, E., Heinen, J., Ferree, J.: Los Angeles museum. https://unframed.lacma.org/2021/12/03/nfts-and-museum-part-5-art-collections-blockchain. Accessed 31 Aug 2022

49. https://greg.org/archive/2022/07/19/objet-daw.html. Accessed 14 Sept 2022

50. https://consgedda.esteri.it/consolato_gedda/en/la_comunicazione/dal_consolato/2019/10/inaugurazione-mostra-leonardo-da.html. Accessed 14 Sept 2022

51. Oxborrow, I.: https://www.thenationalnews.com/business/2022/05/18/dubais-museum-of-the-future-to-launch-its-first-nft-collection/. Accessed 18 Aug 2022

52. Okunytė, P.: https://dailycoin.com/dubai-aims-to-become-metaverse-capital-of-the-world/. Accessed 10 Sept 2022

53. CH Ligon.   https://www.coindesk.com/layer2/metaverseweek/2022/05/25/why-is-south-korea-throwing-money-at-the-metaverse/. Accessed 10 Sept 2022

54. The Morpheus project. https://www.morpheus.art/. Accessed 31 Aug 2022

55. Vastari Labs. https://labs.vastari.com/about-us. Accessed 31 Aug 2022

56. Deakin, T.: https://www.museumnext.com/article/iconic-moments-developing-an-nft-mar ketplace-for-museums-around-the-world/. Accessed 31 Aug 2022

57. He,   Y.:   https://fortune.com/2022/04/28/museums-history-gamification-nfts-metaverse-tech-art-yizan-he/. Accessed 31 Aug 2022

58. Egyptian GODs NFT game. https://linktr.ee/egyptiangods, https://twitter.com/Egyptiang odsnft. Accessed 11 Aug 2022

59. Egypt Tours 2000 about file. http://www.touregypt.net/egypt-info/magazine-mag03012001-mag6.htm. Accessed 31 Aug 2022
60. Bibliotheca Alexandrina and The Alexandria & Mediterranean Research Center, "Heritage Preservation: Tangible Heritage: International Augmented Med (I AM)". https://www.bibalex.org/alexmed/Projects/Details.aspx?ID=98f32266-8aff-4060-a07a-e7d84383293c. Accessed 29 Aug 2022
61. Chen, M.: https://jingculturecommerce.com/national-museums-liverpool-crypto-connections/. Accessed 14 Sept 2022
62. Glithero-West, L.: Performing Tut, Tutankhamun Exhibition, @UoBEgyptology. https://twitter.com/heritage_lizzie/status/1542850475548098560. Accessed 3/7/2022
63. Hammady, R., Ma, M., AL-Kalha, Z., Strathearn, C.: A framework for constructing and evaluating the role of MR as a holographic virtual guide in museums. Virtual Real. **25**(4), 895–918 (2021). https://doi.org/10.1007/s10055-020-00497-9
64. Singer, A.: https://cointelegraph.com/news/does-the-metaverse-need-blockchain-to-ensure-widespread-adoption. Accessed 4 Aug 2022
65. https://trc-leiden.nl/trc/index.php/nl/textiel-momenten/1410-tutankhamun-s-wardrobe. Accessed 26/7/2022
66. https://www.prnewswire.com/news-releases/truesy-a-curated-nft-gallery-and-marketplace-for-culture-and-fashion-301277983.html. Accessed 3 May 2022
67. https://www.cnbc.com/2021/12/22/here-are-the-companies-building-the-metaverse-meta-roblox-epic.html. Accessed 3 May 2022
68. Macdowell, M.: https://www.voguebusiness.com/technology/the-baby-birkin-nft-and-the-legal-scrutiny-on-digital-fashion. Accessed 3 May 2022
69. Metaverse beyond the hype: multidisciplinary perspectives on emerging challenges, opportunities, and agenda for research, practice and policy. Int. J. Inf. Manage. (2022)
70. Stefan, B.H., Cathi, L.: World Economic Forum. https://www.weforum.org/agenda/2022/02/metaverse-monetization-business-guide/. Accessed 12 Aug 2022
71. Cathi, L.: World Economic Forum. https://www.weforum.org/agenda/2022/05/how-to-build-an-economically-viable-inclusive-and-safe-metaverse/. Accessed 12 Aug 2022
72. https://www.xrtoday.com/virtual-reality/what-is-blockchain-and-what-does-it-have-to-do-with-the-metaverse/. Accessed 4 Aug 2022
73. Canorea, E.: https://www.plainconcepts.com/nft-blockchain-metaverse/. Accessed 4 Aug 2022
74. Clarke, O.: https://kqeducationgroup.com/european-institutions-contemplate-the-metaverse-and-its-policy-challenges-osborne-clarke/. Accessed 24 Aug 2022
75. Xuannu, Inking a Smart Contract, Crypto Coven NFT game. https://cryptocoven.mirror.xyz/A622VSRm8-9oLzc8l3oFGmfnFUZQmDQ3Wx3ObhSlhsc. Cited in Women in Blockchains WIB. Accessed 15/3/2022
76. Martin, J., Kellar, C.H.: A Technical Deep Dive Into and Implementation of Non-Fungible Tokens in a Practical Setting. In: COMS 6998–006: Foundations of Blockchains (2021). https://timroughgarden.github.io/fob21/reports/r8.pdf
77. https://worldvirtualtours.online/the-extraordinary-life-of-hatshepsut-daughter-sister-wife-of-pharaoh-and-pharaoh-herself. Accessed 13 Aug 2022
78. https://vi-seem.eu/2018/07/19/virmuf-virtual-museum-framework-for-exhibiting-digitized-collections/. Accessed 6 Sept 2022
79. Beyer, E.J.: https://nftnow.com/features/hit-hard-by-the-pandemic-museums-turn-to-nfts-to-survive/. Accessed 31 Aug 2022
80. Eitzman, R.: https://www.mandiant.com/resources/blog/nft-storage-and-availability-risk-worth-considering. Accessed 17 Sept 2022
81. https://www.galaxy.com/research/insights/a-survey-of-nft-licenses-facts-and-fictions/. Accessed 24 Aug 2022

82. Hayward, A.: https://decrypt.co/107827/bored-apes-moonbirds-misled-buyers-nft-ip-rig hts-galaxy-digita. Accessed 20 Aug 2022
83. https://twitter.com/Lakoz_/status/1555570398267412480. Accessed 1 Sept 2022
84. Jennings, M., Dixon, C.: The Can't Be Evil NFT Licenses, a16x crypto, https://a16zcrypto. com/introducing-nft-licenses/. Accessed 1 Sept 2022
85. Lim, J., Yun, H., Ham, A., Kim, S.: Mine yourself!: A role-playing privacy tutorial in virtual reality environment. In: CHI Conference on Human Factors in Computing Systems Extended Abstracts, CHI EA 2022, New York, NY, USA Association for Computing Machinery (2022)
86. Sykownik, P., Maloney, D., Freeman, G., Masuch, M.: Something personal from the metaverse: goals, topics, and contextual factors of self-disclosure in commercial social VR. In: CHI Conference on Human Factors in Computing Systems, CHI 2022, NY, USA. Association for Computing Machinery (2022)
87. https://www.securitymagazine.com/articles/98142-9-security-threats-in-the-metaverse. Accessed 23 Aug 2022. The original report: https://www.trendmicro.com/vinfo/us/security/news/cybercrime-and-digital-threats/metaworse-the-trouble-with-the-metaverse#newnav menu-mobile. Accessed 26 Aug 2022
88. Claburn, T.: https://www.theregister.com/2022/08/18/metaguard_promises_protection_f rom_metaverse/. Accessed 23 Aug 2022
89. AdNauseam, a tool to confuse Google's ad network. https://adnauseam.io/. Accessed 26 Aug 2022
90. Buterin, V.: https://ethresear.ch/t/how-obfuscation-can-help-ethereum/7380. Accessed 26 Aug 2022
91. Nair, V., Garrido, G.M., Song, D.: Exploring the Unprecedented Privacy Risks of the Metavers. arXiv:2207.13176v1. [cs.CR], 26 July 2022. The product: https://rdi.berkeley. edu/metaguard/. Accessed 25 Aug 2022
92. Gottsegen, W.: https://www.coindesk.com/layer2/2021/12/20/nft-forgeries-arent-going-away/. Accessed 19 Aug 2022
93. Mazur, M.: Non-Fungible Tokens (NFT). The Analysis of Risk and Return. Elsevier Science, SSRN. https://papers.ssrn.com/sol3/papers.cfm?abstract_id=3953535. 31 Oct 2021
94. WIB, NFT Trading and Risk Management. https://twitter.com/i/spaces/1MnGnkwWrgYJO. Accessed 26 Aug 2022
95. https://360virtualbusinesstours.com/360-virtual-business-tour-faqs/how-much-does-it-cost-to-make-a-virtual-tour/. Accessed 6 Sept 2022
96. Lee, H.K., Park, S., Lee, Y.: A proposal of virtual museum metaverse content for the MZ generation. Digit. Creativ. 33(2), 79–95 (2022). https://www.tandfonline.com/doi/abs/10. 1080/14626268.2022.2063903
97. Resta, G., Dicuonzo, F., Karacan, E., Pastore, D.: The impact of virtual tours on museum exhibitions after the onset of covid-19 restrictions: visitor engagement and long-term perspectives (2021)
98. ElSayed, O., Aziz, H.: Virtual tours a means to an end: an analysis of virtual tours' role in tourism recovery post COVID-19. J. Travel Res. (2021). https://journals.sagepub.com/doi/full/10.1177/0047287521997567
99. Fotiadis, A., Polyzos, S., Huan, T.C.T.-C.: The good, the bad and the ugly on COVID-19 tourism recovery. Ann. Tourism Res. (2020). https://www.ncbi.nlm.nih.gov/pmc/articles/PMC7832145/
100. Entriken, W., Shirley, D., Evans, J., Sachs, N.: https://eips.ethereum.org/EIPS/eip-721. Accessed 28 Aug 2022
101. https://ethereum.org/en/developers/docs/standards/tokens/erc-721/. Accessed 28 Aug 2022

102. MAS.S62, lec.17, Tadge Dryja, "Coinjoin, Signature Aggregation, Pdf: https://ocw.mit.edu/courses/mas-s62-cryptocurrency-engineering-and-design-spring-2018/c879ebcc6179 2c1df2a0f0a610350c24_MAS-S62S18-lec17.pdf. Slides 5–7, Video: https://youtu.be/BFw c2XA8rSk. mins

103. https://developers.cardano.org/docs/native-tokens/minting-nfts/. Accessed 29 Aug 2022

104. Lavrova, A., Iakushkin, O.: NFT performance and security review. In: Computational Science and Its Applications – ICCSA 2022 Workshops: Malaga, Spain, 4–7 July 2022, Proceedings, Part I (2022). https://doi.org/10.1007/978-3-031-10536-4_15

105. https://github.com/cardano-foundation/CIPs/blob/8b1f2f0900d81d6233e9805442c2b42aa 1779d2d/CIP-NFTMetadataStandard.md. Accessed 30 Aug 2022

106. Feng, S., et al.: StateSnap: a state-aware P2P storage network for blockchain NFT content data. In: Algorithms and Architectures for Parallel Processing: 21st International Conference, ICA3PP 2021, Virtual Event, 3–5 December 2021, Proceedings, Part III, pp. 3–18 (2021). https://doi.org/10.1007/978-3-030-95391-1_1

107. https://solana.com/developers/nfts. Accessed 29 Aug 2022

108. https://gist.github.com/jcnelson/8c5f89c29192166a4a37f2b807ed1431. Accessed 9 Sept 2022

109. Liddell, F.V.: The Crypto-Museum: Investigating the impact of blockchain and NFTs on digital ownership, authority, and authenticity in museums. A thesis submitted to the University of Manchester for the degree of Doctor of Philosophy in the Faculty of Humanities (2022)

110. Lielacher, A.: https://cryptonews.com/exclusives/nfts-on-bitcoin-yes-thats-a-thing.htm. Accessed 29 Aug 2022

111. Mirza, J.: https://www.gfinityesports.com/cryptocurrency/bitcoin-nft/. Accessed 30 Aug 2022

112. Mena. https://www.egyptindependent.com/cbe-remittances-of-egyptians-abroad-hit-dlrs-31-9-bln-in-fy-2021-22/. Accessed 31 Aug 2022

Author Index

© ICST Institute for Computer Sciences, Social Informatics and Telecommunications Engineering 2023
Published by Springer Nature Switzerland AG 2023. All Rights Reserved
W. Meng and W. Li (Eds.): BlockTEA 2022, LNICST 498, p. 177, 2023.
https://doi.org/10.1007/978-3-031-31420-9

Printed in the United States
by Baker & Taylor Publisher Services